ABOUT ISLAND PRESS

Island Press is the only nonprofit organization in the United States whose principal purpose is the publication of books on environmental issues and natural resource management. We provide solutions-oriented information to professionals, public officials, business and community leaders, and concerned citizens who are shaping responses to environmental problems.

Since 1984, Island Press has been the leading provider of timely and practical books that take a multidisciplinary approach to critical environmental concerns. Our growing list of titles reflects our commitment to bringing the best of an expanding body of literature to the environmental community throughout North America and the world.

Support for Island Press is provided by the Agua Fund, The Geraldine R. Dodge Foundation, Doris Duke Charitable Foundation, The Ford Foundation, The William and Flora Hewlett Foundation, The Joyce Foundation, Kendeda Sustainability Fund of the Tides Foundation, The Forrest & Frances Lattner Foundation, The Henry Luce Foundation, The John D. and Catherine T. MacArthur Foundation, The Marisla Foundation, The Andrew W. Mellon Foundation, Gordon and Betty Moore Foundation, The Curtis and Edith Munson Foundation, Oak Foundation, The Overbrook Foundation, The David and Lucile Packard Foundation, Wallace Global Fund, The Winslow Foundation, and other generous donors.

The opinions expressed in this book are those of the author(s) and do not necessarily reflect the views of these foundations.

BLUEPRINT FOR *GREENING* AFFORDABLE HOUSING

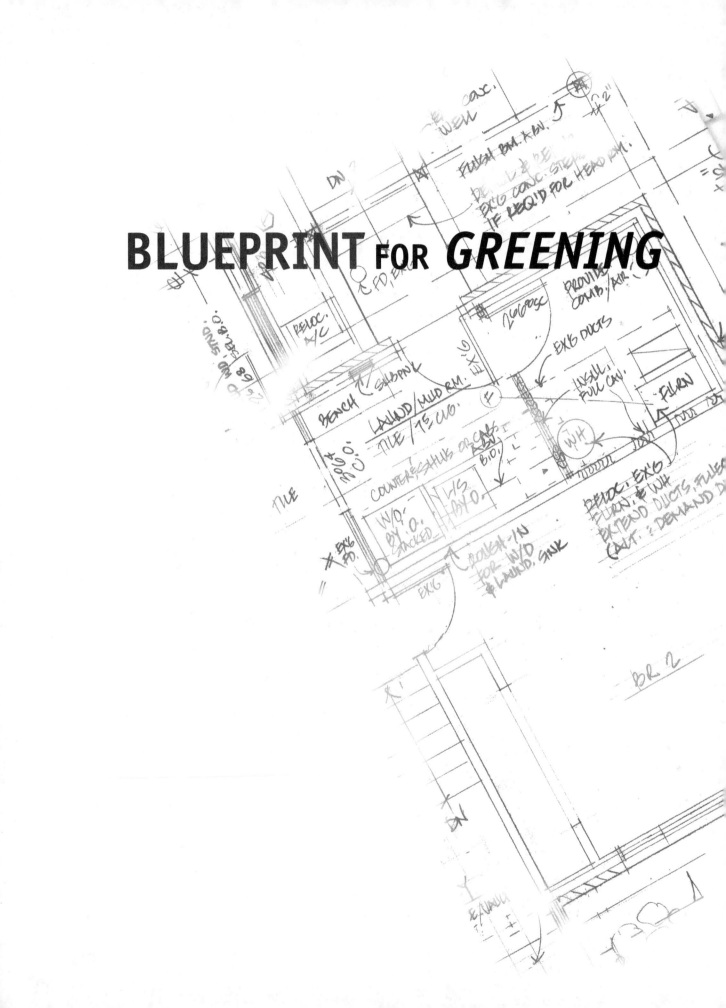

BLUEPRINT FOR GREENING

AFFORDABLE HOUSING

GLOBAL GREEN USA

Edited by WALKER WELLS

with TED BARDACKE, PAMELA CEPE,
JENIFER SEAL CRAMER, LISA MCMANIGAL DELANEY,
MIRIAM LANDMAN, WALKER WELLS

Foreword by: MATT PETERSEN

 **ISLAND**PRESS
WASHINGTON · COVELO · LONDON

Library of Congress Cataloging-in-Publication Data

Blueprint for greening affordable housing / author, Global Green USA ;
edited by Walker Wells ; contributors, Ted Bardacke ... [et al.].
    p. cm.
  Includes bibliographical references and index.
  ISBN-13: 978-1-59726-138-8 (cloth : alk. paper)
  ISBN-10: 1-59726-138-6 (cloth : alk. paper)
  ISBN-13: 978-1-59726-139-5 (pbk. : alk. paper)
  ISBN-10: 1-59726-139-4 (pbk. : alk. paper)
  1. Ecological houses—Design and construction. 2. Housing. I. Wells,
Walker. II. Bardacke, Ted. III. Global Green USA.
  TH4860.B59 2007
  728'.1047—dc22
                                    2006100957

Printed on recycled, acid-free paper ✸

Design by Joan Wolbier

Architectural Drawing by Harold Roger Bresnick

Manufactured in the United States of America
10 9 8 7 6 5 4 3 2 1

Keywords: Green building, affordable housing, LEED HOME rating system, Enterprise Foundation Green
Communities Program, integrated design process, solar energy, indoor air quality, Energy Star

CONTENTS

ACKNOWLEDGMENTS

Global Green would first like to extend deep thanks to Warren Karlenzig for his valuable contributions as author of the original version of this publication, as well as Lynn Simon, David Roodman, and all the other contributors to that edition.

We would also like to recognize the many contributions of Global Green's dedicated staff, past and present, who have helped develop the Greening Affordable Housing Initiative and the concepts and information included in this book: Mary Luevano, Matt Petersen, Walker Wells, Ted Bardacke, Pamela Cepe, Max Wolf, Glen Boldt, Adam Greenfield, Melissa Susman, Alex Pugh, and Denise Lofman; as well as architects Bruce Hampton, Fred Pollack, and Bill Roschen, who have all been sources of support, encouragement, and expertise throughout the years. We also thank the staff of A Community of Friends, Community HousingWorks, First Community Housing, Jamboree Housing, Los Angeles Community Design Center, Mercy Housing California, and South County Housing from whom we have gained so much knowledge and expertise over the years, and Jeanne Peterson and Bill Pavão for their help in shaping the criteria governing the distribution of low-income housing tax credits in California.

Our thanks also go to the many people who provided valuable information, insights, and images for the twelve case studies presented in this book.

We are much indebted to our peer reviewers for giving us their time, expertise, and valuable suggestions: Dana Bourland, Enterprise Community Partners; Angie Brooks, Pugh + Scarpa Architecture; Carlton Brown, Full Spectrum NY; Ed Connelly, New Ecology, Inc.; Cathy Craig, LISC; Bill Edgerton, The Oak Hill Fund; Bert Gregory, Mithun; Bruce M. Hampton, Elton+Hampton Architects; Betsy Hands, homeWORD; Julia Lynch, Full Spectrum NY; Greg Maher, LISC; Janis Mamayek, Icon Architecture; Brandon Mitchell, Full Spectrum NY; Emily Mitchell, U.S. Green Building Council; Rosalba Navarro, Mercy Housing; Brian Ng, U.S. Environmental Protection Agency; Jeff Oberdorfer, First Community Housing; Fred Pollack, Van Meter Williams Pollack; Darren Port, State of New Jersey Department of Community Affairs; Joanne Quinn, Office of Housing City of Seattle; Rob Rich; Jonathan F. P. Rose, Jonathan Rose Companies; Jennifer Somers, LISC; and Fred Wacker, The Home Depot Foundation.

Our special thanks go to Heather Boyer of Island Press, and to Lisa McManigal Delaney, for helping us to stay focused and to put all the pieces of this broad-reaching book together!

Finally, we wish to thank The Home Depot Foundation and the United Technologies Corporation Sustainable City Program for their support of the *Blueprint*, as well as the many supporters, past and present, of the Greening Affordable Housing Initiative.

FOREWORD

These are exciting times for green building. Over a decade ago, when the first edition of this book was published, a number of designers and builders were starting to embrace resource-efficient or "green" building, yet precious few of their efforts focused on affordable housing.

When I joined the newly formed Global Green in the mid-nineties, we had a mandate from President Mikhail S. Gorbachev, founder of our international parent organization Green Cross International: to foster a value shift in patterns of consumption to help create a sustainable future. It was clear to me then, and it remains so now, that in looking at environmental solutions, we must address poverty. But I cannot tell you how many times I've heard that sustainable building practices are luxuries for the virtuous and wealthy few. Or the other refrain, "Why should we experiment on the poor?"

In fact, the opposite, could not be truer: If we can lower energy costs for low-income families, improve their indoor air quality, and connect them to mass transit, we can improve the lives of those who need it most. We simply do not have time to perpetuate the misperception that sustainable building practices are luxuries for the virtuous and wealthy few. By making green building *affordable* we make it *accessible*—if you can build green affordable housing, every building can be green.

But allow me to back up. When I was four years old, or so my father tells me, I saw some trash in the park, left over from a busy weekend, and said "Dad, we have to take care of our planet!" Growing up in Modesto, California, I watched agricultural land and open space disappear for suburban developments. It disturbed me, yet I knew people needed a decent place to live.

In 1991, I began what has become a long relationship with Habitat for Humanity when I volunteered for the organization after moving to Los Angeles for graduate school. Amongst my public administration course readings, I self-selected Paul Hawken's seminal work, *The Ecology of Commerce*—I still have the worn copy full of highlighted passages. Not only did Paul highlight green building, at its core was a message that struck a cord: Whole systems thinking instead of linear solutions to problems! Of course!

Around that time, I joined the Steering Committee for Habitat's Jimmy Carter Work Project in Los Angeles. You can imagine my thrill at being appointed chair of the "green team"! It was a committee of one, and I appointed myself, but it was an important start.

Despite my best efforts and enthusiasm, barriers abounded in trying to "green" the weeklong blitz build. The materials committee would only use a green product if it was donated, the architecture committee had aesthetic objections, the construction committee's volunteers were used to building a certain way, and so on. I took green building pioneer John Picard to meet with the committee chairs. Still, there was little progress until I met David Snell, who was in charge of education at the Jimmy Carter Work Project at Habitat's world headquarters in Georgia. I talked to David about how the Carter project might work differently, and he was intrigued.

In 1994, Diane Meyer Simon asked me to join the newly formed Global Green USA, providing a professional platform from which to pursue an endeavor with Habitat. Not surprisingly, when the organization's first work plan was presented to the board in 1995, it included the goal of influencing Habitat for Humanity and focusing on affordable housing. The plan was approved and Global Green took its first steps toward greening affordable housing.

Reconnecting with David Snell, we quickly identified two opportunities for collaboration between Global Green and Habitat for Humanity. First was a work site recycling plan for the July 1995 Jimmy Carter Work Project. Working with our consultants April Smith and Sid Wales, we insured that everything such as food, construction waste, and hazardous materials was properly disposed of, recycled, composted, or sent to the wood shop at a local high school.

Second, we announced a partnership between Habitat for Humanity International and Global Green USA to identify ways to incorporate green practices into both the design and construction of Habitat projects nationally. The first step in our partnership was holding the Habitat for Humanity and Global Green USA Environmental Initiative Symposium in December 1995. It was said we had one most impressive gathering of green building and sustainability experts in one room at the time: Bob Berkebile, William McDonough, Bill Browning, Gail Lindsay, Steve Loken, John Knott, Dennis Creech, Lynn Simon, and so many others.

The event's goal was to create a plan for Habitat to be good stewards for God's gifts, and improve the lives of the homeowners. I believed we could improve lives and make housing truly affordable and that lower energy costs and significant health benefits could help to transform neighborhoods. The result of the event was the formation of the Habitat Green Team and commitment by Habitat for Humanity International to support green in the work of the many affiliates. This commitment is being borne out today in the way energy efficiency and healthy building practices are integrated into the ambitious Operation Home Delivery for the rebuilding of hurricane-damaged Gulf Coast communities.

Our focus then turned to Los Angeles, where, in 1997, we invited experts in affordable housing design, community development, and green building to participate in a Green Affordable Housing Symposium. At the Symposium four teams explored how to green several affordable projects that were midway through design, including developments led by the Los Angeles Community Design Center, the Housing Authority of the City of Los Angeles, Habitat, and the Lee Group (whose project evolved into the Village Green, where President Clinton launched the PATH Initiative). A concurrent policy team produced recommendations for leaders in local, state, and federal government. The discussion, ideas, and recommendations generated at that event were the foundation for the first edition of this book.

Over the past decade our work has grown to encompass a broad spectrum of research, technical assistance, education, and policy development endeavors. Through the leadership and contributions of Lynn Simon, Mary Luevano, Ted Bardacke, and in particular Walker Wells, Global Green has become a national leader in greening affordable housing and sustainable community development.

But more importantly others have joined us in our commitment to transform communities including Enterprise Community Partners, LISC, NeighborWorks, the U.S. Green Building Council, Habitat for Humanity–International, Southface Energy Institute, AIA Housing Committee, the cities of Los Angeles, San Francisco and Santa Monica, and the States of California and Louisiana. The funding community has also provided essential support and we are grateful for the support of The Home Depot Foundation, the Oak Hill Fund, Blue Moon Fund, Marisla, Turner, David & Lucille Packard, and San Francisco foundations, the U.S. Department of Energy, and United Technology Corporation's Sustainable Cities Program.

In the early days of the Green Affordable Housing Initiative, we faced a great learning curve; thankfully today it is more broadly understood that the construction and maintenance of buildings accounts for 40 percent of the world's energy use, a major portion of overall resource use, and is a major contributor to climate change.

As the case studies in this volume demonstrate, the concept of green affordable housing is not an oxymoron; but rather, it is at the core of a new axiom for community development. To make affordable housing truly affordable, we must embrace green building in all affordable housing. To make green building truly accessible, we must learn to apply it universally in affordable housing.

Green affordable housing also provides us with the unique opportunity to engage an entirely new constituency—designers, developers, community advocates, and policy makers—in the broader, all-encompassing challenge of global warming. We can and must embrace this chance to tackle the enormous challenge of global warming while improving a sizable corner of the world—our communities and our most at-risk citizens—if we are to turn it around for the sake of future generations.

MATT PETERSEN
President and CEO, Global Green USA

CHAPTER 1

Making the Case for Green Affordable Housing

The greening of affordable housing forges a strong link between social justice and environmental sustainability, and connects the well-being of people with the well-being of the environment, thus building on the core social and economic values of affordable housing development.

Housing is a basic human necessity—one that is explicitly identified in the United Nations Universal Declaration of Human Rights.[1]

AFFORDABLE HOUSING

One of the most pressing issues facing communities throughout the United States is the lack of safe, decent, and affordable housing. As wages stay stagnant while housing costs rise,[2] a growing number of low-income men, women, and families[3] are unable to find a place to live that meets the conventional definition of affordability—housing for which residents pay no more than 30 percent of their gross income toward rent or mortgage payments.[4]

In response to the unmet need for housing accessible to low-income individuals and families, a community of nonprofit and for-profit developers, social service organizations, neighborhood and charity organizations, lenders, financiers, and government agencies has emerged over the past forty years to produce and operate what is now commonly referred to as "affordable housing." As a broadly used term, affordable housing includes rental, for-sale, co-, and transitional housing that is income restricted and usually developed through one or more forms of public subsidy. Affordability is achieved by setting the monthly rent or mortgage payment in accordance with the resident's income, rather than at market rates.

The most common types of affordable housing are:

• Rental housing for very low-, low-, and moderate-income individuals and families
• For-sale housing for very low-, low-, and moderate-income individuals and families
• Housing for people with special physical or mental health needs

- Housing for people transitioning out of homelessness or medical or psychiatric institutions, or for emancipated foster youth leaving the family foster care system
- Housing for seniors
- "Sweat-equity" or self-help homes

Affordable housing developers rely on a variety of financial programs administered by federal, state, and local public agencies financial institutions and philanthropic organizations to realize their projects. This assistance is often in the form of tax credits, debt with preferential rates or terms, mortgage guarantees, and grants. While this book outlines a green building process and recommended practices that apply to all types of affordable housing, we emphasize the most common type of affordable housing developed in the United States—income-restricted rental housing funded through a combination of tax credits, preferential debt, grants, and other public subsidies.

WHAT IS GREEN BUILDING?

Green building is the process of creating buildings and supportive infrastructure that reduce the use of resources, create healthier living environments for people, and minimize negative impacts on local, regional, and global ecosystems.

The construction and operation of affordable housing projects, like other building types, consume large quantities of resources, resulting in adverse effects on the natural environment. For example, the annual impacts of building construction and operation in the United States include the following[5]:

- 40 percent of U.S. energy use
- 35 percent of U.S. carbon dioxide production, a major contributor to global warming
- 30 percent of wood and raw materials
- 25 percent of water use
- 20–40 percent of solid waste

In addition, over 30 percent of buildings have poor indoor air, which is cause for concern given that people spend about 90 percent of their time indoors.[6] Many building products have negative impacts on human health through the release of toxins, either during the manufacturing process or after installation. Volatile organic compounds (VOCs), many of which are known carcinogens, are common in pressed wood products, paints, solvents, and adhesives. One of the most common VOCs, formaldehyde, is present in most particleboard, melamine, medium-density fiberboard, and plywood used for cabinetry and trim. Other VOCs, such as acetone, benzene, toluene, and perchloroethylene, can impact the nervous and respiratory systems, especially in vulnerable populations such as children and the elderly, and alone or in combination with mold, dust, and pet dander, be a trigger for asthma.[7] Building operation also has health implications. For example, burning coal to generate electricity releases mercury into the atmosphere; which eventually finds its way into the oceans, then into fish, and finally into our bodies when we eat the fish. Elevated mercury levels in pregnant women harm brain development in hundreds of thousands of unborn children annually.[8] Conventional building often burdens low-income families and property managers with high monthly utility bills and significant ongoing maintenance and replacement expenses.

As affordable housing developers across the country become aware of these environmental, health, and economic issues, they are turning to green building as a way to lower operating costs, create healthier living environments, and minimize local, regional, and global environmental impacts. Examples of a diverse range of affordable housing projects from across the country can be seen in the photographs in this chapter.

Green building addresses five core issue areas: (1) smart land use; (2) water efficiency and management; (3) energy efficiency; (4) resource-efficient materials; and (5) healthy indoor environmental quality. See chapter 3, where these core issues are discussed in more detail. Some specific strategies include the following:

- Building in communities with existing services and infrastructure
- Reusing centrally located land and rehabilitating historic buildings
- Locating projects close to public transit and community amenities to reduce car dependency
- Producing the most compact and efficient units possible to reduce material use and the amount of space needing heating and cooling
- Reducing construction waste through materials reuse or recycling
- Reducing energy consumption through well-designed buildings and efficient appliances and fixtures
- Reducing water consumption both indoors and in landscaping
- Improving the quality and reducing the volume of stormwater
- Using materials that do minimal harm to people and the environment during manufacture, use, and disposal
- Increasing durability by minimizing moisture penetration.
- Improving indoor air quality through good ventilation and use of nontoxic materials and finishes

FIGURE 1.1. Faison Mews Historic Rehabilitation (Camden, NJ). *Photo courtesy of Darren Molnar-Port, NJDCA-NJ Green Homes Office* **FIGURE 1.2.** Cambridge Co-Housing (Cambridge, MA). *Photo courtesy of Bruce M. Hampton, AIA*
FIGURE 1.3. Colorado Court (Santa Monica, CA). *Photo courtesy of Pugh + Scarpa Architects* **FIGURE 1.4.** El Paseo Studios (San Jose, CA). *Photo courtesy of First Community Housing*

- Reducing the heat island effect through reflective roof and paving and planting trees.
- Establishing maintenance practices that reduce use of pesticides, fertilizers, and harmful cleaning chemicals.

THE BENEFITS OF GREEN BUILDING TO AFFORDABLE HOUSING

Sustainability has three core components—economics, social equity, and the environment. Affordable housing diretly addresses two of those aspects: economic stability and social equity. Integrating green building enables developers to address the third environ-

FIGURE 1.5. PVC-Free House (New Orleans, LA). *Photo courtesy of Bruce M. Hampton, AIA* FIGURE 1.6. Riverview Homes (Camden, NJ). *Photo courtesy of Darren Molnar-Port, NJDCA-NJ Green Homes Office* FIGURE 1.7. Betty Ann Gardens (San Jose, CA). *Photo courtesy of First Community Housing* FIGURE 1.8. Magnolia Circle (South DeKalb, GA). *Photo courtesy of Southface Energy Institute*

mental component that has not traditionally been seen as an integral part of affordable housing development.

A green building approach is consistent with the mission of most affordable housing developers, and most community development corporation mission statements include language about ensuring that low-income people have access to safe, decent, and affordable housing. For example, Mercy Housing California gives its mission as "to create and strengthen healthy communities through the provision of quality, affordable, service-enriched housing for individuals and families who are economically poor." California's Eden Housing states its mission as "to build and maintain high-quality, well-managed, service-enriched affordable housing commu-

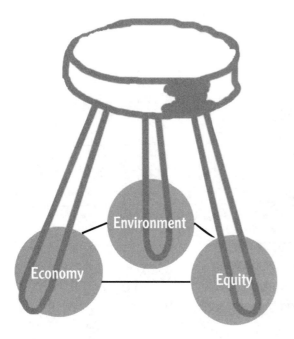

FIGURE: 1.9. Green building can link the three components of sustainability.

nities that meet the needs of lower-income families, seniors, and persons with disabilities."

Though neither mission statement has explicit language addressing the impact of the building itself on the well-being of residents, the core concepts need only be expanded slightly to do so. The definition of *safe* housing should include provision of a living space that is healthy, not just physically secure. *Decent* should include the assurance that low-income families are not disproportionately exposed to toxic materials, mold, extremes of heat or cold, or noise. *Affordable* should include the ongoing costs of utilities and maintenance, not just the purchase price or monthly rent. Finally, the idea of *community* should include a connection to the natural environment.

Combining green building and affordable housing offers a number of direct and indirect benefits to residents and owners of affordable housing and to the larger community. The spheres of benefits green building provides to affordable housing are depicted in Figure 1.10. Direct benefits include utility cost savings, healthier living environments, and increased durability. Utility costs for low-income families can be up to 25 percent of expenses after rent or mortgage payments[9]—more than what is spent on education or health care[10]—as compared to approximately 5 percent of net income for middle-class families. Energy and water savings enable low-income residents to shift financial resources to higher-priority items such as more nutritious food, health care, and education, or to move up financially by saving toward the purchase of a home. Locating projects close to transit helps reduce the financial and environmental impacts of driving and vehicle ownership. Avoiding the need for a second car can save a family approximately $3,200 annually.[11] The health benefits are also crucial, given studies that show a higher rate of asthma among low-income children and attribute asthma incidents to aspects of the indoor environment.[12] Healthy residents also lessen the burden on the overall health care system.

Other, less direct benefits of green affordable housing include support for regional issues such as solid waste management through construction waste recycling programs or use of recycled-content materials, and improved water quality through on-site treatment and retention of stormwater. Global benefits include reduced energy use, thus lowering the amount of carbon dioxide—one of the main climate change gases—entering the atmosphere, or forest preservation by using sustainably harvested wood.

Because projects are typically owned and operated by the same organization for at least fifteen years (the compliance period for the federal low-income housing tax credit),

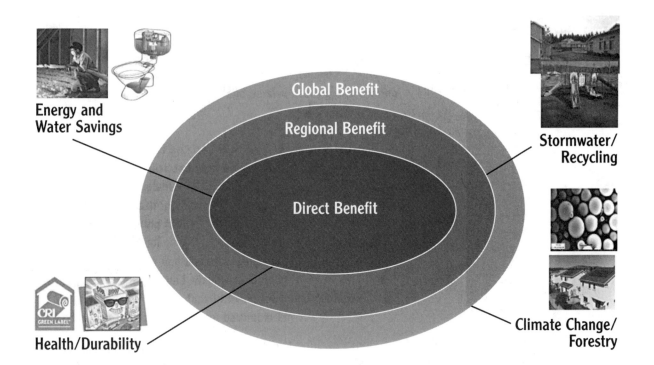

Energy and Water Savings

Global Benefit

Regional Benefit

Direct Benefit

Stormwater/ Recycling

Climate Change/ Forestry

Health/Durability

and often much longer, affordable housing developers are able to use a long-term-life-cycle approach to design, which is one of the core tenets of green building. With this time horizon, a high-efficiency boiler with a seven- to ten-year payback is a viable choice, as the owner would capture at least five to eight years of savings. But the same system would likely not be a viable choice for a market-rate developer with a time horizon of three years or less.

Being able to look at benefits over the long term gives affordable housing developers the unique opportunity to view the full range of green building strategies and their associated benefits in a comprehensive way in order to focus on those that are the best fit for the developer, the residents, the community, and the larger environment.

FIGURE 1.10. Green building provides multiple spheres of benefits, from the individual to the global sphere.

THE ROLE OF THE BLUEPRINT

The goal of this book is to provide in one location the information needed by a developer, designer, public agency staff, housing advocate, lender, or other housing stakeholder seeking to incorporate green strategies into an affordable housing development. To that end, Chapter 1 describes the specific benefits green building brings to housing developments, and delineates the points of compatibility and overlay between green and affordability approaches. To demystify green building, Chapter 2 offers a detailed outline of the integrated design process, and Chapters 3 and 4 provide specific recommendations for best practices in green design, construction, and operation. Chapter 5 explains how to

TABLE 1.1. MOVING TO SUSTAINABLE AFFORDABLE HOUSING

	EQUITY	ECONOMICS	ENVIRONMENT
Affordable Housing Often Provides:	A safe and decent living environment Social services and programs	Stable housing costs to increase the economic stability of families and neighborhoods. Opportunity for people of all incomes to live in a community	Transit- and service-proximate locations that reduce air pollution
Green Building Closes the Gap by:	Providing healthier indoor environments—especially important for seniors and children Encouraging physical activity through walking and bicycling Protecting the health of construction and manufacturing workers	Reducing residents' utility costs, thus allowing spending to shift to higher-priority items such as health care, education, and building equity Providing operation and maintenance savings to developers, thus allowing development of more units or provision of additional services	Using land efficiently through urban infill and brownfield redevelopment Using passive energy and integrated infrastructure to reduce need for natural resources Specifying efficient systems and appliances that save water and energy and help mitigate climate change

pay for the green features, through both existing and new sources of financing and by using a life-cycle approach to design and budgeting. Case studies that span the many types of affordable housing projects show how to put all the pieces together.

By providing practical information drawn from actual projects and the experiences of Global Green staff over the past decade, we hope this book will be a catalyst enabling individuals, organizations, and agencies to make the commitment to go green.

NOTES

1. United Nations Universal Declaration of Human Rights (1948), Article 25.1, www.un.org/Overview/rights.html (accessed January 4, 2007).
2. Danilo Pelletiere, Keith Wardrip, and Sheila Crowley, *Out of Reach, 2005* (Washington, DC: National Low Income Housing Coalition, 2005), www.nlihc.org/oor2005.
3. Low-income individuals are defined as those earning 60 percent or less of the area's median income, adjusted for family size, per Internal Revenue Code 42.
4. U.S. Department of Housing and Urban Development, www.hud.gov (accessed October 2006).
5. U.S. Department of Energy Center of Excellence for Sustainable Development, Smart Communities Network, Green Building Introduction, www.smartcommunities.ncat.org (accessed January 12, 2007).
6. U.S. Environmental Protection Agency, Office of Air and Radiation, *Report to Congress on*

Indoor Air Quality, vol. 2, *Assessment and Control of Indoor Air Pollution,* EPA 400-1-89-001C (Washington, DC: EPA, 1989), 1, 4–14.

7. K. Rumchev, J. Spickett, M. Bulsara, et al., "Domestic Exposure to Formaldehyde Significantly Increases the Risk of Asthma in Young Children," *European Respiratory Journal* 20 (2002): 403–8; K. Rumchev, J. Spickett, M. Bulsara, et al., "Exposure to Volatile Organic Compounds Found to Be Important in the Cause of Childhood Asthma," *Occupational and Environmental Medicine* 61 (2004): 92.

8. Leonardo Trasande et al., "Public Health and Economic Consequences of Methyl Mercury Toxicity to the Developing Brain," *Environmental Health Perspectives* 113 (2005): 590–96.

9. Enterprise Community Partners, Green Communities Initiative Training, 2006, Los Angeles, CA, September 12, 2006.

10. U.S. Bureau of Labor Statistics, *Consumer Expenditures in 2004* (Washington, DC: Bureau of Labor Statistics, 2004)

11. Based on 32.2 cents per mile for a subcompact car (*Cost of Owning and Operating Automobiles, Vans, and Light Trucks—2001* [Washington, DC: Federal Highway Administration, 2001]) and assuming 10,000 miles annually.

12. James Krieger, et al., "The Seattle–King County Healthy Homes Project: Implementation of a Comprehensive Approach to Improving Indoor Environmental Quality for Low-Income Children with Asthma," *Environmental Health Perspectives* 110, suppl. 2 (2002): 311–22.

CHAPTER 2

The Integrated Design Process

An integrated approach to green building is crucial to the success of any green project. Green building strategies should be incorporated into a project from the very beginning of the development process. This means considering the green building implications when reviewing potential sites and developing the initial pro forma financial analysis. Identifying the green options early gives time to check for consistency with the requirements of the expected local, state, and federal funding sources and to identify additional sources if needed. The long-term ownership of most affordable housing means that the developer is often responsible for the operation of the project for many years. Good early decision making is critical in obtaining the greatest benefit from the green measures and ensuring that the building systems and materials continue to provide benefits over the long term.

The key components of the integrated design process are as follows:

- *Start early:* Explore green strategies from the very beginning of the project's budgeting, programming, and conceptual design process.
- *Foster collaboration:* Engage all members of the design and development team in the green building conversations.
- *Make a commitment:* Convey and reiterate the importance of following green principles and the integrated design process.
- *Set clear goals:* Provide specific direction on how the project should perform.
- *Enable feedback:* Establish a communication structure that allows continuous review of the green concepts as the project is refined.
- *Analyze costs:* Review costs on an ongoing basis to ensure that the savings generated by integration are captured in the project financials.
- *Follow-through:* Carry the green concepts into the plans, specifications, construction practices, and operations.

Using an integrated approach requires investment of additional collaboration and design time at the beginning of a project to thoroughly consider and react to the many green options and interrelationships. The cost of integrating green building into a proj-

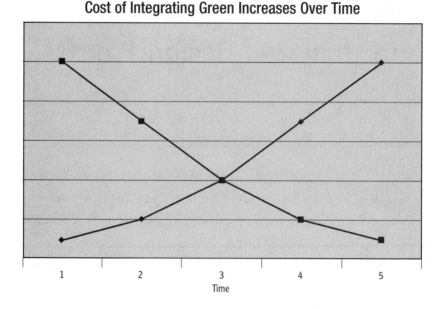

Cost of Integrating Green Increases Over Time

Time

ect increases over time as the project moves through the various phases of design (see Figure 2.1). In the long run, an integrated approach ensures that the design components work together effectively and efficiently, to satisfy project goals ranging from energy efficiency to healthy indoor air to environmental protection.

For first-time green builders, the integrated design process will be unfamiliar, and the team may need time to get comfortable with the process before becoming fully engaged. But even for experienced green developers, there are always new design strategies, systems, or materials to explore. In either case, a well-structured process that builds on past experiences, local examples, and national resources, and which is led by a knowledgeable green building advisor or committed member of the design team, will generate innovative and viable ideas for improving building performance while minimizing additional costs.

How Is the Integrated Design Process Different?

The conventional design process is linear and focused on problem solving, through the introduction of specialized knowledge. The design effort is typically driven by the architect, who makes a large number of critical project decisions, often using generalized experience from previous past projects, traditional rules of thumb, or standard assumptions. The dominant goal at the early stage of a project is meeting the program—providing a predetermined number of dwelling units, community areas, leasable commercial space, and parking spaces. Many of the fundamental aspects of the project—height, massing, orientation, allocation of space, and location of uses—are decided by the architect and developer without input from other professionals.

Other members of the design team are usually brought into the process only after the major design direction is established. Once engaged, the team members are expected to solve detailed problems related specifically to their expertise. For example, the structural engineer determines how to support the building; the mechanical engineer identifies how to heat, cool, and ventilate the spaces; and the landscape architect is asked to beautify what remains of the site after the building and infrastructure needs have been met. With each of the professionals on a separate, discrete path, there are few, if any, opportunities for a comprehensive evaluation of the project. Introducing proposals that would have a building-wide effect—such as changing the shape of the building to reduce the overall need for structural elements, or locating landscaping to amplify natural breezes—is difficult, and new information that emerges during later stages of design is often presented as a problematic disruption of the linear process, rather than as an opportunity. Lack of coordination during construction can result in late-change orders and additional time spent on resolving last-minute modifications to the plans.

The integrated process is iterative, value and systems based, and focused on performance. Throughout the design process, team members are brought together in a series of analysis and decision-making meetings or clusters. The process starts at the planning stage, in which potential sites are considered, the size of the units is determined, and budgets are established. This is the time to address many fundamental green building issues—such as reducing vehicle use, maximizing natural daylight and ventilation, increasing energy and water efficiency, generating on-site energy, managing stormwater—before the site plan and unit or home layout are determined and initial concepts are presented to the local government or the community.

Once the basics of the project are established and a schematic design of the building is complete, the next step in the integrated design process is for the entire project team to participate in a charrette, or collaboration-focused meeting, to discuss community context, orientation, massing, stormwater strategies, space allocation, structural systems, mechanical systems, budget, and construction logistics. The charrette is structured around questions, instead of pure problem solving. If we reduce the width of the building to improve ventilation, can we reduce the size of the heating and cooling equipment? What impact does a narrower building have on the structural system? In the charrette, all participants are expected to contribute to the full conversation and not limit their comments or suggestions to their area of expertise.

After the charrette, additional focused follow-up meetings are held to review energy modeling cost estimates, final plans, and specifications. Cost information is developed on an ongoing basis, so the conventional value engineering process[1]—in which major components of the project are often cut to reduce costs—is avoided. Instead, the team identifies ways to create the greatest value by comparing different options and identifying trade-offs between green strategies in an ongoing iterative fashion. By shifting effort forward in the process and looking at the building holistically and systematically, integrated design minimizes costly late-stage design changes.

It is also essential to establish a way to link the phases of the design process, so that ideas identified during the planning stage are able to make their way into the finished project. For this transfer of information to occur, someone must be designated as responsible for the green building aspects of the project. Often the developer's project manager is given this role as they may be the only person involved in all phases of the project and be the one who understands the financial implications of each decision.

THE BUILDING AS A SYSTEM

For buildings to provide safe, comfortable, and affordable shelter, they must rely on a number of "systems" that address the building's structure, ventilation, plumbing, temperature control, safety, and durability. All of these individual systems need to be seen as contributing to the overall building "ecosystem," rather than as disconnected pieces and parts. The integrated design process uses a systems approach to view the building from a holistic perspective. To design an efficient system, it is essential to understand the various components and how they interact.

The first relationship to consider is between the building, its site, and the surrounding neighborhood. While often described as the passive component to design, decisions at this point set the framework for the entire project. Patterns of foot traffic hydrology, microclimate, topography, solar exposure, prevailing winds, direction of views, and the social needs and patterns of the building users should be documented at the outset. These factors should then guide and shape building orientation, form, and massing. In

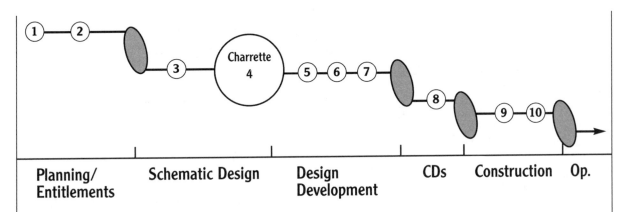

Integrated Design Process

Planning/Entitlements Schematic Design Design Development CDs Construction Op.

many cases, the desire to be compatible with existing development patterns takes precedence over other factors. The challenge is to integrate the environmental parameters into the overall equation.

The first rule of green design is to reduce demand through passive systems, then provide the smallest and most efficient active systems possible. Passive strategies include using the structure's thermal mass to store and radiate heat in the winter; designing building forms and spaces to maximize cross-ventilation for summer cooling; and using air buoyancy (hot air rises) to pull fresh air into and out of the building. Active systems should then be integrated with the passive systems to provide any additional heating, cooling, or ventilation needed.

The building materials themselves, both structural and finish products, should interact efficiently with the major building systems to promote energy efficiency, remove excess moisture, and prevent exposure of the occupants to environmental toxins. Finally, the building must be operated in a way that delivers the benefits intended by the design. This means regular maintenance of systems, upkeep of building materials, and preventing the introduction of new toxins in the form of cleaning or repair products.

THE GREEN DESIGN TEAM

The design team should, at a minimum, include the owner, the architect, a knowledgeable heating, ventilating, and air-conditioning (HVAC) designer, and an experienced contractor. For larger projects, a mechanical engineer, structural engineer, civil engineer, landscape architect, construction manager, and property manager are also needed. If the design team does not have green building expertise, a green building consultant should be included. When selecting team members, requests for pro-

FIGURE 2.2. The integrated design process continues throughout the course of developing a project, from design to construction.

Legend
1. Project definition
2. Program and site selection
3. Massing and orientation
4. Charrette
5. Research
6. Cost analysis
7. Materials and systems decisions
8. Specification review
9. Contractor orientation
10. Requests for information and HERS testing

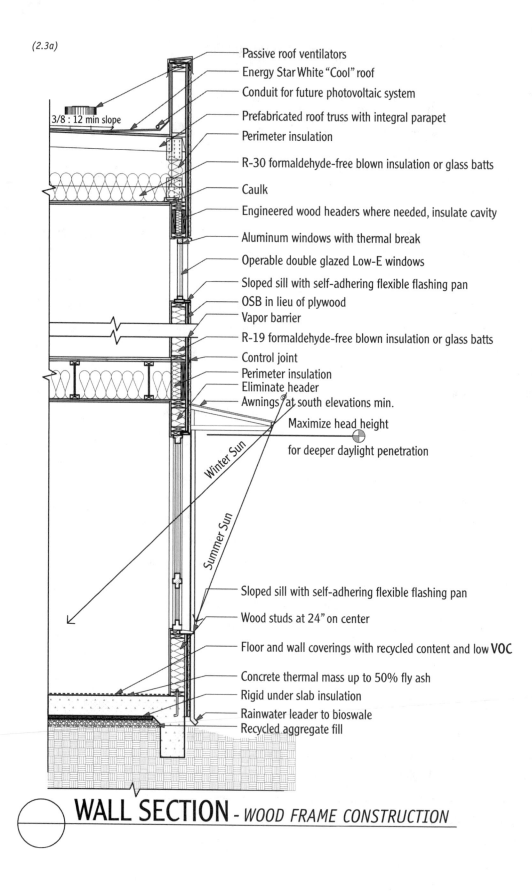

(2.3a)

3/8 : 12 min slope

Passive roof ventilators

Energy Star White "Cool" roof

Conduit for future photovoltaic system

Prefabricated roof truss with integral parapet

Perimeter insulation

R-30 formaldehyde-free blown insulation or glass batts

Caulk

Engineered wood headers where needed, insulate cavity

Aluminum windows with thermal break

Operable double glazed Low-E windows

Sloped sill with self-adhering flexible flashing pan

OSB in lieu of plywood

Vapor barrier

R-19 formaldehyde-free blown insulation or glass batts

Control joint

Perimeter insulation

Eliminate header

Awnings at south elevations min.

Maximize head height

for deeper daylight penetration

Winter Sun

Summer Sun

Sloped sill with self-adhering flexible flashing pan

Wood studs at 24" on center

Floor and wall coverings with recycled content and low **VOC**

Concrete thermal mass up to 50% fly ash

Rigid under slab insulation

Rainwater leader to bioswale

Recycled aggregate fill

WALL SECTION - *WOOD FRAME CONSTRUCTION*

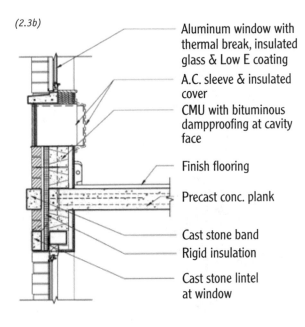

(2.3b)

Aluminum window with thermal break, insulated glass & Low E coating

A.C. sleeve & insulated cover

CMU with bituminous dampproofing at cavity face

Finish flooring

Precast conc. plank

Cast stone band

Rigid insulation

Cast stone lintel at window

FIGURE 2.3. The above cross sections show how the various envelope elements can be integrated to achieve an enclosure that is thermally effective, avoids moisture intrusion, and also allows for flow of fresh air into the living space and exhaust of stale air to the exterior. While the specific design approach and material relationships differ between concrete masonry (2.3b) and wood frame construction (2.3a), similar practices such as the effective placement of insulation, providing continuous drainage plain, thorough flashing, and planning for ventilation apply to both construction types.

Figures courtesy of Dattner Architects (2.3a) and Van Meter Williams Pollack (2.3b)

posals (RFPs) or requests for qualifications (RFQs) should specify what type of green building experience is required.

If at all possible, select and retain the contractor through a negotiated bid process. This approach allows the developer to select a builder with experience in green construction and to integrate the contractor into the project team at the early stages of design. Selecting a contractor early on helps to ensure that the people responsible for building the project are knowledgeable about the green design elements, allows the contractor to participate in the give-and-take of the design process, and provides a way to get ongoing feedback on the costs and practicality of various options. If a public bid is required, use a two-step contractor selection process that focuses first on qualification and then allows the prequalified general contractors to submit competitive bids. To gain expertise on construction and cost-related issuesduring design, retain a construction management consultant or other professional with experience in construction to participate in the green design charrette and provide cost estimates during design.

THE CHARRETTE

A charrette is an intensive, facilitated workshop that involves all team members, lasts from three to four hours to a day or more, and aims to create a clear vision for how the project will be developed, including how the green building elements will be incorporated. When a group of people with diverse experience are brought together in an environment that is both structured and open-ended, the opportunities for green design are explored in a thorough, creative, and effective way.

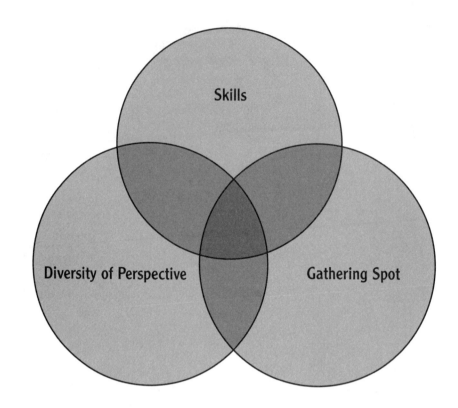

Who Should Attend the Charrette?

All members of the design team should attend the charrette, as well as the property manager, and, if possible, representatives from the local utilities and permitting and funding agencies. Involving community representatives and potential residents is also useful to gain insight into the character of the neighborhood and the needs of residents. Each participant should bring unique expertise and an open mind to the discussion. Through dialogue, the trade-offs and synergies between the concepts and concerns that emerge during the charrette can be fully explored, and strategies can be identified for how to best meet the project's green goals.

One person should be designated to facilitate the charette. The facilitator should be knowledgeable about green building strategies and rating systems and be familiar with the architectural design process. If possible, the facilitator should have working knowledge of affordable housing development and construction practices. The facilitator's role is to guide the participants through an exploration of the project, making sure that critical green issues are addressed in the time allotted for the charette. It is beneficial for the facilitator to speak with the developer and the architect prior to the charette to identify any critical technical, financial, or design issues that need to be emphasized. During the charette, the facilitator is responsible for guiding the conversation, listening to the participants, engaging all the participants in the discussion, and accurately documenting decisions made, unresolved issues, and areas that need further research or analysis before a decision can be made.

Format and Schedule of the Charrette

A green design charrette requires at least a half day and, if the project is in a very early stage and many alternate approaches are being discussed, may require up to two days. The room should be set up to encourage collaboration—either a round table or multiple tables arranged in a square. General rules of order—such as having only one person speak at a time so everyone can hear, having people raise their hand if they want to speak, and forbidding side conversations—should be established up front. Establish a culture of collaboration by making it clear that all ideas are valued and by encouraging people to make suggestions outside of their specific area of expertise or to propose creative solutions that do not appear to fit within conventional industry practices.

Either prior to or as the first component of the charrette, the development team should visit the site to become familiar with the patterns of local winds, rainfall, solar exposure, relationships to nearby buildings, and ambient noise. Walking around the neighborhood can reveal off-site factors that might affect the development, such as traffic and pedestrian circulation patterns and the location of neighborhood amenities and services. Site visits allow team members to imagine how the development would affect the appearance of the neighborhood, and how to place the buildings to take advantage of the site's inherent benefits.

To start the charrette, the project developer and architect should describe the overall objectives of the project—what types of families or individuals will be served and how the project fits into other types of housing or social services in the surrounding neighborhood—and any major regulatory or community issues. The architect should outline the general approach for the project in terms of how the buildings could be located; the number, size, and placement of the dwelling units; the number and location of parking spaces; and any façade or other design features being considered.

The next step is to identify and document the overall goals of the green building effort in a concise statement. At a minimum, the project goals should include reducing utility bills for tenants, increasing durability for the owner, and creating healthier environments for residents. Other goals could include providing tenants with a way to interact with nature, assisting in fundraising for the project, supporting larger community-wide greening efforts, or providing features in the project that make it more palatable to the neighbors or elected officials. The goal statement then provides direction to the design team in setting more specific performance criteria and evaluating various strategies, systems, or materials for inclusion in the project.

Through the course of the charrette, the goal statement should be refined into clear, specific, and measurable performance criteria. Examples of the performance criteria include:

- *Neighborhood connections:* Bicycle racks should be installed for 50 percent or more of the dwelling units; safe walkways should be created through the development; clear connections should be provided to public sidewalks leading to neighborhood facilities.
- *Energy efficiency and renewable energy use:* Building code requirements for energy efficiency should be exceeded by at least 15 percent; at least 10 percent of annual electricity needs should be provided through on-site energy generation.
- *Resource efficiency:* A set number or value of recycled-content materials should be used; 50 percent or more of the construction waste should be recycled; water use should be reduced by at least 15 percent.
- *Durability:* Improve the durability of units through the incorporation of products with long-term warranties.
- *Indoor air quality:* Introduction of toxins should be avoided to the greatest extent possible; only materials with no added urea formaldehyde should be used; sufficient introduction of fresh air into the living space, and regular removal of stale air should be provided.

Using Rating Systems to Guide the Charrette Discussion

Guidelines and rating systems provide a way to structure the charrette and to move efficiently through the various topics of green building. There are many good green building rating programs used in various parts of the country. Examples include Seattle's SeaGreen program (Washington); the city of Portland's Green Affordable Housing guidelines (Oregon); Alameda County Waste Management Authority's New Home Construction and Multifamily green building guidelines (California); EarthCraft's

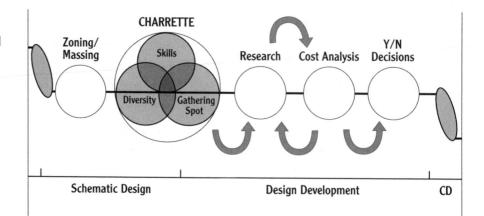

FIGURE 2.5. The charrette is followed by research and cost analysis to support decision making around the most effective green strategies.

Traugott Terrace (Seattle, Washington)
Archdiocesan Housing Authority

Traugott Terrace was built to provide "clean and sober" housing in Seattle, Washington. The project includes 38 studio and one-bedroom apartments for very low-income individuals, as well as 12 transitional single-room occupancy (SRO) units and common spaces.

The entire project team held an initial charrette to determine the project's green building goals (in hopes of obtaining the LEED (Leadership in Energy and Environmental Design) incentive funding provided by Seattle City Light). Participants included the design team, the developer, client representatives, Seattle Housing Authority, and the local utility. The charrette provided the opportunity for the entire team to establish its goals and strategies for green building, as well as the chance to create buyoff among all parties.

As the design progressed, based on its initial goals, the team was able to incorporate various strategies that enabled the project to become the first LEED-certified affordable housing project in the country. Although the funding to pursue a LEED certification did not arise until midway through the construction documents stage, the team attributed their ability to achieve LEED certification at such a late stage to critical decisions made early. Without the charrette and initial goal-setting it would have been difficult to achieve LEED certification.

Single and Multifamily programs used in Georgia and other parts of the Southeast; and New Jersey's Green Homes program.

The two national rating systems that best apply to affordable housing are the Green Communities Initiative criteria developed by Enterprise Community Partners and the Leadership in Energy and Environmental Design (LEED) rating systems for new construction (LEED NC) and for homes (LEED for Homes) developed and administered by the U.S. Green Building Council. While each program is slightly different in terms of the types of measures recommended and how different green items are allocated points (or credits in the LEED ratings system), each addresses the five core categories of green building—site, water, energy, materials, and indoor environmental quality. These categories and specific strategies are discussed in more detail in Chapter 3.

In the charrette, the facilitator can describe the intent behind each of the points and explain what design strategies would be needed for the project to earn the points. It is essential, however, for the facilitator to keep in mind what the goals are for the project and to avoid having the rating system either dominate the charrette process or lead the team to choose items that are not a good fit for the project just for the sake of earning credits.

The remainder of the charrette is used to determine how to best meet the performance standards—drawing on the expertise and experience in the room—with the goal of identifying several robust possibilities for integration and synergy, such as the following:

- Designing the building to have a narrow footprint (50 feet or less) and exterior walkways and stairs, thus creating a situation in which natural ventilation and ample daylight nearly eliminate the need for mechanical cooling or artificial lighting during the day.
- Designing the HVAC system around a central boiler, which produces hot water for both domestic use (sinks, tubs, and showers) and space heating through either a radiant (wall or floor mounted radiators) or forced-air system. This approach both eliminates the need for individual hot-water heaters and removes two sources of combustion (the water heater and the furnace) from the individual dwellings, thus reducing venting requirements and eliminating the potential for exposure to combustion gases.
- Designing the landscaping to reduce stormwater runoff through grading the site to direct water toward recessed areas, or paving walkways and fire access lanes with permeable materials, thus reducing the cost of stormwater infrastructure.
- Placing the laundry rooms or management office in a central location to increase interaction among neighbors, help build a sense of community, and improve safety.

During the charrette, the design team and developer should also anticipate the type of postoccupancy maintenance that will be provided and how the residents will use the building, given their demographic characteristics and the past experience of the developer. To that end it is important to solicit input from property management and maintenance personnel. If the building's design intent does not match the level of maintenance to be provided, or the ability of the residents to maintain their units, the benefits expected in design may not be achieved or may quickly diminish. The intent of certain features such as programmable thermostats, occupancy sensors, and automatic bathroom fans may even backfire if residents and maintenance staff are not informed about what the features are or how to use them. Chapter 4 provides more information on operations and maintenance issues.

Concluding the Charrette

After the performance criteria and/or items in the selected rating system have been discussed and decisions have been made about applicability to the project (yes, no, or maybe), the facilitator should make sure that the notes about the discussion and decisions made are clear. Responsibility for follow-up research, cost analysis, and energy or daylight modeling should be determined and agreed upon by the team members, with due dates established. A follow-up meeting should be tentatively set for a date within the next one to three months (depending on the status of the project). Within a week after the charrette, a copy of the checklist with the notes and responsibility assignments should be sent to all team members. In the weeks and months ahead, the charrette summary and checklist of green building items becomes a working document to guide team members and track the green building items as the project moves through design development and into construction documents.

POST-CHARRETTE FOLLOW-UP

Post-charrette follow-up is as important as the charrette itself. There is a tendency to feel that the green issues were fully addressed during the charrette. In truth, many decisions must be made as the project moves into the design development and construction document phases. Chapter 3 provides detail on recommended best practices in green affordable housing design and outlines many of the interrelationships between building systems, materials, air quality, and environmental protection that should be taken into consideration. Major efforts following the charrette are research into the viability and cost of various green strategies identified in the charrette. After the research has been completed, decisions can be made about the final pool of green strategies, systems, and materials.

Research, Analysis, and Decision Making

During the charrette it is common to identify a number of items as "maybes." Immediately after the charrette, the team should focus on determining whether these items are or are not a good fit for the project. Making these decisions requires research into whether the item is truly applicable to or feasible for the project and what additional costs are involved. Of particular importance are the major building systems. The mechanical engineer or green building consultant should prepare an initial energy analysis using RemRate, EnergyPlus, or other ResNet-compliant modeling software. Two or three optional approaches for the major energy systems and building envelope should be modeled to determine what approach is most energy-efficient. Combining this information with cost data from the contractor enables the project manager to give direction to the architect, mechanical engineer, and structural engineer about what system to pursue.

Research on specific structural, insulation, and roofing products should also take place shortly after the charrette and before the completion of design development. Specification of the exact products for paint, flooring, and other finishes does not need to occur until the construction document phase, but it is still important to prepare an initial list during design development in the event that material choices have an impact on other aspects of the building. For example, deciding to use exposed concrete in public corridors instead of carpet is an excellent way to reduce overall material use, dramatically reduce maintenance, and provide additional thermal mass in the structure, but modifications to the floor assembly may be needed to avoid excess sound transmittance.

Near the end of design development, a follow-up meeting should be held to review the green items and identify whether any additional research or analysis is needed before final decisions can be made about what strategies, systems, and materials will be incorporated into the project. At this point, enough technical and cost information should be available to make decisions about trade-offs—for instance, which has more lasting overall value: High-efficiency windows or a Cool Roof? A more efficient boiler or photovoltaic panels? Dedicated kitchen and bathroom ventilation or no-VOC (no volatile organic compounds) paint? This also the time to look for additional synergies: Can the excavation needed for below-grade parking be used to improve the financial viability of a geothermal system? Can the HVAC components be downsized because the building has a tight envelope and is designed for natural ventilation for most of the year? Can the number of storm drain inlets and the amount of piping be reduced or eliminated all together by providing a bioswale or green roof? Once these issues have been thoroughly reviewed, adjustments should be made to the plans and project cost estimates.

Construction Documents and Specifications

The construction documents dictate what the contractor is expected to include in the project, so it is essential that the green items are included in the specifications. The draft specifications should be reviewed to check consistency with the selected performance criteria or rating system. Effective specifications provide detail clarification regarding the green aspects—percentage of recycled content material, flow rate per minute, maximum levels of VOCs—to avoid substitutions during construction of materials that are similar but that lack the green qualities. Other items, such as construction waste recycling and construction air quality management, need to be included in the general section of contractor requirements.

For the items that the owner would like to specify but which have not been included in the plan because of cost concerns, a useful approach is to specify a limited number (7-10) of "add alternates." Both a conventional and an alternate green product are specified, and the contractor obtains costs for both. The owner then has the option of making a choice at the time the product needs to be purchased rather than when the drawings are completed. This approach works best for finish materials that are purchased and installed near the end of the project.

The person responsible for the green items should stay engaged during the construction process to provide clarification on what certain materials are and where to source products, and to assist the contractor with verification or documentation of credits earned in a rating program.

CONCLUSION

Integrating green building practices—from the mission of the organization to the project specifications—requires a thoughtful and thorough process. The stakeholders involved must come to the process with an open mind and willingness to view the design and development process from a different vantage point. Conducted well, the integrated design process is a powerful tool for rethinking how we design housing and how to better align the projects with the desire for safe, decent, affordable, and environmentally sustainable housing.

NOTE

1. True value engineering identifies ways to achieve the same goal at less cost and could be compared to a design/build effort based on performance standards.

CHAPTER 3

Best Practices in Green Design

Green building encompasses a wide range of design practices, building systems integration, product specification, and construction techniques. This chapter outlines the green building practices that are most applicable to affordable housing. Generally, affordable housing projects utilize readily available, low- to medium-cost materials and systems. Custom products, such as cast-in-place recycled glass terrazzo, or elaborate energy system approaches, such as nighttime ice production, displacement ventilation, or double-glazed facades, that may be found in commercial buildings or custom residential projects are not usually considered because of cost and a desire to maintain simplicity in operations and maintenance. The challenge is to identify opportunities for innovation through the integration of good architectural and mechanical system design with thoughtful and strategic selection of materials, appliances, lighting, and equipment.

We describe the best practices in green design in five main categories: (1) location and site, (2) water conservation, (3) energy efficiency and renewable energy, (4) resource-efficient materials, and (5) health and indoor air quality. These categories are similar to the structure of the U.S. Green Building Council's Leadership in Energy and Environmental Design (LEED) rating system and encompass the issues addressed in the Enterprise Community Partners' Green Communities Initiative criteria; EarthCraft's Single and Multifamily programs; Alameda County Waste Management Authority's New Home Construction and Multifamily green building guidelines; and many other guidelines in use around the country.

While each of the green building topic areas is described separately here, it is important to follow the integrated design process described in Chapter 2, and to keep in mind that the various design strategies have interrelated impacts. For example, designing for natural daylight both improves livability and reduces electricity use, and well-located trees can both shade buildings in the summer and reduce stormwater runoff year round. The integrated design process is the best way to capture these synergies and to identify green building practices that derive the greatest benefit at the lowest additional cost. Furthermore, these strategies are only effective if they stay functional over the long term. Chapter 4 outlines how to put a maintenance and operations plan in place so that the benefits continue to accrue to the tenants and owners well into the future.

Specific practices are highlighted in this chapter, based on the decade of experience by Global Green staff members in providing technical assistance to affordable housing developers and their design teams. The recommended practices are generally cost-effective, provide clear benefits, and are compatible with the type of construction and maintenance common in the full range of affordable housing developments—from single-family houses to high-rise senior or SRO developments. However, each project is unique and the design team should combine local knowledge with guidance provided by green building rating systems, energy models, materials databases, and other tools to determine the most appropriate strategies for a given project type, resident population, and financial structure. The recommended best practices in this chapter are organized generally to follow the sequence of the design and development process.

SITE SELECTION AND DESIGN

Site selection sets the framework for many future choices related to green building. The type of development that surrounds the site; the shape and orientation of the site; the context of nearby urbanized, agricultural, or natural areas; and local climate conditions all establish a unique set of conditions that should be folded into the green building dialogue.

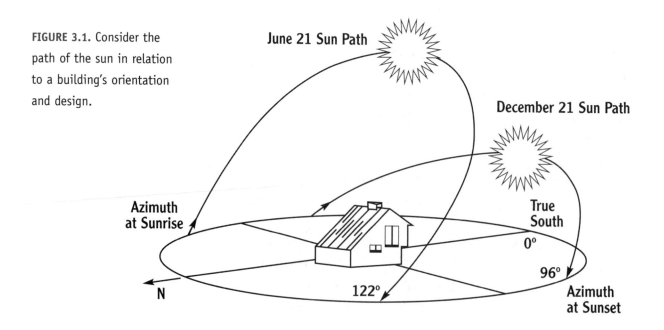

FIGURE 3.1. Consider the path of the sun in relation to a building's orientation and design.

Consider the following factors when visiting potential sites:

- *Solar exposure:* In the Northern Hemisphere, the south side of a building receives the most sun, providing free heat and light to the building. Eastern and western exposures also experience solar gain, with more heat usually experienced on the west.
- *Topography features:* Slopes and patterns of landforms such as ridges, swales, and lowlands can be used to reduce the intensity of winter winds or summer sun or to capture stormwater.
- *Hydrology and soils:* Existing drainage patterns reveal how water moves through the site. This information, combined with data on the quality and porosity of soils, is essential when planning for rainwater capture, stormwater management, and environmentally friendly wastewater treatment. Existing wetlands can be preserved or restored to filter surface runoff and provide natural habitat.
- *Microclimate:* Two sites within the same city or region can differ significantly due to microclimate effects caused by adjacent buildings, parking lots, or topography. Tall buildings can create urban wind tunnels, parking lots can absorb and radiate heat, and low-lying areas can generate cooler temperatures or increased humidity. Knowledge of these issues should influence building massing and the locations of entrances, courtyards, and windows.
- *Services and transit:* Nearby services such as stores, churches, schools, and hospitals, and public transit will enable residents to tend to daily needs more easily and cost-effectively.

FIGURE 3.2. The Annie Mitchell development in Aspen, CO, includes trails and roads leading to bike and pedestrian trails into town.

Photo courtesy of Lisa McManigal Delaney

A site adjacent to existing development, with access to existing infrastructure and proximity to services and public transportation, is preferred. But not all sites can meet these criteria. Rural housing is often built on more remote sites or in agricultural communities where higher-density development is uncommon or not permitted and transit service is infrequent or not provided. In either situation, understanding how site selection impacts on residents' ability to access jobs or services and on the developer's ability to make the most efficient use of the land should lead developers and public agency staff to give each potential site serious consideration before the decision to go forward with a specific location is made.

URBAN INFILL

Infill development adds value to established neighborhoods by reusing structures already on the site, placing new buildings in existing communities, and developing underutilized parcels. In many instances, new development makes better use of the land by converting land that had low-intensity activity, such as parking lots or storage, to medium- or high-density housing. Potential infill sites can be vacant, developed below the level permitted by code, or can contain abandoned or obsolete buildings.

Infill projects reduce the need for driving, slow the development of greenfield sites such as prime agricultural land and open space, and reduce the need to invest in new infrastructure at the city or town perimeter. While infill development offers many benefits, suitable sites can be hard to find, the assembly of multiple small parcels can be time consuming, and the permitting and construction process is often more complicated. However, greenfield development often passes the costs of sewer, water, and road extension to taxpayers, and the provision of schools, fire protection, and emergency services to less dense areas is often more costly to local governments. Greenfield development also has higher environmental impacts, such as fragmenting wildlife habitat and exacerbating stormwater volume and water quality issues with new roads, driveways, and at-grade parking.

Many infill sites are classified as "brownfields"—parcels that are either contaminated by previous uses or carry the possibility of contamination and the associated legal concerns. Contamination on brownfields may be from waste dumping or from leaks of stored diesel fuel, gasoline, pesticides, or other chemicals into the soil or groundwater. Brownfield sites may also lack adequate infrastructure and transportation access. The presence of pollutants is identified through a Phase I environmental site assessment (ESA), and if needed, a Phase II ESA, which includes soil or water testing and lays out a plan for remediation consistent with applicable local, regional, state, and federal agencies. Even when contamination can be mitigated to meet state and federal standards, community groups may express concerns about the health effects of living on former brownfields. Federal and state brownfield grants, loans, and tax incentives can be used to offset some of the costs associated with assessment and remediation.

Another common type of infill parcel is "grayfields"—economically obsolescent retail or commercial areas that may not be contaminated but which require demolition or reuse of existing structures, rezoning, and upgrades to roads and utility capacity. Development of brownfield and grayfield parcels revitalizes urban neighborhoods by putting unused or underused parcels to more productive, community-beneficial uses.

CONNECTING TO AND BUILDING COMMUNITY

An affordable housing project should be an integral part of its surrounding neighborhood and add value to the community fabric. The building should be placed to contribute to the character of the street, and if possible include a community space, daycare, small store, or other facility that can be used by members of the greater community. Projects that include joint use of facilities, such as a recreation facility shared by residents and a nearby school, help add to the integration of the residents with the surrounding community. Such projects also reduce the need to develop other facilities nearby that serve duplicative uses.

The walking or cycling route to the nearest community services and transportation stop should be identified, to ensure a safe path of travel to and from the development. A general rule of thumb is that people will walk fifteen minutes or a quarter mile to a bus stop, and thirty minutes or a half mile to a subway or commuter rail line.

The safety of residents should be given serious consideration so that security measures and green strategies do not conflict. For example, if residents keep their windows closed for fear of intruders, natural ventilation strategies are negated. To reconcile these competing concerns, locate exterior circulation and outdoor areas to be visible from within buildings; orient kitchens, living rooms, or laundry facilities toward courtyards so residents can keep an eye on public areas; provide one or two designated entrances so that staff and residents are able to monitor who enters and leaves the building; and design hallways, stairways, and other common spaces to be easily observable from the exterior. If necessary, install security screens on ground-floor windows and doors so residents can benefit from natural ventilation without sacrificing security. Consider providing playground equipment or community garden plots—giving residents reasons to use common spaces and providing a method of building community among the residents. Most importantly, take cues from surrounding buildings to identify successful ways to handle security concerns.

INTEGRATING AFFORDABLE WITH THE SURROUNDING COMMUNITY

Chestnut Court (West Oakland, California)
BRIDGE Housing Corporation

Located in West Oakland, Chestnut Court is a HOPE VI project that uses careful site design and programming to fit into and enhance its urban neighborhood. Completed in May 2003 by BRIDGE Housing Corporation, the one-block project consists of 72 new residential units in flats as well as townhomes located above mixed-use spaces including retail, community services, and childcare. The design of the site and community spaces increases the sense of community through numerous details. A new private street connects pedestrians to tuck-under parking as well as common outdoor spaces, including a playground and basketball court. The aesthetic of the surrounding industrial and loft neighborhood of busy Grand Avenue is echoed through large windows, corrugated metal siding, and exposed concrete piers. Adjacent small private homes are acknowledged through a smaller scale of buildings on the side streets. Access to public transportation is easy, as Chestnut Court is located at two major bus thoroughfares.

WATER QUALITY

Every building site is part of a watershed. Water that falls onto a development's roof, parking lot, and landscaping eventually flows into adjacent low-lying areas, creeks, rivers, lakes, or oceans. Disturbing topsoil, removing permeable surfaces, and introducing chemical fertilizers and pesticides, motor oil, vehicle coolant, and pet waste all have negative impacts on water quality and the vitality of the local watershed. Chemical pollutants, increased sediment, and altered water temperature can disrupt water ecosystems and lead to unhealthy conditions for fish, animals, and humans. Increased stormwater volume, created by paving over permeable surfaces, can overwhelm the capacity of the storm drainage system (causing flooding) or water treatment infrastructure (resulting in the release of polluted water).

Stormwater infrastructure varies from region to region and from city to city. Many East Coast cities have combined stormwater and sanitary sewer systems. The benefit of combined systems is that stormwater goes to a treatment facility prior to being released into nearby rivers, lakes, or the ocean. During periods of intense rainfall, however, the treatment facility may be overloaded, resulting in the release of both stormwater and partially treated sewage. In combined-system locations, the most critical strategies are to reduce the volume of water and to slow the rate at which water enters the storm sewer to prevent overloading.

Most West Coast cities—San Francisco being one exception—have separate sewer and stormwater systems. The separation usually prevents system overloading, although some rainwater can still enter the sewer system through cracks in underground pipes. However, stormwater is usually not filtered or treated before it flows into the nearest body of water. In locations with separate systems, the most critical strategy is to remove contaminants from stormwater, either naturally or mechanically, before the water leaves the development site. The first half inch of water from each storm event—the first flush—is the most important to address, as this water contains the greatest number of pollutants from roofs, paved areas, and landscaping. In locations where the storm drain system is outdated or underdimensioned, it is also important to reduce the volume of water leaving the development site to prevent neighborhood flooding.

Practices to improve water quality include:

- During construction use U.S. Environmental Protection Agency (EPA) or local best management practices such as minimizing the area of soil disruption, preserving topsoil, installing silt fences, and providing traps or filters on adjacent storm drain inlets.
- Maintain the permeability of unbuilt portions of the site. Permeable surfaces such as gravel, decomposed granite, mulched landscape beds, and turf areas let rainwater percolate into the soil. Microorganisms in the soil then filter water as it moves slowly down to the water table.

- In parking areas, pave only the drive aisles with hard surfaces, using gravel or turf for the parking spaces. For areas that require a hard surface, consider using pavers, porous asphalt, or porous concrete instead of conventional asphalt or concrete. Pave little-used vehicular areas, such as overflow parking and emergency access lanes with porous surfaces. Slope parking areas to drain toward landscaped areas, or provide grease traps and filters at drainage collection areas.

- For pedestrian surfaces such as walkways and patios, use pavers, gravel or other aggregate, decomposed granite, or wooden planks.

- Direct stormwater runoff into recessed areas and vegetated swales for percolation and biofiltration. Route down spouts into gravel pits or other natural infiltration areas. When integrated into the site and landscape design, these systems reduce the need for conventional curb openings, pipes, and filters, thus lowering overall project costs.

- Capture a portion of stormwater to reduce the flow rate during storm events and to reduce the use of potable water for irrigation. Cisterns and rain barrels are common approaches for water storage. Green roofs also store and filter water via the soil medium and allow excess water to be released slowly over several days. A green roof can capture and retain up to 75 percent of a 1-inch rainfall in the plants and growing medium.[1]

- Plant trees to reduce peak stormwater flow by capturing water in the leaf canopy, branches, and trunk. One hundred trees can retain about 100,000 gallons of rainfall annually that would otherwise run off into the drainage system.[2]

- Design irrigation to avoid overspray onto paved areas by using drip emitters, bubblers, or microspray sprinkler heads. Irrigation systems that spray onto sidewalks and roads can carry high concentrations of fertilizer, pesticides, pet droppings, and other pollutants into the storm drainage system. In many locations, dry-weather runoff is more contaminated than wet-weather flows.

LANDSCAPING

Properly designed landscaping cuts water costs, reduces soil erosion, captures stormwater, and produces food. For the landscape to provide functional as well as aesthetic benefits, the design of the site should be considered in tandem with the building design. The following practices and strategies should be considered:

- Preserve existing trees, shrubs, and topsoil whenever possible. If excavation is required, remove and store uncontaminated native topsoil for later use in landscaping and drainage filtration systems. Fence the full area of any preserved

FIGURE 3.3. The bioswale system at Nuevo Amenecer helps improve the quality of water draining off the site.
Photo courtesy of South County Housing

FIGURE 3.4. The New York City–based nonprofit organization Earth Pledge assists affordable housing developers and designers in designing and installing green roofs, such as this one on the Rheingold Gardens development in Brooklyn, NY.
Photo courtesy of Earth Pledge

trees' root zone (roughly the same size as the crown) during construction to avoid root compaction damage from heavy machinery.

- Consider the path of the sun and the location of both new and existing buildings when designing landscaping. Place shade- or sun-tolerant plants as appropriate and locate trees to shade buildings from summer sun. Trees can also shade parking lots, play areas, and sidewalks, thus reducing the ambient temperature of the entire development.

- Use native plant species, which are better adapted to local pests, soil, and climate. Native gardens can create pockets of biodiversity by providing food and shelter for native insects and birds. Thoughtful plant selection and use of native and drought-tolerant species can result in a reduced water use of over 30 percent as compared with conventional landscaping, especially in the arid West and Southwest.

- Edible landscaping or community gardens are a way to provide a functional landscape that provides both an aesthetic benefit and a fresh, healthy food source for residents.

- Design landscaping with security in mind. Consider a two-tiered system, consisting of trees higher than 10 feet combined with groundcover lower than 2 feet, thus providing shade and natural greenery while denying cover for criminal activity and loitering.

- Do not plant trees or shrubs with poisonous leaves or fruit, as children are present at most developments.

- Provide space to capture stormwater runoff, utilizing the site's natural hydrology.
- Use lawn or turf in limited, high-value locations, such as children's play areas or adjacent to a community space.
- Slope landscape areas away from building foundations to prevent moisture buildup in foundations or basements.

BUILDING ORIENTATION AND MASSING

The orientation and massing of the building has a major impact on the viability of other green strategies such as passive heating and cooling, natural ventilation, use of natural daylight, and solar hot water or photovoltaic systems. The basic approach is very simple: create thin buildings oriented with the long side of the structure facing south. A south-facing orientation provides the greatest solar access, which can then be put to maximum use through the placement and sizing of thermal mass, windows, roof overhangs, window awnings, and solar systems. A chiefly south-facing building limits the façade area exposed to low (and thus difficult-to-control) morning and evening sun.

The basic shape and mass of the building should further promote green objectives. Narrow floor plates—less than 50 feet in width—are optimal for utilizing natural cross-ventilation for cooling and passive solar systems for heating. Open floor plans assist in natural ventilation and daylight strategies. Exterior walkways and stairways reduce the amount of space that needs to be heated or cooled. Courtyards create a pocket of cool air that can augment the natural flow of air through dwelling units. Balconies can shade windows below, and roof overhangs can both provide shade and direct water away from the building foundation.

FIGURE 3.5. The Nueva Vista project in Santa Cruz, CA, features narrow buildings in a courtyard design, a daycare facility, and reuse of an included public street.

Photo courtesy of Van Meter Williams Pollack

PASSIVE HEATING AND COOLING

Passive heating and cooling utilize the heat created by the sun to warm living spaces; prevailing winds and air buoyancy (warm air rises) to provide natural ventilation; and the cooling effect that trees and plants provide through a combination of shade and evapotranspiration to reduce the need for mechanical heating, cooling, or ventilation systems. Passive solar design possibilities are often overlooked during site selection and building design, in urban areas, as the incorrect assumption is that passive solar systems are impractical in a dense, constrained setting. Passive solar gains can be captured in the mass of the overall building, in stairwells, or on the sides of buildings with good solar exposure. Also, the benefits of solar radiation are not limited to locations with a large annual percentage of sunny days, as solar gain can still occur on overcast days or when outdoor temperatures are well below freezing.

Taking advantage of the sun's free heat reduces the need for and the cost of operating conventional heating equipment. Passive solar systems use thermal storage materials such as concrete or masonry that are strategically placed to absorb the heat of the sun during the day and then release it during the cooler nighttime hours. Such systems may require additional building mass, increased insulation, and possibly more involvement by occupants or maintenance staff to open or close window blinds at certain times.

Direct thermal mass is mass that is in the path of sunlight, such as floors adjacent to south-facing windows. Concrete or tile floors are the most commonly used material, with darker materials generally absorbing more heat. Indirect thermal storage is mass that receives little direct sunlight but which can absorb ambient heat during hot parts of the day and release it at cooler times. Indirect thermal mass can be placed anywhere in a building, and can be any color. A thin layer of concrete can be added to upper floors, for instance.

Passive ventilation reduces the need for air-conditioning and fans, and improves indoor air quality by supplementing mechanical ventilation during temperate periods. Strategies include designing window location and floor plans for cross-ventilation; using awnings, louvers, horizontal fins, or trees to block direct sun on windows; and minimizing window exposure to low-angle afternoon summer sun. Recommended passive heating and cooling strategies include the following:

- Optimize the amount of south-facing windows adjacent to thermal mass.
- Orient buildings to capture prevailing winds.
- Place smaller window openings on the sides of buildings that face prevailing winds and larger openings (doors, larger windows) on the opposite sides to increase pressure differentials and facilitate cross-ventilation.
- Provide overhangs or shading devices on the south-side roof lines of buildings to shade windows, doors, porches, and patios from hot midday sun. Overhangs on

the east and west sides of buildings are much less effective because of the long sun angle in the morning and evening.

- Consider use of operable exterior blinds or other shading devices on west-facing windows in hot climates.
- Landscape with deciduous trees to provide shade in the hot parts of the year and capture warmth in the winter. Shade is most needed on the west side of a building, which receives sun on hot afternoons.
- Place trellises or arbors on or adjacent to buildings so climbing plants can shade patios, walkways, and windows.
- In warm climates, use exterior cladding and roofing materials with high reflectivity (light-colored) to reduce solar gain.
- Install an a light-colored ENERGY STAR® or Cool Roof to reduce heat transfer into attics or top-floor living units.

FIGURE 3.6. Window overhangs, such as these on the Bellevue Court project in Trenton, NJ, can be a design element while also providing shading to cool a building.

Photo courtesy of Darren Molnar-Port, NJDCA-NJ Green Homes Office

BUILDING ENVELOPE

After the benefits of orientation and massing have been maximized, the next area to address is the building envelope. The building envelope includes the walls, vapor barrier, insulation, windows, doors, roof, foundation, structure, and flooring. A well-designed envelope should protect structural members from moisture buildup, reduce thermal transfer and air infiltration, bring in daylight, and prevent pest problems. One of the greatest challenges is to create a tight, well-insulated envelope to save energy while at the same time providing sufficient window area for natural ventilation and daylight.

In new construction projects, the project should, at a minimum, attempt to achieve certification through the ENERGY STAR Homes program. ENERGY STAR certification can be achieved either by meeting the prescriptive requirements of the most appropriate Builder Option Package (BOP) for the project, or by demonstrating, through a computer simulation, that the project is at least 15 percent more efficient than the current International Energy Conservation Code (IECC). In addition to meeting criteria for envelope design and building system performance, achieving ENERGY STAR certification requires that the project be field inspected and tested by a qualified Home Energy Rating System (HERS) rater. The role of the HERS rater is to verify that the insulation meets the required R-value and is installed correctly, that the ductwork is fully sealed, and that the overall building envelope is free of major leaks or other sources of air infiltration. Many states have programs that offer both technical assistance and financial incentives to projects that achieve ENERGY STAR certification.

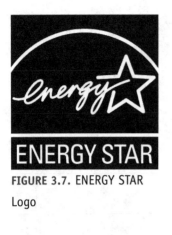

FIGURE 3.7. ENERGY STAR
Logo

FIGURE 3.8. Look for
windows that have been
certified by the NFRC.

Image courtesy of the National
Fenestration Rating Council

Whether the decision to pursue ENERGY STAR® certification is made or not, the following envelope design strategies should be considered:

- Specify insulation in walls, floors, ceilings, and the foundation that meet or exceed the requirements in the International Energy Conservation Code (IECC). Consider use of blown cellulose insulation, which provides high R-value thermal resistance, lower air infiltration, and excellent acoustic performance.

- Select double-paned, low-e (low-emissivity) windows with a U-value (a measure of heat transfer through the glass, usually related to the loss of interior heat) and a solar heat gain coefficient (SHGC, a measure of how much of the solar energy striking the window is transmitted through the window as heat) appropriate for the local climate. Window air leakage (AL) rates should be less than 0.3. The National Fenestration Rating Council (NFRC) should certify ratings, such as on ENERGY STAR windows, which must be NFRC certified in order to receive the ENERGY STAR label.

- Use raised heel trusses and two- or three-stud corners to ensure that sufficient insulation is provided at eaves and corners and that thermal breaks in the envelope are minimized.

- Fill all gaps around windows and doors, between walls and floors, and all penetrations with a low-VOC caulk or foam that is resistant to ultraviolet light. Special attention should be given to seal places where wiring, plumbing, and ducts penetrate floors or exterior walls, and around vent or utility shafts, siding, and windows so that weep screeds and drip holes do not get clogged.

- Use a moisture barrier or install a housewrap to reduce air infiltration.

- Consider the use of structural insulated panels (SIPs), which place foam between two sheets of plywood or oriented strand board (OSB). SIPs have a similar R-value to a framed wall but actually create a better thermal barrier because they provide a more continuous layer of insulation.

- If using steel studs, either provide a thermal break or include a layer of rigid insulation on the exterior. Steel is extremely efficient at transmitting heat, counteracting the effects of insulation, and, under certain conditions, creating condensation on interior walls.

WEATHERIZATION

Every building has gaps in its thermal envelope—exterior walls, windows, doors, roof, and foundation. Even a well-insulated home can lose as much as 30 percent of its heat through small cracks around door and window jambs, thresholds, and frames, which are responsible for the largest waste of energy in residential buildings. Combined, these gaps can be the equivalent of having a 2-foot-wide hole cut in the side of the building.

The cost of a poorly sealed building goes beyond energy losses. Leaks can cause moisture buildup inside of walls, damaging wood framing, electrical systems, and insulation, and creating a condition that fosters mold growth. Sealing a house is the simplest and most cost-effective way to reduce energy use. Seal all visible openings or cracks with a low-VOC exterior grade caulk, weatherstrip doors and windows, and replace or repair gaskets and latches. Caulking and weatherstripping usually pay for themselves in energy savings within one year.

Sealing ductwork can improve equipment efficiency by as much as 20 to 30 percent. In addition to wasting energy, leaky ducts can also result in health problems due to pressure differences between the interior and exterior of a building. If negative pressure is created in living spaces, smoke from fireplaces, combustion gases from furnaces, and fumes from stored cleaning supplies or paint can be sucked back into the building. Reseal accessible joints in ductwork with mastic, patch any punctures, and replace damaged areas. Exposed hot- and cold-water pipes and ductwork should be insulated to avoid energy losses and unwanted condensation.

BUILDING INTERIOR AND FLOOR PLANS

The organization of interior spaces should support the passive design strategies and overall resource conservation. Floor plans should allow for the free flow of air through the unit by creating a line-of-sight connection between the windows expected to provide air input and exhaust. Open, flexible floor plans allow for the dwelling unit to accommodate many different types of tenants and be adaptable over time. The main principles of universal design should be incorporated, in that the design should (1) be useful to people with diverse abilities, (2) accommodate a wide range of preferences and abilities, (3) minimize hazards, and (4) provide appropriate size and space to reach and manipulate items in the home regardless of body size, posture, or mobility. Stacking plumbing, vents, and major structural elements reduces the use of building materials.

BUILDING SYSTEMS

Once the building design is established, the next major area to address is the major building systems. Passive cooling and heating, daylighting, and good envelope design reduces heating and cooling demands placed on building systems, but in most climate zones, some mechanical heating and cooling systems are still needed. Careful selection and sizing of equipment is critical, as heating and cooling account for about 56 percent of the annual energy bill for U.S. residences.[3]

Heating, ventilating, and air-conditioning (HVAC) systems need to be designed with thermal comfort, energy efficiency, life-cycle cost, and the need for healthy indoor air in mind. A well-ventilated living space features the frequent exhaust of indoor air to remove pollutants and reduce moisture and the regular introduction of fresh air.

Historically, many affordable housing units were designed with individual heating and cooling systems. A forced-air furnace or electric-resistance heater, an evaporative swamp cooler or window-mounted air conditioner, and individual 30- to 40-gallon tank hot-water heaters are common. As energy codes have improved and fuel costs have increased, a growing number of projects are turning to central systems for domestic hot-water and space heating. With this approach, hot water is pumped through the building for use in showers and sinks and, when needed, in floor or wall radiators. A central hot-water-based system permits elimination of gas lines to individual units, as appliances and air-conditioning (if provided) can be electric. Another approach is to use a high-efficiency heat pump for both heating and cooling. Either strategy improves energy efficiency and can lower utility costs by 15 percent or more.

Energy modeling is a valuable and effective tool in the decision-making process. Several alternative options for major systems can be defined during the design charrette and then modeled to identify what option is projected to deliver the greatest savings over the life of the systems for the least installed cost.

When considering alternatives for the major building systems, also consider the impacts on utility metering and utility allowances (see Chapter 5). Installing separate electric and gas meters gives residents more incentive to conserve resources. However, master metering provides a way to average out utility costs among residents, which is valuable if the owner is responsible for the bills, as is typical for senior, single-room occupancy (SRO), and special needs developments. Providing multiple meters also requires space and additional piping and wiring. In some locations, submetering is permitted, a choice that offers the energy efficiency of central HVAC systems and the accountability of individual meters.

Recommended strategies include the following:

- Install ceiling fans in the living room and bedrooms to augment air movement in buildings designed with passive heating and cooling principles. In mild climates, fans can help eliminate the need for air-conditioning. In hotter climates, they can reduce the need to use air-conditioning.
- Use RemRate or other Residential Energy Services Network (ResNet) accredited software to simulate building energy demand and estimate equipment needs for low-rise buildings, and EnergyPlus or other DOE-2-compatible software for buildings over three stories.[4]
- Provide at least 15 cubic feet per minute (cfm) of fresh air per occupant, consis-

tent with the American Society of Heating, Refrigerating and Air-Conditioning Engineers (ASHRAE) standard 62.2, to dilute pollutants and prevent moisture buildup.

- Determine the heating and cooling loads of the building using Air Conditioning Contractors of America (ACCA) Manual J.
- Size ductwork using ACCA Manual D and locate ductwork in conditioned spaces. If ductwork must run outside conditioned areas, it should be well sealed and insulated.
- Size the HVAC equipment using ACCA Manual S to prevent the purchase of oversized equipment that may short-cycle (constantly turn on and off), which leads to substandard comfort, buildup of moisture in the equipment, and shorter equipment life.
- Seal ductwork with fiber-reinforced mastic. Do not use cloth duct tape, foil tape, or silicon.
- Balance the air supply being distributed to each room on the basis of the calculated room loads. Make sure return grills and ducts are adequate to maintain the desired airflow, provide balanced flow to each room, and ensure that air has a path to the return grill, even if doors are closed.
- Specify ENERGY STAR®–rated heating and cooling equipment.
- Specify hot-water heaters with an energy factor (EF) of 0.8 or better, and install a drainwater heat recovery unit.
- Test HVAC systems after installation to ensure that the refrigerant charge is correct and the system is balanced.
- Provide thermostats that are easy to use and accessible.
- Consider hydronic radiant heat systems, as an alternate to electric resistance or gas-fired-furnace forced-air systems.
- Consider using whole-house fans for single-family homes in climates with significant swings between afternoon and evening temperatures.
- In the dry Southwest and mountain regions, consider evaporative coolers as an energy-saving alternative to conventional air conditioners.
- In climates with significant heating needs, consider a heat recovery ventilation unit, which transfers heat from the air being exhausted from the dwelling to the air entering the heating system.
- In climates with both a high number of heating and cooling days, consider geothermal heat pumps, which use the constant temperature of the earth to assist in heating and cooling. In the summer, heat is carried away from the building and released into the earth; in the winter, the process is reversed, and heat is pulled from the ground and released into the building.

- Consider using tankless hot-water heaters, alone or, for multiunit buildings, in a series.
- Consider using a solar hot-water system to preheat the water before it enters either the central boiler or individual water heaters.

LIGHTING

The lighting strategy for living spaces and common areas should first maximize the use of available natural daylight and then augment with artificial lighting. In affordable housing, daylighting can be employed both in the units and in stairwells and corridors, thus reducing the owner's operating costs. Of greatest importance is to provide daylight in the living room, kitchen, and other high-use areas of homes and apartments. For stairwells and corridors, use skylights, roof monitors, and windows to meet basic light needs during daytime hours.

When designing the artificial lighting system, keep in mind that the operating expenses over the life of a lighting system can be up to ten times greater than the first cost. Fluorescent light fixtures save up to 75 percent of the electricity costs over traditional incandescent lights. Fluorescent lamps also last up to ten times longer than incandescent bulbs and produce 90 percent less heat.

FIGURE 3.9. A combined hydronic heating system uses warm water stored in the water heater for both domestic use and to provide heat to the units.

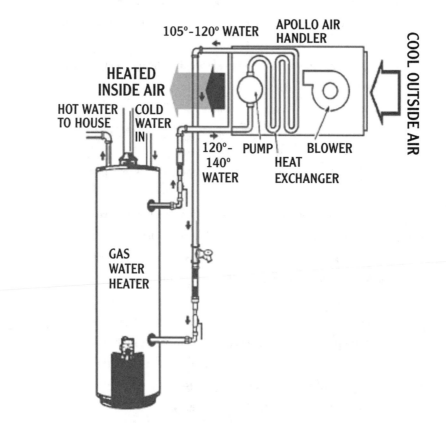

Vistas at Kensington Park (Dallas, Texas)
Carl Franklin Homes

Vistas at Kensington Park is a community of seventeen new single-family homes in an existing neighborhood in Dallas, Texas, that was developed by Carl Franklin Homes in conjunction with the Dallas Affordable Housing Coalition and the City of Dallas Housing Authority. The energy performance of these homes, for entry-level workforce buyers, was greatly enhanced through the use of structural insulated panels (SIPs) and geothermal heating and cooling units, as well as other efficient technologies. SIPs, which are used for both walls and roof structures on the exterior shell of the homes, consist of a core layer of rigid foam insulation sandwiched between two structural skins of oriented strand board (OSB).

Heating and cooling is provided by geothermal heat pumps, which use the more constant temperatures of the below-surface earth to heat and cool circulated air before returning it to the home. In a place like Dallas, with extreme summer temperatures, geothermal heat pumps are a smart choice, as the earth's temperature remains more moderate. The developer's method of using SIPs and geothermal heating and cooling easily qualified the project for the ENERGY STAR® label, while saving residents approximately 50 percent in energy costs as compared with similar conventionally built homes.

The most appropriate type of fluorescent lighting for dwelling units is the compact fluorescent lamp (CFL). Although the initial cost of CFLs is higher than incandescent lamps, the energy savings and reduced maintenance time and expense from lamp replacement make CFLs a cost-effective energy conservation measure. CFLs should be installed in areas with the heaviest use, such as common-area hallways, stairwells, lobbies, and community rooms.

Screw-in CFLs fit into conventional fixtures, just as incandescent bulbs do, and include the ballast with the bulb. Special care should be taken to ensure adequate light levels in order to prevent removal by dissatisfied residents. Most CFLs provide a lumen comparison to assist in selecting the appropriate size. Full-spectrum bulbs of not less than 32 watts should be selected to provide sufficient, good-quality light. Pin-type fixtures consist of the ballast and a socket that can only receive a CFL or other type of fluorescent bulb. The most appropriate places for pin-type fixtures are in the kitchen, bathroom, frequently used ceiling fixtures, and hallway security lighting.

Exit signs should use high-efficiency light-emitting diode (LED) bulbs. These will both reduce energy use by up to 80 percent and lower maintenance costs. One sign alone can save about $15 to $20 annually on electricity costs and can last up to twenty-five years without a lamp replacement.

Lighting controls such as photo sensors, occupancy sensors, and timers save energy by turning lights off when they are not needed. Timers can be located at a light switch, at

FIGURE 3.10. The majority
of residential energy use is
fo heating, cooling, and
appliances.

Electricity Use in Residential Buildings

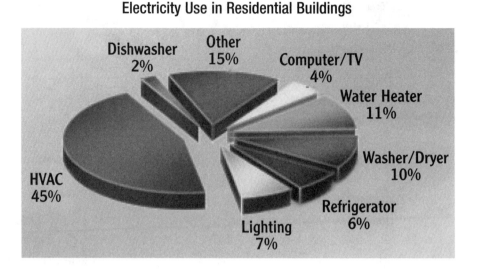

a plug, or in a socket and are an inexpensive way to control the amount of time a light stays on, either inside the home or outdoors. Photo sensors measure the ambient light level in an area and turn on an electric light when the level drops below a set minimum. They are most effective with outdoor fixtures that need to respond to changing levels of daylight during the year. Motion detectors or other occupancy sensors save energy by turning off lights when rooms such as bathrooms or common areas are empty. Dimmers save energy by allowing building occupants to adjust the light output to suit their needs.

APPLIANCES

Appliances account for around 20 percent of an American household's energy consumption, with refrigerators, washing machines, and dryers consuming the most energy. New ENERGY STAR appliances are vastly more efficient than the models of ten or twenty years ago, saving water, energy, and money in operating costs.

Because appliances last a long time (ten to twenty years, depending on the appliance), it is important to buy wisely. If tenants pay their own energy bills, installing energy-efficient appliances helps improve their overall economic situation. If the property owner pays the utility bills, efficient appliances reduce overall operating costs. For example, in Oregon, a partnership between Portland General Electric and Web Service Company, Inc., is supplying approximately 750 energy- and water-efficient Maytag Neptune washing machines to multifamily facilities. These washers are expected to save the apartment owners 1.6 million kilowatt-hours of electric power and 10 million gallons of water annually. The combined electric, water, and sewer bill savings are estimated to be $185,000 a year, or about $250 per machine.[5]

When selecting and specifying appliances, use models that are ENERGY STAR®–certified, which are generally in the top 25 percent of their product class. Currently, refrigerators, clothes washers, and dishwashers are available with ENERGY STAR certification. The ENERGY STAR program provides a full list of ENERGY STAR product specifications to help in selecting energy-efficient products, appliances, HVAC, and lighting equipment. The U.S. Department of Energy (DOE) maintains a website (www.bulkpurchase.net) to enable affordable housing developers to benefit from the cost savings of bulk purchasing of ENERGY STAR appliances.

RENEWABLE ENERGY

In affordable housing, the most practical renewable energy strategy is to capture solar energy for electricity generation or water heating.

Active solar design strategies should be taken up only after passive solar and comprehensive energy efficiency and load reduction approaches have been incorporated, since active systems are typically more costly. Solar water heaters are the most common type of active solar system in affordable housing. Typically, they are mounted on south-facing rooftops and are connected to a gas-fired boiler, with solar used for preheating water.

Photovoltaic (PV) or solar cells convert sunlight directly into electricity. In rental developments, photovoltaic systems are most commonly sized to offset the electricity attributed to the "house meter"—for office and community room; corridor safety lighting; exterior building, parking lot, and landscape lighting; and garage exhaust fans. For a fifty-unit rental development, a PV system designed to provide all the annual electric needs of the common area would likely have a size of 25 to 70 kilowatts (kW), or eight to twenty-five times what is typical for a single-family house. Less common are projects that include PV systems that offset the electricity use of the individual dwelling units. One example of a project that powers both common areas and the dwelling units is the Solara in Poway, California, which also meets the California Energy Commission's zero-energy criteria. Other projects are preparing for future PV or hot-water systems by installing conduit and plumbing during construction to enable easy installation at a later date. PV installations in home ownership projects are usually 1.5 to 5 kW, which can offset 40 to 90 percent of electricity use, depending on home size and the occupant's energy use. While the cost of PV systems often appears to be prohibitive, state rebate programs, federal tax credits, innovative financing (such as including the cost of the PV system in the mortgage for the house or leasing the system), and anticipated increases in energy costs can make these systems a cost-effective investment for owners with a ten-year or longer time horizon.

FIGURE 3.11. Installation of photovoltaic panels on the Nuevo Amenecer Apartments in Pajaro, CA.

Photo courtesy of Pamela Cepe

WATER CONSERVATION

Water is used in housing developments for landscaping, cooking, bathing, laundry, toilet flushing, mechanical and ventilation systems, and landscape irrigation. In households nationally, indoor use accounts for approximately 40 percent of annual water use, with 60 percent used for outdoor purposes. On average, an individual in the United States uses 70 gallons of water a day.

The long-term ownership and centralized management structure typical of affordable multifamily rental housing supports the use of water savings features both indoors and in landscaping. Water is commonly master metered, with the bill being paid by the owner. In homeownership projects and rental projects with individual water meters, the savings from lower water bills can be combined with energy savings to increase family income.

Installing water-conserving systems and fixtures can considerably reduce water use in buildings. The current water consumption guidelines (measured in gallons per minute or gallons per flush) for bathroom sink and kitchen faucets, showerheads, toilets, and urinals were established by the Energy Policy Act of 1992. Most manufactures offer fixtures and toilets that use less water than the federal standards, and many utility companies offer rebates for the installation of low-flow water fixtures.

Reducing water consumption also reduces the use of other resources. For example, reducing water use in showers and faucets also reduces the amount of gas or electricity needed for hot-water heating. See Table 3.1 for a list of recommended water flow rates for various household water fixtures.

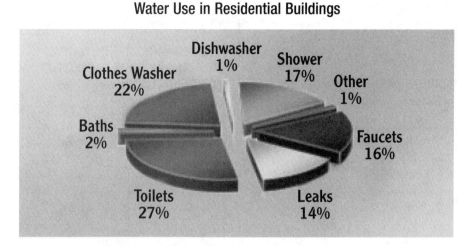

Water Use in Residential Buildings

Dishwasher 1%
Shower 17%
Clothes Washer 22%
Other 1%
Baths 2%
Faucets 16%
Toilets 27%
Leaks 14%

FIGURE 3.12. Toilet flushing and clothes washing comprise nearly 50 percent of residential water use.

Another water-saving measure is to use reclaimed water for landscaping and toilet flushing. For projects served by the Irvine Ranch Water District in Southern California, it is standard practice to install "purple pipe" to provide reclaimed water to the landscaping and "double pipe" to provide reclaimed water to toilets and urinals. The City of Irvine has installed reclaimed water distribution lines on many major boulevards, making it easy to serve most projects with reclaimed water. In locations without ready access to a municipal supply of reclaimed water, the remaining option is to treat the water at the building site. This approach is usually deemed too costly for affordable housing projects except in remote locations.

Recommended practices for reducing water consumption indoors include:

- Install flow restrictors between the supply line and the kitchen and bathroom faucets to limit water waste if faucets are left running while residents are shaving or doing the dishes.
- Install showerheads and faucets that use less water than current federal standards (see Table 3.1).
- Install high-efficiency (HET) or dual-flush toilets that use less than 1.3 gallons on average per flush, as compared to 1.6 gallons per flush for current models.
- Specify front-loading ENERGY STAR® clothes washers, which use 35 to 50 percent less water per load as compared with conventional, top-loading washers. Front-loading washers also remove more water with a faster spin cycle, thus reducing drying time. ENERGY STAR dishwashers also use less water than conventional models.[6]
- Use locally provided reclaimed water for landscaping. Consider providing separate supply lines to toilets for reclaimed water use in toilet flushing.

TABLE 3.1. COMPARISON OF EPA 1992 STANDARDS VERSUS SUGGESTED WATER-CONSERVING FIXTURES

CURRENT EPA 1992 STANDARDS *gallons per minute (gpm) or* *gallons per flush (gpf)*		GREEN COMMUNITIES INITIATIVE AND LEED FOR HOME SUGGESTED SPECIFICATIONS *gallons per minute (gpm) or* *gallons per flush (gpf)*	
Bathroom Sink	2.0 gpm	Bathroom Sink	1.5 gpm
Kitchen Sink	2.0 gpm	Kitchen Sink	2.0 gpm
Shower	2.5 gpm	Showerhead	2.0 gpm
Toilet	1.6 gpf	Toilet	<1.3 gpf

RAINWATER HARVESTING AND REUSE

Station Place Tower (Portland, Oregon)
REACH Community Development

FIGURE 3.13. Station Place Tower in Portland, OR, includes an innovative strategy for using rainwater captured from the roof.

Photo courtesy of REACH Community Development

Completed in February 2005, Station Place Tower in Portland, Oregon, is a mixed-income, affordable housing development for seniors built by REACH Community Development. The development is located on a three-block reclaimed brownfield site in the now fashionable Pearl District near transit and essential city services in downtown Portland. In addition to 176 units of senior housing, the fourteen-story tower of glass and steel consists of 26,000 square feet of commercial space and a five-floor parking garage.

Station Place gives Portland's overtaxed stormwater and sewer system a reprieve. An innovative design channels rainwater into a separate plumbing system that provides water for some of the building's toilets, saving an estimated 250,000 gallons of water a year. All of the roof's rainwater is captured and stored in a 20,000-gallon tank on the first floor, treated, and then pumped to the first six floors. The developer received a $70,000 grant from Portland's Green Investment Fund to offset the cost of installing the system. It is the largest rainwater harvesting and reuse system for a residential building in Portland and demonstrates the viability of green building practices for affordable housing.

RESOURCE-EFFICIENT MATERIALS

The most effective way to reduce the environmental impact of the materials used in a building is simply to use less. This is known as "materials source reduction." One straightforward technique is to use structural materials, like concrete, as the finished surface. Specifying highly durable materials (ones that will not need replacing often) is another effective strategy. Tile, for instance, lasts much longer than carpeting.

Another technique is to rethink assumptions about how materials are used. In residential construction, wood is a large component of the materials flow into a project and a major contributor to the waste stream coming out of it. "Optimum value engineering" (OVE, also known as "advanced framing") reduces the need for framing lumber by spacing framing members at 24 inches on center as compared with the conventional 16 inches on center, using two-stud corners with drywall clips, locating windows next to structural studs, using "in-line framing" to reduce the need for double top plates and headers, and eliminating large-diameter wood in nonstructural locations. Applying OVE can reduce wood use by up to 30 percent and reduces the amount of waste wood ending up in landfills.

Even after source reduction techniques have been used to their full potential, many building materials will still be needed. Materials that are reclaimed, have recycled content, or come from rapidly renewable sources should be specified whenever possible. Recommended practices include the following:

- Use salvaged materials from other buildings, such as the windows, doors, flooring, siding, or large beams.
- Specify landscaping amendments, aggregate, and backfill with recycled content.
- Use engineered lumber instead of conventional lumber for framing. Engineered lumber is made from fast-growing, small-diameter trees, thus helping to preserve old-growth forests. Engineered lumber also resists warping, cracking, and splitting better than dimensional lumber. If possible, specify engineered lumber made with glues that are free of urea formaldehyde.
- Use manufactured roof trusses, floor trusses, and wall panels instead of traditional stick frame construction. Factory assembly can reduce lumber use by more than 25 percent, and nearly eliminates waste in the field. Premanufactured materials may cost slightly more but, because they are easier to assemble, save labor.
- Use drywall, insulation, carpet, and ceramic tile with recycled content.
- Consider products made from recycled plastic for decking, roofing, fences, and other nonstructural functions.
- If purchasing new lumber, check to see if wood certified by the Forest

Stewardship Council (FSC) is available. FSC wood comes from well-managed forests and is sustainably harvested.

- Use fly ash to replace 15 percent or more of the Portland cement in concrete. Fly ash is by-product of burning coal that is often sent to landfills. Using fly ash in concrete puts an industrial waste to good use, saves the energy needed to manufacture cement, and results in a harder and more durable final product. Use of fly ash requires coordination with both the structural engineer and contractor, as higher levels of fly ash require slightly longer curing times before reaching the required strength, and the workability of fly ash concrete is impacted more by changes in temperature.

- Use carpet tiles so that small damaged areas can be replaced instead of the entire carpet. Installation is critical to prevent uneven seams that can lift or damage tiles prematurely.

- Specify board made from agricultural by-products, such as wheat board, for cabinetry, trim, and furniture.

FIGURE 3.14. Example of OVE framing markups for the Carrier House built by Hartford Area Habitat for Humanity.

Figure provided by Bruce M. Hampton, AIA

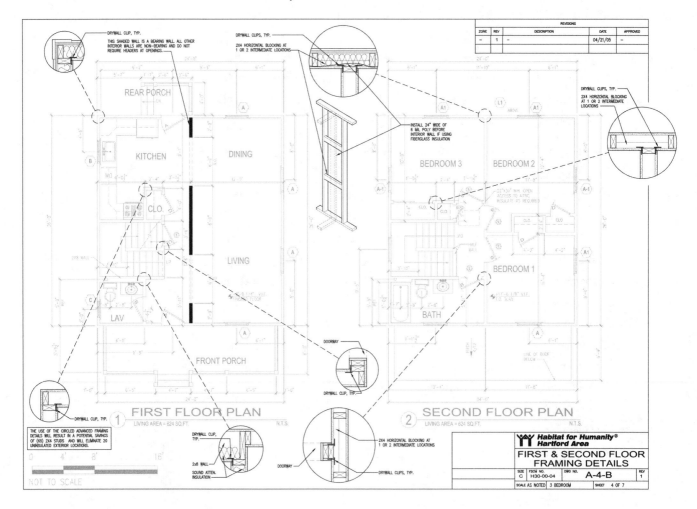

FIGURES 3.15 AND 3.16. The Carrier House project by the Hartford Area Habitat for Humanity features OVE using engineered lumber. *Photo courtesy of buildingctgreen.com*

REUSING SALVAGED WOOD

Nageezi House (Nageezi, New Mexico)
Stardust Center

When building the Stardust Center's Nageezi House on the Navajo Reservation in New Mexico, the builders reused materials wherever possible, starting with the original house. The Nageezi House is a home built for an elderly Navajo couple to replace their dilapidated home. The builders attempted to reuse as much material from the old home as possible. For more information on the Nageezi House, see the Case Studies section, where this project is discussed at length. Once dismantled, its usable lumber became the new home's decking and trellis, as well as the framing for doors and windows. The home's doors and windows came from demolished homes in the Phoenix area. The seven large juniper logs that make up the hooghan and native stone used to

FIGURE 3.17. The builders of the Nageezi House in New Mexico attempted to incorporate salvaged wood whenever possible. *Photo courtesy of ASU Stardust Center*

pave the hooghan courtyard were also gathered locally. The roof's structure is comprised of local timber culled from Arizona forests via local fire prevention programs. Too small in diameter to use as conventional lumber, millers consider these timbers a waste material, and typically use them for composting. The designers used these 8-inch round timbers spaced on 4-foot centers, supporting a composite roof comprised of two layers of oriented strand board (OSB), with 5 inches of rigid insulation in between and metal roofing on top.

The Stardust Center's next project, the Guadalupe House, also uses small-diameter timbers from the Navajo Reservation in northern Arizona. A small Navajo-owned start-up, Southwest Traditional Homes, provided logs that would have otherwise been mulched or burned as a waste product.

CONSTRUCTION WASTE REDUCTION

Builders can reduce construction waste by reusing materials on-site, sorting waste, or contracting with a mixed-load hauler.

Recommended practices are:

- Define waste management goals in bid solicitations. For instance, the solicitations can specify an overall waste recycling/reuse goal of 50 percent or more and provide targets for categories such as wood products, concrete, and steel. Bid packages should supply contact information for local recyclers.
- Have the contractor draw up a draft waste management plan immediately after a bid is awarded.
- Prior to the start of construction, the general contractor should submit a final waste management plan that contains: (1) lists of materials that can be recycled, reused, or returned to manufacturers, including cardboard, paper, packaging, clean dimensional wood and palette wood, land-clearing debris, bricks, concrete masonry units (CMUs), metal from banding, stud trim, ductwork, piping, rebar, roofing, drywall, carpet and pad, paint, asphalt roofing shingles, rigid foam, glass, and plastic; (2) lists of available alternatives to landfilling for each material, such as crushing, grinding, or diverting to a collection and sorting facility; (3) who will be responsible for the waste management effort; and, (4) procedures for materials handling, management on-site, transportation, and distribution of the plan to the developer, architect, job supervisor, subcontractor, and construction manager.

INDOOR ENVIRONMENTAL QUALITY AND HEALTH

Elements in many building products, such as volatile organic compounds (VOCs), mold, and dust, contribute to respiratory ailments and asthma. This is of particular concern because studies have shown that up to 26 percent of all emergency room visits are asthma related.[7] Young children and the elderly are particularly susceptible to indoor air pollution. Children have higher respiratory rates and are closer to pollutant sources, such as carpeting and furniture. VOCs such as formaldehyde, acetone, benzene, xylene, and toluene are emitted by many kinds of carpet, paint, adhesives, solvents, insulation, and furniture. Unsafe levels of these chemicals in indoor air are often signaled by strong odors and health problems such as headaches, dizziness, skin irritation, nose and throat discomfort, fatigue, or nausea. Flooring materials made of polyvinyl chloride (PVC) can also leach phalates over time, which can mix with household dust and enter the respiratory system.

An equally serious indoor air quality (IAQ) problem is leaks and condensation on pipes or inside HVAC systems, which can create environments in which mold, mildew, dust mites, and insects can thrive. Damp drywall inside a kitchen or bathroom wall is an ideal location for mold growth, so keeping moisture out of kitchens and bathrooms is a high priority.

To prevent IAQ problems, first reduce the sources of pollution by keeping construction materials dry and by flushing out a building with fresh air for at least a week prior to occupancy. Second, provide natural or mechanical ventilation to remove pollutants and introduce fresh air into living spaces. Finally, maintenance procedures should keep systems operating to the design specifications and prevent the use of new pollutants in maintenance or cleaning. The ENERGY STAR® Indoor Air Quality Package provides a comprehensive approach to improving air quality in residential buildings.

In addition to air quality issues, factors that impact the quality of the living environment are thermal comfort, acoustics, the presence of natural daylight, and access to views (especially views of trees or landscaped areas).

Recommended strategies for improving indoor environmental quality include the following:

- Specify low-VOC interior paint consistent with Green Seal (65-11) standards.
- Use formaldehyde-free insulation.
- Use natural linoleum, rubber, or concrete instead of vinyl composite tile or sheet goods.
- Specify composite wood products (particleboard, melamine, medium-density fiberboard) for cabinets and countertops that are free of added urea formaldehyde.
- If using carpet, select a low-looped pile that meets the Carpet and Rug Institute (CRI) Green Label standards for both carpet and pad.
- Minimize the amount of dirt and other pollutants that are tracked indoors by providing entry mats or grills at doorways.
- Use low-VOC caulks and adhesives.

- Vent all kitchen range hoods directly to the outside. Recirculating range models are ineffective in removing odors, smoke, combustion by-products, and moisture.

- Direct-vent and provide either a humidistat or hard-wired timer for bathroom fans.

- Provide at least 15 cubic feet of fresh air per minute (cfm) per occupant, consistent with the American Society of Heating, Refrigerating and Air-Conditioning Engineers (ASHRAE) standard 62.2 to ensure that adequate fresh air is brought into the space to dilute pollutants and prevent moisture buildup within the building envelope.

- Install at least one carbon monoxide monitor per dwelling unit.

- Place ventilation intakes away from exhaust fans.

- Install MERV 8 or better air filters in ducted ventilation systems

- Provide sealed-combustion, power-vented furnaces and hot-water heaters.

- Provide constant exhaust through rooftop "scavenger fans" or an "always-on" low-speed fan in each unit with dedicated exhaust to the roof or exterior.

- Provide natural daylight in bedrooms, kitchens, and other frequently used rooms.

- Improve acoustic performance by using blown cellulose or cotton batt insulation and sealing around all plumbing and electrical penetrations.

VENTILATION FOR GOOD INDOOR ENVIRONMENTAL QUALITY

229 East Third Street project (New York, NY)
Lower East Side Mutual People's Housing Association

New York–based architect Chris Benedict has designed a unique ventilation system for multifamily buildings. This system was recently used in the 229 East Third Street project, a new building designed by Benedict and developed and owned by the Lower East Side Mutual People's Housing Association. The system works by treating each unit as its own independent "vessel" that is air sealed from all other units and public spaces.

Careful attention to air tightening is critical to good results. The architect identified where incoming fresh air should come from, and then did air sealing to prevent leaks from other places. The system reduces an unwanted stack effect (warm air rising up through a tall building, pulling cold air in at the bottom of the building), which makes residents of lower floors cold and overheats residents near the top.

Specially designed "trickle vents" in the bedroom windows pull in fresh air, which is then drawn out through small, quiet, always-on fans in the kitchen and bathroom. The air moves through each apartment slowly and steadily, which helps maintain a constant humidity level and temperature. Besides providing healthy indoor environmental quality, the ventilation system offers additional benefits: it increases soundproofing and fireproofing between units, improves air quality because air isn't shared among units, and saves energy by not leaking air.

TOP 25 LOW COST GREEN BUILDING PRACTICES————————————————————

1. Locate close to transit and services
2. Reduce parking and provide secure bicycle storage
3. Design for natural ventilation and passive heating and cooling
4. Design for natural daylight
5. HVAC sizing
6. Permeable surfaces on site
7. Trees to shade east and west elevation
8. Low-water use plants
9. Flyash or slagash in concrete
10. Advanced framing (OVE)
11. Light-colored roof
12. Seal all plumbing and electrical penetrations
13. Proper flashing around windows and doors
14. ENERGY STAR® ceiling fans in living room and bedrooms
15. Timer delay or humidistat on bathroom fan
16. Formaldehyde-free insulation
17. ENERGY STAR or pin-type fluorescent lighting
18. ENERGY STAR appliances
19. Low-water use plumbing fixtures
20. Recycled-content insulation, carpet, drywall, etc.
21. Formaldehyde-free cabinets or fully sealed cabinets and counters
22. Low-VOC paint
23. CRI carpet
24. Carbon monoxide detector
25. Provide owners or tenants with information on green features

SUMMARY

By carefully considering each decision in the design process, from how the building is oriented to what type of carpet is specified, the operating efficiency, comfort, and health of the dwelling units can be greatly improved while reducing impacts in the environment. The Box above contains a list of our recommended "Top 25" low-cost green building practices. These strategies serve as a baseline of green building practices that are appropriate for affordable housing and can be implemented on a tight budget.

For the systems and materials to provide the expected benefit, it is essential that the plans and specifications clearly state not just the product but what specific green features are desired. Later, when substitutions or change orders occur, having clear documentation will ensure that the green aspects are not overlooked. Diligent construction management will ensure the green items are incorporated per the plans and specs and thus able to deliver benefits to the owner and the future tenants or owners.

NOTES

1. Earth Pledge website, www.earthpledge.org (accessed September 18, 2006).
2. U.S. Department of Agriculture, Southern Region, "Benefits of Urban Trees," Report R8-FR71 (Washington, D.C.: U.S. Department of Agriculture, September 2003), 5.
3. U.S. Department of Energy, www.eere.energy.gov (accessed January 8, 2007).
4. For more information on RemRates see www.archenergy.com and for EnergyPlus see www.eere.energy.gov/buildings/energyplus.
5. Portland General Electric Press Release, June 17, 2002.
6. ENERGY STAR website, www.energystar.gov (accessed September 18, 2006).
7. G. Thurston, K. Ito, P. Kinney, and M. Lippmann, "A Multi-Year Study of Air Pollution and Respiratory Hospital Admissions in Three Results for 1988 and 1989 Summers," *Journal of Exposure Analysis and Environmental Epidemiology* 2 (1992): 429–50.

CASE STUDIES

Model Developments of Green Affordable Housing

The following section provides twelve case studies detailing green affordable housing projects that have made comprehensive and integrated attempts to thoroughly incorporate green building. These case studies were selected from a list of recent green affordable housing projects that we were personally aware of, plus others we discovered by combing through various resources, such as submissions to the American Institute of Architects' Show You're Green Award and the Home Depot Foundation's Awards of Excellence in green affordable housing. The "Master List of Green Affordable Housing Projects" includes summary information on these projects.

In selecting the twelve projects for the case studies included in this book, our intent was to provide a snapshot of green affordable housing that was geographically diverse and that represented the variety of types of affordable housing. The project list contains summary information about projects and basic information for obtaining more information about each given project. The case studies attempt to the tell the story of the project while also providing detailed descriptions and comprehensive information on the project's design, finance, and its notable green features, as well as the lessons learned and challenges faced in the development process.

The processes for inclusion of a project in the master list and for the selection of the case studies were by no means scientific, and the exclusion of any particular project is not intended as an indicator of a project's sustainable attributes.

PROJECT NAME	LOCATION	DEVELOPER/OWNER
Featured Case Studies		
Arroyo Chico	Santa Fe, NM	Santa Fe Community Housing Trust
Brick Hill Cottages	S. Portland, ME	Avesta Housing
Faison Mews	Camden, NJ	Pennrose Properties
Greenway Park Cohousing	Chicago, IL	Woodlawn Development Association
High Point	Seattle, WA	Seattle Housing Authority
Linden Street Apartments	Somerville, MA	Somerville Community Corporation
Maverick Landing	Boston, MA	Trinity East Boston Development
Nageezi House	Nageezi, NM	Arizona State University Stardust Design Center
Orchard Gardens	Missoula, MT	homeWORD
Plaza Apartments	San Francisco, CA	San Francisco Redevelopment Agency
Portland Place	Minneapolis, MN	Project for Pride in Living
The Street Where Dreams Come True	South Atlanta, GA	Atlanta Habitat for Humanity
More Projects from Across the Country		
Annie Mitchell Homestead	Aspen, CO	City of Aspen/ASW Realty
1400 on 5th	New York, NY	Full Spectrum New York
20th Street Apartments	Santa Monica, CA	Community Corporation of Santa Monica
228 E. Third Street	New York, NY	Lower East Side People's Mutual Housing Association
Affordable Green Homes	Franklin County, MA	Rural Development, Inc.
Azotea Senior Apartments	Alamogordo, NM	Tierra Realty Trust

SUMMARY	CONTACT INFORMATION
Workforce housing project that includes 17 single-family homes that are resource efficient	Santa Fe Community Housing Trust: www.santafecommunityhousingtrust.com
5 buildings renovated into 43 units, workforce housing, historic preservation	Avesta Housing: www.avestahousing.org
51 units of senior housing that involved the preservation of a historic building	Pennrose Properties: www.pennrose.com
10 units of cohousing that involved a systemic approach to providing well insulated homes	Woodlawn Development Associates: Pat Wilcoxen, Phone (773) 643-7495
800 low-income units in a HOPE VI mixed-income community	Seattle Housing Authority: www.seattlehousing.org
42 units of rental housing on a remediated brownfield intended for very low-income families	Somerville Community Corporation: www.somervillecdc.org
411 units in a mixed-income development	Boston Housing Authority: www.bostonhousing.org
Culturally appropriate single-family home in the Navajo Nation that includes passive solar design and salvaged wood	Arizona State University Stardust Design Center: www.asu.edu/stardust/design.htm
35-unit project on the rural fringe that made extensive use of local materials	homeWORD: www.homeword.org
An SRO project in a redevelopment area that provides stability and a healthy building for the formerly homeless	San Francisco Redevelopment Agency: www.sfgov.org/sfra
47 units in a 2-block revitalization	Project for Pride in Living: www.ppl-inc.org
10 bungalows on infill sites where the project created green spaces	Atlanta Habitat for Humanity: www.atlantahabitat.org
39 one-bedroom units of workforce housing	City of Aspen Housing Office: www.aspenhousingoffice.com
High-rise urban development including 85 units	Full Spectrum NY: www.fullspectrumny.com
Energy-efficient rehabilitation of 2 buildings	Community Corporation of Santa Monica: www.communitycorp.org
New York City project that includes a unique ventilation system to help provide a healthy indoor environment	Lower East Side People's Mutual Housing Association: www.lespmha.org
Rural homeownership project; recipient of the Home Depot Foundation 2005 Award of Excellence for Housing Built Responsibly	Rural Development Incorporated: www.ruraldevelopmentinc.org
60 units of housing for low-income seniors	Azotea Senior Apartments: Phone (505) 437-5465

PROJECT NAME	LOCATION	DEVELOPER/OWNER
Betty Ann Gardens	San Jose, CA	First Community Housing
Bridgeton Revitalization	Bridgeton, NJ	New Jersey Green Homes Office
Brookview Senior Housing	Poway, CA	San Diego Interfaith Housing Foundation
Cabrini First Hill Apartments	Seattle, WA	Cabrini Mission Foundation
Chestnut Linden Court	Oakland, CA	BRIDGE Housing Corporation
Clara Vista Townhomes	Portland, OR	Hacienda Community Development Corporation
Cobb Hill Cohousing	Hartland, VT	Jeff Schoellkopf Design
Colorado Court	Santa Monica, CA	Community Corporation of Santa Monica
Columbia Terrace (CAST)	Cambridge, MA	Homeowner's Rehab Inc.
Connor's Cottage	Portsmouth, OH	Portsmouth Metropolitan Housing Authority
Denny Park	Seattle, WA	Low Income Housing Institute
Diversity Houses	New York, NY	Lower East Side People's Mutual Housing Association
East Kelly Avenue Housing	Jackson Hole, WY	Jackson Hole Community Housing Trust
El Paseo Studios	Santa Clara, CA	First Community Housing
Emeryville Resourceful Building	Emeryville, CA	Emeryville Resourceful Building Project
Erie Ellington	Boston, MA	Hickory Consortium
Folsom/Dore Apartments	San Francisco, CA	Citizens Housing Corporation
Gold Dust Apartments	Missoula, MT	homeWORD
Highland Gardens	Denver, CO	Perry Rose LLC

SUMMARY	CONTACT INFORMATION
76 units of family housing close to nature and community services	First Community Housing: www.firsthousing.org
HOPE VI project that restored the community's connection to a nearby river	New Jersey Green Homes Office: www.state.nj.us.dca/dh/gho
102 unit complex for low-income seniors in the generally affluent north San Diego County area	San Diego Interfaith Housing Foundation: www.sdihf.org
50 units of senior housing, including 10 set aside for formerly homeless seniors, near downtown Seattle	Cabrini Mission Foundation: www.cabrinifoundation.org
Project that includes apartments, townhomes, single-family homes, and ground-floor retail spaces	BRIDGE Housing Corporation: www.bridgehousing.org
44 2- and 3- bedroom units targeting large families; first LEED for Homes certified project on the West Coast	Hacienda CDC: www.haciendacdc.org
Cluster of cohousing for 20–25 families in Vermont that preserves farmland while increasing density	Sustainability Institute: www.sustainabilityinstitute.com/cobbhill
Urban infill project that includes 44 SRO units; certified LEED Gold	Community Corporation of Santa Monica: www.communitycorp.org
Rehabilitation of 42 units in 3 buildings whose affordability was at risk	Homeowner's Rehab Inc: www.homeownersrehab.org
20 units of senior housing part of the adaptive reuse of an historic building	Portsmouth Metropolitan Housing Authority: www.pmha.us
50 units of housing in a mixed-use development	Low Income Housing Institute: www.lihi.org
44 units of housing for families earning 30–50% less than AMI	Lower East Side People's Mutual Housing Association: www.lespmha.org
28 units built using modular construction for families in Jackson Hole	Jackson Hole Community Housing Trust: housingtrustjh.org/homes
98-unit SRO complex targeting individuals earning 30–55% of AMI	First Community Housing: www.firsthousing.org
3 units on an infill site composed of a single-family house and duplex	Architects, Designers, Planners for Social Responsibilty: www.adpsr-norcal.org
Includes 50 units of affordable housing and a community building	Hickory Consortium: www.hickoryconsortium.org
98 SRO units for low- and very low-income individuals, some with special needs; certified LEED Gold	Citizens Housing Corporation: citizenshousing.org
18 units for low-income individuals and families in a historic neighborhood	homeWORD: www.homeword.org
New, compact mixed-use development with 291 units in a range of housing types. Forty percent of the senior housing and 20 percent of the apartments are affordably priced.	Jonathan Rose Companies: www.rose-network.com

PROJECT NAME	LOCATION	DEVELOPER/OWNER
HIP Artists' Housing	Mt Rainier, MD	Housing Initiative Partnership, Inc.
Indian Wells Villas Senior Housing	Indian Wells, CA	City of Indian Wells Redevelopment Agency
Jacob's Place	Bronx, NY	Fordham Bedford Housing Corporation
James Wood Apartments	Los Angeles, CA	1010 Development Corporation
Johnson Creek Commons	Portland, OR	Sustainable Communities NorthWest
Magnolia Circle Apartments	Decatur, GA	Initiatives for Affordable Housing
Melrose Commons II	Bronx, NY	Melrose Commons II LLC
Murphy Ranch	Morgan Hill, CA	First Community Housing
New Homes for South Chicago	South Chicago, IL	Claretian Associates
New San Marco	Duluth, MN	Center City Housing
New Shiloh Village Senior Living	Baltimore, MD	Unity Properties Inc. and Enterprise Homes Inc.
NextGen Homes	Carbondale, CO	Fenton Development LLC
Northgate Grandview Apartments	Oakland, CA	Resources for Community Development
Nueva Vista Family Housing	Santa Cruz, CA	Mercy Housing
Oleson Woods	Portland, OR	Community Partners for Affordable Housing
Orange Place Cooperative	Escondido, CA	Community HousingWorks
Pantages Apartments	Seattle, WA	Stickney Murphy Romine Architecture
Positive Match	San Francisco, CA	San Francisco Redevelopment Agency

SUMMARY	CONTACT INFORMATION
Blighted building converted into 12 units of artist housing	Housing Initiative Partnership: www.hiphomes.org
90 units for low- and very low-income seniors	Indian Wells Redevelopment Agency: www.cityofindianwells.org
9 units of housing on a former parking lot	Fordham Bedford Housing Corporation: www.fordham-bedford.org
2 buildings with 61 units and a daycare for 24 children near downtown Los Angeles	1010 Development Corp: http://www.1010dev.org
15-unit apartment complex rehabilitated for low and very low-income families	Sustainable NorthWest: www.sustainablenorthwest.org
84 units of housing for low-income seniors; certified by Southface Energy Institute's EarthCraft House program	Initiative for Affordable Housing: www.affordablehousingatl.org
30 triplexes as part of homeownership project in high-cost urban area	GreenHome NYC: www.greenhomenyc.org
100 affordable family townhomes close to transit and services	First Community Housing: www.firsthousing.org
Energy-efficient homes for low- and moderate-income families	Claretian Associates: www.claretianassociates.org
70 units and supportive services serving Duluth's formerly homeless residents on a redeveloped urban infill site	Center City Housing Corporation: www.centercityhousing.org
80 units for seniors with incomes 30–60% below AMI	New Shiloh Baptist Church: www.newshilohbaptist.org/village.html
Two 3-bedroom low-energy demonstration homes	NextGen Homes: www.nextgenhomes.net
42 units of low-income units for large families	Resources for Community Development: www.rcdev.org
48-unit urban infill project that includes community space and services open to the public	Mercy Housing: www.mercyhousing.org
32 units, including townhomes and flat-style units, close to a preserved wetlands area providing residents a natural environment to enjoy	Community Partners for Affordable Housing: www.cpahinc.org
32 units of multigenerational, cooperative townhomes	Community HousingWorks: www.chworks.org
Adaptive reuse of old building into 49 units, which includes 11 units of transitional housing	Delrdige Neighborhood Development Association: www.dnda.org
7 apartments featuring support services for HIV-positive individuals and their families in the adaptive reuse of an historic building	San Francisco Redevelopment Agency: www.sfgov.org/sfra

PROJECT NAME	LOCATION	DEVELOPER/OWNER
Renaissance at Rosemary Park	Bonita Springs, FL	Bonita Springs Housing Development Corporation
Ripley Gardens	Minneapolis, MN	Central Community Housing Trust
Riverwalk Point	Spokane, WA	Spokane Neighborhood Action Program (SNAP) & Sustainable Housing Innovation Project (SHIP)
Phillips Creek Project	Milwaukee, OR	Clackamas Community Land Trust
Powelton Heights	Philadelphia, PA	1260 Housing Development Corporation
Taino Plaza	South Bronx, NY	South Bronx Overall Economic Development Corporation
The Helena	New York, NY	Durst Org & Rose Associates
Timothy Commons	Santa Rosa, CA	Burbank Housing Corporation
Tompkins Park North Homes	New York, NY	Northeast Brooklyn Housing Development Corporation
Traugott Terrace	Seattle, WA	Archdiocesan Housing Authority of Western Washington
Twin Oaks	Madison, WI	Wisconsin Environmental Initiative & Habitat for Humanity Dane County
University Estates	Atlanta, GA	University Community Development Corporation (UCDC)
Vistas at Kensington Park	Dallas, TX	Carl Franklin Homes
Washington Park	Chicago, IL	East Lake Management
Waterfront Housing	Burlington, VT	Housing Vermont
Wentworth Commons	Chicago, IL	Harley Ellis Devereaux
Wisdom Way Solar Village	Greenfield, MA	Rural Development Inc.

*Some projects may still be under construction.

SUMMARY	CONTACT INFORMATION
39 single-family homes for sale to families earning low and moderate incomes	Bonita Springs Housing Development Corporation: Phone (239) 495-7100
Adaptive reuse of 3 historic buildings plus new construction of 3 new buildings to provide 60 units (52 rental and 8 homeownership)	Central Community Housing Trust: www.ccht.org
110 units of affordable housing for low-income individuals and families	Spokane Neighborhood Action Program & Sustainable Housing Innovation Projects: www.ship.snapwa.org
14 for-sale units as part of a community land trust	Clackamas Community Land Trust: www.clackamaclt.org
New construction of 48 one-bedroom units, including units for disabled formerly homeless persons	1260 Housing Development Corporation: www.pmhcc.org
105 low-income family units in a mixed-use building on a redeveloped industrial site	Curtis+Ginsberg Architects: www.clplusga.com
37 floors with 116 affordable units in a high-rise development on a redeveloped industrial site	Durst Organization: www.thehelena.com
32 units on an infill brownfield site	Burbank Housing Corporation: www.burbankhousing.org
3 units that are part of a larger 9-unit cluster of affordable homes	North East Brooklyn Housing Development Corporation: www.nebhdco.org
50 units of SRO housing; LEED-certified project	Archdiocesan Housing Authority of Western Washington: www.ccsww.org
50 self-help Habitat for Humanity homes as part of a 142-unit subdivision	Habitat for Humanity Dane County: www.habitatdane.org
15 single-family homes in a mixed-income development geared toward households earning 80% or less of AMI	University Community Development Corporation: www.aucenter.edu/ucdc
Scattered urban infill affordable homes built using SIPs construction	Carl Franklin Homes: www.carlfranklinhomes.com
Redevelopment of the Washington Park YMCA into 63 SRO units	East Lake Management: http://www.eastlakemgmt.com
Mixed-income project on a remediated brownfield site containing 40 units; certified LEED project	Housing Vermont: www.hvt.org
51 units for formerly homeless individuals and families, including those with special needs	Harley Ellis Devereaux: www.harleyellis.com
20 net zero homes for low- and moderate-income residents	Rural Development Inc: www.ruraldevelopmentinc.org

Arroyo Chico

Valentine Way and Apache Knoll,
Tierra Contenta Subdivision,
Santa Fe, New Mexico

**WORKFORCE HOUSING / OWNERSHIP / PASSIVE SOLAR /
RAINWATER CATCHMENT**

arroyo A deep gully cut by an intermittent
stream; a dry gulch. A brook; a creek.
chico The common greasewood of the
western United States

Southwest city Santa Fe faces a harsh climate with huge
daily temperature swings, not much shade, a lot of
wind, rocky soil, and high runoff. Nevertheless, the beauty
of the desert and the charm of this historic city have attracted
many to it. As the city has grown over the years, the need for
affordable housing has increased greatly as well.

In the early 1990s, the Santa Fe Community Housing
Trust (SFCHT) arose out of a community planning effort
to address a growing gap in housing. Enterprise
Community Partners helped by providing funds for a com-
munitywide effort to improve affordable housing options in
Santa Fe County. In 1993, the same year that SFCHT was
formed to serve as the umbrella organization for these
affordable housing funds, the city and county of Santa Fe
passed an inclusionary zoning ordinance requiring market-
rate builders to either provide affordable housing units
based on a percentage of the total development or pay an
in-lieu fee into an affordable housing trust fund. SFCHT
became the executor of that trust fund as well as a housing
developer. This trust fund model reduces the initial cost of
for-sale housing and protects the affordability of a home
over the long term.

Taking advantage of the region's enormous solar potential, in 2003 the Arroyo Chico project became the first passive solar affordable project in Santa Fe, considered by the
SFCHT board to be "the culmination of its work to date."
According to Jim Hannan, SFCHT finance director, "the
Arroyo Chico project incorporated some important green
features: passive solar orientation, a very tight building envelope, long-lasting metal roofs, and a low-cost, efficient water
harvesting system. We proved that green building techniques can be incorporated into affordable housing."

Built in a northern New Mexico style, the 17 single-
family houses, each averaging 1,175 square feet, are designed
for maximum passive solar gain, with south-oriented windows, radiant heat in the tile floors, and high levels of insulation. Part of the larger market-rate Tierra Contenta subdivision, the homes are located in a pedestrian-friendly neighborhood next to a city park, a library, a youth facility, and
four schools. Many of the houses are also adjacent to open
space that connects to the Tierra Contenta walking trails.

The trust is unique in its full-service approach to providing housing for low-income people. Its Homebuyer
Training and Counseling program has assisted over 3,500
prospective homebuyers since 1993. Cosponsored by local
lenders, real estate agents, nonprofit groups, and government agencies, the program teaches the "ABCs of Home
Ownership"—evaluating needs, financial eligibility, and
how to be financially savvy first-time homebuyers.
Prospective homeowners must complete the program's four
classes before they are eligible for the trust's housing devel-

opments. For Arroyo Chico, all of the new homeowners were at or below 80 percent of Santa Fe's area median income of $60,000 per year. In recent years, the lack of workforce housing, or housing affordable to professionals

---

> "We proved that green building techniques can be incorporated into affordable housing."
>
> JIM HANNAN
> *finance director, Santa Fe Community Housing Trust*

---

such as teachers, police officers, firefighters, and nurses who provide essential community services, emerged as a concern among housing advocates, employers, business leaders, and policymakers in the Santa Fe area.[1]

GREEN ACHIEVEMENTS

From the very beginning, architect Suby Bowden and her firm pushed for passive solar design in the project. A particular challenge on the small lots was to make sure one property did not shade another. Bowden came up with a site plan that has a unique Z-shaped lot layout, allowing the 17 single-family detached home lots to fit onto the site and still maintain good solar access.

Passive Solar Design: As a part of the passive solar design strategy, there are no windows on the north elevations and minimal windows on the west elevations. The majority of the high-efficiency, low-e windows are on the south side of the homes, and for ease of maintenance can be tilted in for cleaning without removing the screen. Ceramic tiles, used throughout the homes except in the bedrooms, are also a part of the passive solar design, acting as thermal mass sinks.[2] The use of tile instead of the more typical carpeting greatly improves indoor air quality by removing areas where dust, mites, and mold can accumulate. In addition, the team's research showed that

ceramic tile will last two and a half times longer than carpet, with a life span of roughly twenty-five years. The pitched metal roofs, used instead of composite shingles, are expected to last up to fifty years, twice as long as a standard roof.

To ensure a tight building envelope, blown-in cellulose insulation was used in all the houses in place of rigid foam or batt insulation. This insulation has a higher R-value and is made out of recycled newspaper.

With good passive solar design and a tight building envelope, the remaining heat needs are handled with efficient radiant floor heat. SFCHT's Jim Hannan notes that there are three zones in each home, using McLain boilers and Wirsbo tubing. With radiant heat, each object in the room becomes warm, contributing to comfort while avoiding air currents, blowing dust, or cold spots. Hannan says that the trust "did training information sheets for homeowners, particularly for the radiant floor education," as it was a new technology for most people.

PROJECT DETAILS

Project Size:	17 single-family detached homes for sale in three floor plans. Includes 11 three-bedroom units averaging 1,175 sq ft, not counting garage; and 6 two-bedroom homes averaging 1,050 sq ft, for first-time homeowners.
Total Square Footage:	20,000 sq ft
Construction Cost:	$1,784,885
Total Development Cost:	$2,337,477
Average Cost/Unit:	$137,499
Average Cost/Sq Ft:	$116.87
Incremental Cost to Build Green:	0.74%
Average Price of House:	$152,647
Completion date:	August 2003

Project Team

Developer:	Santa Fe Community Housing Trust
Architect:	Suby Bowden and Associates
Development Consultant:	Guy Stanke
Infrastructure and Planning	Tierra Contenta Corporation
Contractor:	Sage Builders

As a part of the larger market-rate Tierra Contenta subdivision, the homes are located in a pedestrian-friendly neighborhood. © *Santa Fe Community Housing Trust.*

Xeriscape and Rainwater Harvesting: A xeriscape approach to the landscaping at Arroyo Chico uses native plants to reflect local character and to reduce maintenance and water use. The landscape also incorporates edible fruit trees, bushes, and grapevines. The necessary outdoor watering, particularly during frequent periods of severe drought, is supplied by one of the most innovative features of Arroyo Chico—the rainwater harvesting system. Downspouts from the roof gutters are connected to a 550-gallon cistern. A hose bib attachment allows homeowners to water individual plants by gravity flow. This system has proved quite successful, and the fruit trees and other landscaping are doing very well, according to Hannan.

Social Aspects of Design: Bowden cites the importance of focusing not only on the energy efficiency and physical health aspects of the design but also on the social side as well. The idea was to make these affordable houses thoughtfully designed *homes* for the families who would live in them. Special effort was made to accommodate growing families. The roofs enclose large attic areas that can be used for storage, and the framing allows for later conversion into additional living spaces such as an extra bedroom and bathroom. Plans illustrating a future expansion were given to the owners.

"The project attracted people who might not have normally been interested in living in an affordable housing community," notes Bowden, even if their income levels gave them access to this option. The project was not marketed as "green" because at the time the term was not well understood. Instead, Bowden used "passive solar and healthy building" to describe the development. The market response to Arroyo Chico was very positive. There was a

SUMMARY OF GREEN FEATURES

Site
- Passive solar site layout for all homes
- Pedestrian-friendly neighborhood close to schools and open space

Water
- Water harvesting system with 550-gal cistern
- Xeriscape and native landscaping design
- Low-flow toilet and shower fixtures

Energy
- Very tight building envelope
- Low-e windows
- High R-value blown-in cellulose insulation
- Passive heating and cooling
- Radiant floors

Materials and Resources
- Recycled-content cellulose insulation
- Mechanical system site reduced through passive heating and cooling

Health and Comfort
- Low-volatile organic compounds (VOC) paint, flooring, and cabinets
- Roofs enclose large attic areas that can be used for storage or converted to living space later on
- Porch with plantable shaded trellis
- Project marketed as "passive solar and healthy building"

Durability and Ease of Maintenance
- Ceramic tile flooring (instead of carpet)
- Metal roof (instead of asphalt shingles)
- Windows tilt in without removing the screen for cleaning
- Architect presentation on how to operate a green home and information sheets given to homeowners

waiting list of more than a hundred SFCHT-prequalified households, including teachers, hospital workers, public workers, the elderly, and some disabled people.

PROJECT FINANCING

The trust purchased the property for $407,390 with its own funds, while Charter Bank supplied a construction loan. The total project cost was $2,337,477, or $116 per square foot. The Federal Home Loan Bank of Dallas provided an Affordable Housing Program grant of $119,000 for predevelopment costs. The homes sold for between $140,000 and $165,000 with an average down payment of $19,000. As a designated Community Housing Development Organization (CHDO), SFCHT received $220,000 from New Mexico Mortgage Finance Agency's HOME fund set-aside for down payment assistance. The Federal Home Loan Bank of Dallas provided additional assistance of $105,000 to provide a soft second mortgage to each buyer. Homeowners were responsible for obtaining their own mortgage financing for the balance of the loan.

According to a study on Arroyo Chico by the Tellus Institute and New Ecology, Inc., the cost increase due to green features was less than 1 percent of the total development costs, while the benefits were much greater. "There were no differences in design costs," says Jim Hannan, and "going

NET COST OF GREENING ARROYO CHICO

	COST	COST/SF	% OF TOTAL DEV COST
Green Design	$64,702	$3.24	2.77%
Traditional Design	$64,702	$3.24	
Green Design Premium	$0	$0	0%
Green Construction	$1,784,885	$89.24	76.36%
Traditional Construction	$1,767,597	$88.38	
Net Cost of Greening	$17,288	$0.86	.74%

from R-19 to R-25 insulation had no cost increase." The value of the green improvements is estimated at nearly "$8,000 per house over a thirty-year time period, or $132,267 for the development as a whole," the study concluded.

The green building strategies used in this project are saving the homeowners $25 to $30 per month in utility bills from November to March, with annual savings of over $125 per year.

LESSONS LEARNED

For architect Suby Bowden, whose firm has done affordable housing projects all over the United States as well as in Dublin, Ireland, the lessons learned and struggles are always the same: "To produce enough units so that it's still affordable, you have to capture the economies of scale." With only 17 units in this project, this kind of economy was hard to pull off; Bowden wanted to make it a bigger project. During construction, for example, prices on the highly insulated windows escalated in cost. The contractor wanted to substitute vinyl windows, which, as Bowden notes, "are not a green solution."[3] In addition, the team designed a simple-to-maintain, long-lasting steel porch that could host a shade trellis. However, during construction, steel costs increased enormously, so the team ended up substituting wood. The project team learned that they needed to be nimble and prepared with information on alternative materials or solutions in the event that their first choices became too expensive or were not available.

PROJECT FINANCING

FUNDING SOURCES	AMOUNT
Equity	
Santa Fe Community Housing Trust (Property acquisition)	$407,390
Federal Home Loan Bank of Dallas– Affordable Housing Program (grant)	$119,000
Debt	
Charter Bank (construction financing)	$1,811,087
TOTAL	**$2,337,477**

Another problem Bowden noted was the lack of general contractors in the area who were familiar with green techniques at the time. With a county population of 120,000, "the small community doesn't yet have the capacity to support green products or building," she says. Her firm is now working on building a green building–friendly contractor community.

In the end, Bowden commented that "people are very happy with their homes" and that the project represents a wonderful mix of people, with various ages and family sizes. For many of the buyers, Arroyo Chico represented their only chance to purchase a new home in the Santa Fe area. According to the trust's annual report, forty-two-year-old homeowner Lisa Hernandez said, "I had been thinking about buying a home for more than four years before I actually was able to do it. The night we closed, my kids made me camp out in the house with no furniture!"

"The Arroyo project has held up well," says Jim Hannan, "although some people have built porches that block the passive solar opportunity." The SFCHT has gone on to do other green projects, such as the 30-unit ElderGrace project, also in Santa Fe, a conscious-aging cohousing development whose members dedicate themselves to spiritual growth, mutual support, respect for the environment, and service to others.

CONTACTS

Developer: Santa Fe Community Housing Trust
Jim Hannan, finance director: 505-989-3960

Architect: Suby Bowden Architects
Suby Bowden, project architect: 505-983-3755

SOURCES

Bowden, Suby, of Suby Bowden Architects, personal interview by Jenifer Seal Cramer, July 19, 2006, and e-mail correspondence, July 2006.

The Costs and Benefits of Green Affordable Housing, a publication of New Ecology, Inc., the Tellus Institute, and the Green CDCs Initiative, 2005, www.fraserinstitute.net/ssg/uploads/resources /affordable%20housing/final_cb_report.pdf.

City of Santa Fe Affordable Housing: www.santafenm.gov/ community-services/index.asp.

ElderGrace, Santa Fe Community Housing Trust's recent green cohousing community for older residents: www.eldergrace.org.

Fogarty, Mark, "Affordable Housing Scene in Santa Fe Heats Up with a Rising Number of Solar Powered Developments," *New Mexico Business Weekly*, March 29, 2002, www.bizjournals.com/albuquerque/stories/2002/04/01/focus3.html.

Hannan, Jim, finance director, Santa Fe Community Housing Trust, personal interview by Jenifer Seal Cramer, June 2, 2006, and e-mail correspondence, June 2006.

Santa Fe Community Housing Trust, "Annual Report: Jan. 2002–June 2003."

NOTES

1. Workforce housing is aimed at middle-income professionals such as teachers, police officers, firefighters, nurses and medical technicians, who provide essential community services. Workforce families are usually younger and often include children. Although no uniform income guidelines have yet been set, workforce housing is generally affordable to households earning incomes within the range of 60–120 percent of area median income. The lack of workforce housing is typically of great concern in areas with expensive real estate markets or in resort areas. Workforce housing is also often located in or near employment centers, as one antidote to traffic congestion and lengthy commutes stemming from sprawl.

2. Thermal mass sinks temper the intensity of the heat during the day by absorbing the heat. At night, the thermal mass radiates heat into the living space.

3. According to the Healthy Building Network, vinyl is a highly toxic product that contaminates our houses, bodies, and the environment.

Brick Hill Cottages

Westbrook Street and Red Oak Drive,
South Portland, Maine

**HISTORIC RENOVATION / WORKFORCE HOUSING /
MAINE GREEN HOUSING PROGRAM PILOT**

In 2000, the state of Maine started working with the city of South Portland on redevelopment of a site formerly occupied by the Maine Youth Center. The buildings had been abandoned for more than three years and were in a growing state of disrepair. The unique property, located on a hill with mature landscaping and a river wrapping around it, includes the former administration building, called "the castle," five "cottages" that were used as dormitory-style housing, and a historic barn. (These are not cottages in the usual sense, which are small structures; these are three-story brick buildings.) The cottages were designed in 1893 by John Calvin Stevens and are included in the National Registry of Historic Places.

Today transformed campus is an excellent example of workforce housing adaptive reuse and mixed-use development.[1] Working closely with the state of Maine and local community members, the development team produced a smart-growth project complete with affordable housing, green building, office space, community-supported facilities, and preserved open space. The project is ideally located, with close proximity to shopping and access to bus routes, trains, and the airport.

"Within the affordable housing community, this was a unique project," comments Danuta Drozdowicz of Fore Solutions, the green building consultant to the project. "It was the first time that the full team stepped up to the concept of green design. It was amazing who Richard Berman, the developer of the Brick Hill Cottages, and Avesta Housing, the owner and manager, brought into the process. They let the team run with it. In addition, this project informed the Maine State Housing Authority in creating their own green building standards. We went through all the strategies for green. It was a terrific learning

> "Within the affordable housing community, this was a unique project. It was the first time that the full team stepped up to the concept of green design. . . . This project informed the Maine State Housing Authority in creating their own green building standards. We went through all the strategies for green. It was a terrific learning experience for the whole team."
>
> DANUTA DROZDOWICZ
> *Fore Solutions*

experience for the whole team." Jay Waterman, director of Avesta Housing, agrees: "Everyone involved in the cottages—for-profit and nonprofit developers—came from a perspective of wanting to do more than just provide some affordable housing. They wanted to include durability, healthy living, and green building in their project mission."

Because of the ideal location of the site, the state's

Bureau of General Services wanted to keep the land under state ownership and held a competition to gather ideas for redevelopment of the site. Richard Berman was selected to develop the master plan and granted a ninety-year ground lease. His approach was to work "not by stating my own grand vision for the site, but instead by describing a community-based process that would produce a vision for what the community wanted for the site."

Berman worked with community process consultant Ed Suslovik and architecture firm Winton Scott to conduct a public participation process for the master plan. Suslovik designed a four-month process that included three public meetings with stakeholders including people from the neighboring parts of the city, city councilors, and the parents of students who attended a nearby school. At these "Kumbaya meetings," Berman talked about the importance of "(1) communication and (2) communion—trust building." He believes that food should always be served at such meetings and says this "breaking bread" is very important in building rapport and trust in the community.

Out of these meetings came "values" for developing the property. The community called for affordable housing (both rental and for-sale) to help stabilize the neighborhood; mixed-use options for people to be able to work as well as live on-site; open space; historic preservation; and public access to the Fore River. Berman and his development partner, Jim Hatch, brought the green building aspect. A self-described "bit of a hippie," Berman is increasingly concerned about the growing dependence on oil. "I used to be focused on green in my wallet in the past. Now, I'm more focused on preservation of the earth—smart growth coupled with green building projects," he says.

In addition to renovation of the historic cottages and the castle into 43 affordable housing units and 52,000 square feet of office space, respectively, the final master plan features the construction of 66 affordable new rental townhouse units; a new apartment building of 34 affordable units; 79 new market-priced condominium units; a new 70,000-square-foot office building; and renovation of the historic barn into a home for Youth Alternatives, a Maine nonprofit that serves families by providing a play space, conference room, and family center. The plan also calls for public access and open space, including a public square, a trail to a public dock on Long Creek, a children's playground, and a new bus stop. This case study primarily focuses on the renovation of the cottages into affordable housing units.

GREEN ACHIEVEMENTS

From the beginning of the project, developer Richard Berman pledged to incorporate green aspects into the entire development.

Setting Green Goals: Berman hired Fore Solutions, a Portland, Maine–based green building consulting firm, to help the architecture firm Winton Scott frame the green building aspects of the project. The team decided to use the U.S. Green Building Council's Leadership in Energy and Environmental Design (LEED) for Homes standard as a

The community called for preservation of historic "cottages" and affordable housing (both rental and for-sale) to help stabilize the neighborhood.
© *Bernard C. Meyers.*

green guide, but not to pursue certification because of the time and expense required to go through the actual process. Pandika Pleqi, lead architect with Winton Scott, commented that with the help of Fore Solutions, the project incorporated several resource efficiency measures, including a tight building envelope, good insulation, high-efficiency appliances, lighting, energy-efficient windows, and natural ventilation. The team also brought in a third-party engineer, Marc Rosenbaum of Energysmiths.

Saving the Buildings: The first, and biggest, green achievement by the development team was saving all the original historic buildings. The state had completed architectural studies that indicated the buildings should be torn down because of the dilapidated condition. However, developer Richard Berman refused to tear down the structures, explaining, "The uniqueness of the historic buildings will add to the special character of Brick Hill," and saving the buildings worked with his pro forma.

Another goal was to maintain the open space of the campus and to avoid cutting down any trees. The team worked within this framework to preserve the large, central open space and to place new structures strategically around it. No existing trees were cut down. At one point, some people pushed for basket-

PROJECT DETAILS

Project Size

Historic Cottage Renovation:	5 buildings renovated into 43 units (1, 2, and 4 bedrooms) and one common space for laundry and community meetings
New Townhouses:	66 affordable housing units. Developer: Deep Cove LLC (Richard Berman and Jim Hatch). Owner/manager: Avesta Housing
New Apartment Building:	34 affordable housing units. Developer: Deep Cove LLC (Richard Berman and Jim Hatch). Owner/manager: Avesta Housing
Historic Barn:	Leased to nonprofit Youth Alternatives to serve families by providing a play space, conference room, and family center
Historic Castle:	52,000 sq ft of office space, fully leased in 2006. A number of residents work for the current tenants. Developer: Castle Brook LLC (Richard Berman and Dirk Thomas)
New Condo Project:	79 market-rate units. Developer: Heron's Cove (Richard Berman and Jim Hatch)
New Office Building:	70,000 sq ft. Developer: To be determined; goal of LEED certification
Open Space:	Provisions for public access and open space include a public square and a trail to a public dock on Long Creek; children's playground planned
Site Acreage:	5.36 acres for the cottages and 52 acres for the total site
Construction Cost:	$6,296,387 for the cottages
Development Cost:	$8,842,460 million for the cottages
Completion Date:	Summer 2006 for the cottages

Project Team

Developer:	Richard Berman
Owner/Manager:	Avesta Housing
Architect:	Winton Scott Architects
Process Consultant:	Ed Suslovik
MEP Engineers:	Swift Engineering / System Engineering / Energysmiths
Construction:	Wright-Ryan Construction
Landscape Architect:	Carroll & Associates
Green Building Consultants:	Fore Solutions; Maine State Housing for green guidelines

ball courts in the open space in front of the cottages, but, in the end, the group decided the space would remain open.

Renovation Elements: The decrepit structures were essentially gutted. Even though the cottages are listed on the National Registry of Historic Places, Pleqi said no conflicts came up while trying to balance green goals with those of the historic preservation requirements. For example, energy-efficient vinyl windows were not allowed under historic preservation guidelines, so efficient wood-frame windows were used. These met both green and historic criteria.

The old brick buildings were not insulated. Spray-in Icynene foam insulation was selected to insulate the roof and wall cavities. This type of insulation provides a protective barrier against outdoor allergens and pollutants while minimizing air leakage for increased energy efficiency and a healthier indoor environment. It maintains its performance with no loss of R-value over time. Pleqi conducted a special inspection of the insulation process to ensure that it would not harm the buildings.

Systems: The units have individual heating, ventilating, and air-conditioning (HVAC) systems rather than a central system, allowing residents to control their own space conditioning and therefore their own energy consumption. Radiant flooring was discussed but quickly dismissed because the old substructure and beams made its use impractical. A great deal of time was spent looking at provisions for make-up air,[2] and the team determined it was not possible to use air-to-air heat exchangers. A Panasonic exhaust fan system was selected for each cottage's ventilation system. It was set to run on a schedule to ensure good exhaust of the building.

WASTE MANAGEMENT

The selected construction company, Wright-Ryan Construction, Inc., is a member of the U.S. Green Building Council (USGBC) and a founding member of

SUMMARY OF GREEN FEATURES
Utilized LEED for Homes to guide the entire process.

Site
- Preserved of open space and mature landscaping; avoided cutting down any trees
- Reused all historic structures on the site and sensitively infilled site with new buildings
- Located close to mass transit and shopping; added new bus stop
- Included mixed-use and live/work elements as an integral element of the program
- Included central park and children's playground
- Located local nonprofit Youth Alternatives on-site for family support and kid play options

Water
- Low-flow faucets and showerheads
- Water-efficient appliances

Energy
- Icynene insulation system used to improve building envelope and reduce energy costs in old brick buildings
- Energy-efficient windows
- ENERGY STAR® appliances
- High-efficiency ventilation system with fan controls installed

Materials and Resources
- Low-volatile organic compounds (VOC) materials used for adhesives, glues, sealants, primers, and paints
- Aggressive construction waste management plan diverted an average of 67% of waste away from landfills and to recycling facilities, representing 1,003 tons of construction waste

Health and Comfort
- Icynene insulation system, which has no harmful emissions and does not breed mold
- Indoor air quality program
- Community-supportive process embraced during design and development
- Community room and shared laundry space for cottages

the USGBC Maine chapter. Wright-Ryan used the large redevelopment project as an opportunity to implement an aggressive construction waste management plan, diverting an average of 67 percent of waste away from landfills and to recycling facilities. This practice kept more than 1,003 tons of construction waste out of landfills.

PROJECT FINANCING

"The development had a good financial arrangement and partnership—one of the best for-profit developers on the front end who could put up the at-risk capital, then exit via Maine's largest nonprofit developer, Avesta, coming in for the long-term rental and operations of the project," says Jay Waterman of Avesta Housing. Through the process these partners discovered their shared values for the development.

Unique to Brick Hill development, developer Richard Berman proposed a transparent financial process. Berman told the state he would "report every cent spent on the project every year." This financial transparency was coupled with his concept of financial partnership with the city and the state. After developer fees and a return on the equity investment of 25 percent, any additional profits are to be split equally between Berman, the city of South Portland, and the state of Maine. By "making them partners," Berman says, he reduced his risk by encouraging the city and state to take active roles in ensuring the success of the development. This strong relationship and active communication among project partners helped the team to earn much needed funding sources, including Community Development Block Grant (CDBG) funds from the Department of Housing and Urban Development, and to help South Portland to become the first city in Maine to utilize tax increment financing to fund an affordable housing development. Tax increment financing (TIF) is a method of public financing that uses increases in municipal tax revenue in a designated area to finance the development of projects in that area.

With regard to savings, Waterman notes, "While we did not do energy modeling on this project, I expect that about $400 per unit per year will be saved in heating and electric costs given the insulation and systems we have installed, compared to typically developed projects we have in the Avesta portfolio."

LESSONS LEARNED

Many lessons were learned from the developer, the architect, and the owner/manager in the process of creating the Brick Hill Cottages project. One of the main accomplishments of this particular team was to come together in helping to frame and launch the Maine Green Housing program.

Community Process

"Some developers are afraid of community process—they don't want to give up control," Berman says. He feels that there is actually less risk with more community process, because one has the "benefit of hearing from more players. For example, opportunities for subsidies come up. It may take a bit more time for this kind of process, but there's less risk in the end." Less risk means it makes more financial sense. "You do have to know what you are doing in the process, but you will be rewarded," Berman notes.

Lessons from the Cottages Will Support the Whole Development: Jay Waterman of Avesta Housing commented that there were lessons learned that translated to the other parts of Brick Hill with regard to specific green features at the

PROJECT FINANCING

FUNDING SOURCES	AMOUNT
Equity	
General Partner Capital	$254,460
Federal Home Loan Bank of Boston AHP (grant)	$300,000
Low Income Housing Tax Credit	$6,006,000
Debt	
Bangor Savings (Federal Home Loan Bank of Boston AHP Advance for permanent loan)	$1,100,000
Maine State Housing Authority RLP	$600,000
Tax Increment Financing	$582,000
Total Sources	**$8,842,460**

cottages. "We will definitely pursue some of the aspects of the cottages design in the future phases," he says—for example:

- Open cell foam insulation will be pursued for its prevention of air infiltration and sound attenuation as well as high R-value.
- Significant money will be saved in both construction costs and operating costs if a flat roof is used instead of a pitched roof. Operating costs saved include monitoring the sprinkler system in attics; flushing glycol loops in cold spaces in attics; preventing the potential for ice damming if the space does get warm air circulating; and melting roof snow from within.
- Waterproofing brick is accomplished more from a good mortar and pointing than from any sealer that is put over the brick.
- High ceilings in older buildings absolutely need ceiling fans to help keep air circulating and to push heat down to residents in the winter.

Renovation: Architect Pandika Pleqi comments that "the biggest lesson learned was that we could take these old buildings that were in such bad shape and transform them, giving them life for hopefully another 100 years." Each building was unique and thus had to be handled individually. "It was a challenge and an achievement," she says. "We were lucky to have Wright-Ryan on board as the contractor from the very beginning. They have good experience in green building and so everyone was able to work together. It was a very cordial team." Pleqi is also pleased with how the team was able to infill the site sensitively with new buildings while maintaining the original character.

CONTACTS

Developer: Richard Berman
207-772-3225, rberm@rcn.com

Architect: Winston Scott
Pandika Pleqi, project architect: 207-774-481

Owner/Manager: Avesta Housing
James Waterman, director: 1-800-339-6516

SOURCES

Berman, Richard, developer, personal interview by Jenifer Seal Cramer, July 24, 2006, and e-mail correspondence, July 2006.

Drozdowicz, Danuta, Fore Solutions, personal interview by Jenifer Seal Cramer, July 6, 2006.

Hatch, Jim, developer with Richard Berman, e-mail correspondence with Jenifer Seal Cramer, July 2006.

McGowan, Myranda, and Benjamin Smith, "A Case Study of the Brick Hill Development in South Portland," Maine Muskie School of Public Service, University of Southern Maine (May 2005).

Pleqi, Pandika, Winston Scott Architects, personal interview by Jenifer Seal Cramer, July 19, 2006, and e-mail correspondence, July 2006.

Staddard, Allison, Wright-Ryan Construction, Inc., personal interview by Jenifer Seal Cramer, June 13, 2006, and e-mail correspondence, June–July 2006.

Waterman, James, Avesta Housing, personal interviews by Jenifer Seal Cramer, June 10 and July 26, 2006, and e-mail correspondence, July–August 2006.

Wright-Ryan Construction, Inc. "Brick Hill Project" information sheet, spring 2006.

NOTES

1. Workforce housing is aimed at middle-income professionals such as teachers, police officers, firefighters, nurses, and medical technicians, who provide essential community services. Workforce families are usually younger and often include children. Although no uniform income guidelines have yet been set, workforce housing is generally affordable to households earning incomes within the range of 60–120 percent of area median income. The lack of workforce housing is typically of great concern in areas with expensive real estate markets or in resort areas. Workforce housing is also often located in or near employment centers, as one antidote to traffic congestion and lengthy commutes stemming from sprawl.

2. Make-up air prevents negative pressure problems due to air exhausted from a building and can also be heated (or cooled) to provide clean, comfortable working conditions.

Faison Mews

Park and Baird Boulevards,
Camden, New Jersey

SENIOR HOUSING / REHABILITATION AND INFILL NEW CONSTRUCTION / NEW JERSEY GREEN HOMES PROGRAM

Park Boulevard in Camden, New Jersey is one of the three main thoroughfares of the Parkside neighborhood (named for the three local parks, Red Hill, Forest Hill, and Farnham parks). One of the neighborhood landmarks is the historic Pearlye Building. Originally constructed in the late 1800s as an apartment building, the structure was dilapidated after having been abandoned for over fifteen years. In 1998 a community group, Parkside Business and Community in Partnership (PBCIP), approached a local developer, Charles Lewis, with Pennrose Properties about rehabilitating the property. Lewis expressed interest but noted that the building would only yield ten or eleven apartments, too small for the firm to take on, so he began looking for a way to augment the project. He found that the adjacent, 1950s-era Parkview Apartments were also abandoned. By combining the properties, the project became economically viable.

Pennrose Properties, in a joint venture with the Camden Redevelopment Agency and PBCIP, worked to have the city condemn both the Parkview and Pearlye buildings so they could move forward with redevelopment of the three small, connected properties.

Once the property was assembled, the team began working with the neighborhood in community meetings to plan the redevelopment of the site. A need for senior housing was identified immediately. Local residents generally owned their homes, but as they got older, these larger homes often became too much for these seniors to manage on their own.

Residents wanted an option to stay in the neighborhood to be close to friends and because the area is well located. Shopping is close by and links to the Rand Transportation Center provide easy access to downtown Camden, downtown Philadelphia, and connections to New York.

The landmark Pearlye building was rehabilitated and connected with a three-story breezeway to a new building to form the Faison Mews project.
© *Kitchen & Associates Architectural Services.*

By 2004, the buildings acquisitions were fully assembled, and the development team closed on the financing. In 2005, work started with the architects and moved quickly through the planning phase. It was decided that three of the buildings on the site with less architectural value would be demolished, but the historic Pearlye Building would remain. Working in conjunction with the New Jersey Green Homes Office (NJGHO—part of the New Jersey Department of Community Affairs, Division of Housing), the resulting project, called Faison Mews, produced 51 units of deed-restricted[1] green affordable housing for independent seniors age sixty-two and older. The landmark Pearlye Building was rehabilitated and connected with a

The architecture of the new building reflects many of the characteristics of the adjacent historic building.
© *Kitchen & Associates Architectural Services.*

three-story breezeway to a new building. The architecture of the new addition reflects many of the characteristics of the historic building with its tile roof and brick-and-siding façade. "At the ribbon cutting, a huge crowd of 250 people showed up. Everyone was thrilled with the project," Charles Lewis says.

GREEN ACHIEVEMENTS

In addition to the inherent green achievement of rehabilitating the Pearlye Building and developing the new building on an infill site as described above, the Faison Mews team, working closely with the New Jersey Green Homes Office (NJGHO), made great strides in greening the whole project. Working with Darren Port at the NJGHO, the team applied the New Jersey Affordable Green (NJAG) program matrix to guide the decision-making process for the project. Experts from the program help the develop-

PROJECT DETAILS

Project Size:	51 units of affordable senior housing (for independent seniors age sixty-two and older). One rehabilitated historic landmark building and one new building with connecting three-story breezeway in which the laundry and community room are located. The historic Pearlye Building was originally constructed in the late 1800s and holds 12 of the 51 units.
Total Development Cost:	$8.95 million
Project Started:	November 2004 (official date; some planning began years earlier)
Completion Date:	March 2006

Project Team

Developer:	Pennrose Properties in a joint venture with the Camden Redevelopment Agency and Parkside Business & Community in Partnership
Architect:	Kitchen & Associates
Contractor:	Domus
Structural Engineer:	Bevan Lawson
MEP Engineer:	Mark A. Hagan, PE
Civil Engineer:	CES
Green Building Consultant:	Darren Port, Andrew Shapiro, and Robert Wisniewski of New Jersey Green Homes Office (part of New Jersey Department of Community Affairs, Division of Housing)

ment/architectural team to understand green options and trade-offs. Port notes that "sometimes charrettes [special design workshops] are held to work on a project to ensure an integrated design process." Also, experts conduct trainings for contractors and offer monitoring during construction and basic commissioning to ensure the green goals are accomplished. All of these offerings were a part of the Faison Mews project as well. For their Affordable Green program, in 2006 the New Jersey Department of Community Affairs Office was awarded the USDOE/EPA ENERGY STAR® Partner of the Year Award for Excellence in Energy-Efficient Affordable Housing.

Some of the highlights include a rainwater collection system; access to daylighting with views for every unit; green materials selection with attention to durability, recycled content, and indoor air quality (IAQ) impacts; a construction waste management plan; and proper attention during construction to ensure good IAQ. All units are also New Jersey ENERGY STAR rated.

Developer's Green History: Prior to the Faison Mews project, Pennrose had worked with the NJGHO under the Sustainable Development pilot program on another project. Charles Lewis notes that Pennrose likes to be "on the cutting edge," so they were excited to be part of this earlier pilot effort. For this first project, they selected energy-efficient appliances, recycled products or less product, and other low-environmental-impact options. They went through the pilot project, and "it worked—and was very workable," according to Lewis. The developer tried things they hadn't done before, such as framing 2-by-6-foot lumber at 24 inches on center, thereby saving on lumber and adding extra space for insulation. Lewis said they faced resistance from their contractor and paid a premium initially, but ultimately, the reduction in materials ended up costing the contractor less. Now, they use this framing technique all the time and save resources. These lessons were the foundation for the Faison Mews project.

Materials: Andrea Garland, an architect with Kitchen and Associates Architectural Services, a woman-owned architecture, planning, and interior design firm based in Collingswood, New Jersey, was the project architect. Garland was very pleased with her company's green achievements on the project and tracked them on the program's matrix: "Our firm's participation in the New Jersey Green Homes program for the Faison Mews senior housing project has established a great new outlook on building green. This process has resulted in a conscientious selection of materials and methods. Many standard materials such as flooring, paints, cabinets, siding, et cetera, are available using recycled materials or less hazardous chemicals and pollutants.

> "People look at environmentalists as nuts. But I've found this green program to be very reasonable, very understandable, and it worked well."
>
> CHARLES LEWIS
> Pennrose Properties

Specifying particular site materials such as cisterns, site furnishings such as recycled content benches, recycled parking bumpers, and native plantings also contributes to building green and will create a better environment for the user." She notes that in most instances, these items were found to be of excellent quality and had only between a 2 to 5 percent upcharge from typical specified items.

Systems: Each of the 51 units in the Faison Mews project has an individual ENERGY STAR heating and cooling system and a 95-percent-efficient gas water heater. These units are power vented to ensure proper ventilation and to avoid backdrafting. With regard to the building envelope, Garland says that "it was difficult with the older Pearlye Building to achieve airtightness—and we ended up using a

SUMMARY OF GREEN FEATURES

Site

- Rehabilitation of building and new development on infill site
- Secure on-site courtyard with room for resident gardens
- Access to nature trails at nearby urban park
- Within ½ mile of transit, including bus
- Native landscaping

Water

- Rainwater collection system
- High-efficiency drip irrigation
- Storm sewer inlets labeled with info on water protection
- Low-water-use toilets
- Water management system developed for existing Pearlye Building

Energy

- Access to daylighting and views for every unit
- All units New Jersey ENERGY STAR® rated
- High-performance (low solar heat gain coefficient, low-e) windows
- Cellulose insulation in walls and attic
- High-energy-factor water heater[1]
- Airtight drywall approach to air control leakage with Energy and Environmental Building Association (EEBA) details
- ENERGY STAR hard-wired fluorescent lighting in high-use areas
- ENERGY STAR refrigerators
- EEBA window detail and flashing[2]

Materials and Resources

- Recycled materials utlized, including acoustical ceiling tiles and carpet
- Waste management plan recycled and salvaged construction and demolition debris

Health and Comfort

- Low-volatile organic compound (VOC) paint used for interior finishes and for all sealants and adhesives
- All combustion devices power vented
- Non-formaldehyde-free particleboard in cabinets encapsulated
- Tacked-down recycled-content carpet instead of glued-down carpet
- Under-slab vapor barriers and perimeter slab insulation
- Ducts and HVAC protected from dust during construction
- Building aired out prior to occupancy
- Flexible common space included for meetings and performances in community room

Durability and Ease of Maintenance

- Durable kitchen, bath, and entry flooring (linoleum in kitchen, tile in bathrooms)
- 50-year-plus durable siding (partial brick and Hardiplank fiber cement siding)
- Tenant O&M manual and training
- On-site recycling centers in common areas

---

[1] For the water heater, the energy factor is the portion of the energy going into the unit that gets turned into usable hot water under average conditions.

[2] See Joseph W. Lstiburek, *Water Management Guide,* 2nd ed. (Minneapolis: Energy and Environmental Building Association, 2004). This guide presents a variety of recommendations for minimizing water intrusion into homes (i.e., window and flashing details).

---

lot of foam insulation. A blower door ENERGY STAR® test was conducted to ensure we got it right."

PROJECT FINANCING

The total development costs for Faison Mews were $8.95 million. Financing included funds earmarked for green features from the NJGHO as well as a rebate from the ENERGY STAR program.

Charles Lewis worked back and forth with NJGHO director Darren Port on various cost and selection implica-

tions related to the program. In the end, the program offered $7,500 per unit as a green subsidy to help meet the state's green threshold, resulting in a total subsidy of $382,500 for the 51 units.

Frequent visits by the NJGHO staff meant that the development team "had to always stay on top of the green aspects," according to NJGHO director Darren Port. In the process, some options, however, were cost-prohibitive. For example, the possibility of dual flush toilets was suggested. In the end, the specification to include such toilets couldn't

PROJECT FINANCING

FUNDING SOURCES	AMOUNT
Equity	
Low-Income Housing Tax Credit	$5,884,127
Grants	
New Jersey Department of Community Affairs Balanced Housing Program	$2,070,008
City of Camden HOME Funds	$200,000
New Jersey Affordable Green Funds	$382,500
Federal Home Loan Bank of New York	$250,000
ENERGY STAR® Rebate	$64,850
Other	
Deferred Developer Fee	$99,229
Total Sources	**$8,950,714**

be made, because of additional costs and a longer procurement time. This was an issue because the team had a very tight project timeline based on the tax credit requirements.

LESSONS LEARNED

Developer Charles Lewis says the highlight of the project was that all went "very smoothly." Since Pennrose Properties had previously gone through the state's green program during its pilot phase, he said they knew what to expect and what the state would accept in terms of decision making around the green issues.

Barriers: Architect Andrea Garland says, "In general, the more restrictive lead time and availability of the green materials and specifications were the only negative issue. The materials are not always as readily available, which hampers the schedule, and it is harder to substitute due to the restrictions of the program requirements." Some on-site requirements were harder to control, she noted, such as covering all ductwork during construction. Contractors, when in a hurry, do not want to spend the extra initial time to protect these systems from the dust and debris from construction, she said.

Cost Implications: "There is a fine line between balancing the needs of the Green Homes program with the reality of schedule and cost," Garland says. "This project has been a good example of this need for compromise." She feels it is worth spending slightly more on initial costs as well as the time paying closer attention to construction practices in order to have a more energy-efficient, environmentally friendly building: "If the overall costs are not exorbitant, then why not take the additional steps to build green? The owner of the building will eventually save money on building systems while maintaining an ecologically sound project."

Green Homes Program: Participating in the Green Homes program challenged Kitchen and Associates' typical construction administration process, but the final product is aesthetically pleasing and well received by all involved parties.

"People look at environmentalists as nuts. But I've found this green program to be very reasonable, very understandable, and it worked well," says Charles Lewis. Further, he's observed how many of the energy efficiency elements, such as insulating the foundation, are not really that dramatic to implement. The three construction companies typically used by Pennrose have now changed their ways as well because of these projects and Pennrose's influence. Lewis notes, "What's dramatic is how standard practice has changed in just a few short years."

CONTACTS

Developer: Pennrose Properties, Inc.
Charles Lewis, project developer: 267-386-8672

Architect: Kitchen and Associates
Andrea Garland, project architect: 856-854-1880

Green Building Consultant: New Jersey Department of Community Affairs
Darren Port: 609-984-7607; dport@dca.state.nj.us

SOURCES

Faison Mews two-page marketing flyer from Pennrose Properties, Inc., 2006.

Garland, Andrea, project architect, Kitchen and Associates, personal interview with Jenifer Seal Cramer, June 9, 2006, and e-mail correspondence June–August 2006.

Lewis, Charles, developer, Pennrose Properties, Inc., personal interview with Jenifer Seal Cramer, June 14, 2006.

New Jersey Green Homes Office: www.state.nj.us/dca/dh/gho/index.shtml.

Pearlye Building, old photo: www.state.nj.us/dca/dh/gho/frames/pearlyle.shtml.

Port, Darren, director, New Jersey Green Homes Office, New Jersey Department of Community Affairs, Division of Housing, personal interview with Jenifer Seal Cramer, June 1, 2006, and e-mail correspondence June–August 2006.

Greenway Park Cohousing

6224–26 South Kimbark Avenue, Chicago

**COHOUSING / INTEGRATED ENERGY EFFICIENCY
MEASURES / REHABILITATION OF OLD BUILDING**

Cohousing is a type of collaborative housing that has become increasingly popular in the United States over the past decade. In this model, residents commit to active participation in their community's daily life, as well as in its design and operations. Although individual homes are private spaces with all the features of conventional homes, cohousing projects include shared facilities such as a common house (for shared meals, classes, meetings, etc.), open space, a playground, and outdoor gathering spaces.[1]

In an old building on Chicago's south side, a small cohousing community has been created with a "green" identity that distinguishes it from its neighbors. The project is located in Woodlawn, a neighborhood near the University of Chicago that is undergoing gentrification after decades of building decay. Some longtime residents now struggle to afford to remain in the neighborhood. Woodlawn Development Associates (WDA) viewed this project, Greenway Park, as an avenue to provide affordable housing for local Chicago residents, as well as to strengthen neighborhood cohesiveness and self-sufficiency through the cohousing model.

When WDA purchased the decrepit three-story masonry building (as well as the vacant lot next door), it had been abandoned for six years, and was in need of major rehabilitation. The architect, Sam Marts; the developer; and a core of potential residents made plans to reconfigure the traditional "six-flat" building into a 10-unit affordable cohousing project, including an interior common space and exterior

areas for gardening and recreation. The project involved demolition of all interior walls and finishes, new windows, a new roof, and new heating, electrical, and plumbing systems. Completed in 2000, Greenway Park is comprised of 4 one-bedroom, 4 two-bedroom, and 2 three-bedroom apartments. Four of the units are for residents making no more

Units on the back of the Greenway Park building include large windows, ample balconies, and a ramp accessing ADA-accessible units on the first floor. A grassy area behind the building provides an outdoor gathering spot, with gardens on the side and next door.
© *Woodlawn Development Association.*

than 60 percent of the area median income (AMI), and the other six are designated for those making no more than 50 percent of AMI. (Currently, however, 3 of the units receive an additional subsidy to rent to very low-income residents making no more than 30 percent of AMI.)

Greenway Park is one of the first cohousing projects created exclusively for low-income residents (most such projects are for middle- to upper-middle-class residents, and a few are mixed income) and is structurally a rental project (most cohousing projects raise construction funds by preselling units). Unlike most cohousing projects, it does not yet have a common house, although WDA hopes to build one soon on the adjacent vacant lot. Also, the building is the first affordable housing project in Chicago to have no professional manager. Greenway Park is self-managed by its residents, and future tenants are selected by current tenants (while following fair housing guidelines), with preference given to current residents of the Woodlawn neighborhood. Residents do most of the management entirely on their own, including maintaining shared basement laundry facilities, collecting money, and handling repairs. One resident also serves as a part-time paid management assistant.

The building was initially intended to be mixed income, but lenders' guidelines precluded this from happening. Instead, a larger mixed-income community is slowly growing, spread out over several lots, with plans for future additions. In 2001, WDA renovated two three-flat buildings across the back alley from Greenway Park into 12 for-sale condominiums (on the low end of market rate). WDA is now in the process of developing plans for a shared common house and additional for-sale housing to be built on the lot adjacent to Greenway Park on the south side. The common house would be shared by all three developments, offering a gathering place for community meals, meetings, classes, and possibly guest quarters. WDA is again working with architect Sam Marts and has asked him to include as many green items as possible.

The residents worked with Chicago Botanic Gardens to create gardens behind their building as well as on the vacant lot next door. Supplies were donated, and residents contributed the labor to plant the gardens.
© *Woodlawn Development Association.*

GREEN ACHIEVEMENTS

This project has already served as a learning opportunity in several ways. WDA received funding assistance from the state of Illinois to integrate environmentally responsive features into this project, with the goal of applying lessons learned here to future affordable multifamily projects. Greenway Park's green efforts focused on an integrated approach that incorporated a package of energy-efficient building practices, the deliberate substitution of a variety of green building materials for their more conventional counterparts, and a 2.4 kW rooftop photovoltaic system. Greenway Park Cohousing also served as a core part of a publication titled *Building for Sustainability*, produced by one of its funders, the Chicago Community Loan Foundation (CCLF). Many others interested in affordable green housing have toured the development or learned about the measures undertaken here by reading the case study in CCLF's booklet.

Since WDA believed that long-term affordability meant keeping heating costs low, it decided to focus on improving the building's energy efficiency. Keenly aware that its budget lacked the flexibility to do this, WDA applied to the state of Illinois's Energy Efficient Affordable Housing program (part of the Illinois Department of Commerce and Community Affairs, or DCCA) for an up-front grant of $20,000 to offset incremental costs associated with improved energy efficiency.

Additionally, energy consultant Paul Knight contributed technical expertise and manager of DCCA's program Maureen Davlin later offered to pay the difference of $25,632 if Greenway Park would replace an assortment of products typically used in affordable housing projects with more resource-efficient or green products in an effort to identify and experiment with new products that might be widely applicable in future affordable projects. The collaboration between the state and the project team also led to additional funding for a rooftop photovoltaic (PV) system, to illustrate how PV could be used in affordable housing.

Superior Energy Efficiency Through an Integration of Measures: A high level of energy efficiency was achieved through a package of measures that together produce results that are superior to the sum of their parts. Maureen Davlin, explains that the approach uses "a package of energy-efficient building measures that we want to see incorporated in building rehab. These measures include high insulation levels, air sealing and ventilation, and high-efficiency heating systems. Developers can't pick and choose the energy measures they want. They have to understand that these measures work in concert with each other."

Numerous techniques were used to increase the building's energy performance. For example, a thermal break was created between the inside face and the outside of exterior walls. Rock wool insulation was sprayed into this cavity for a total R-value of 18.6 (much higher than the R-value of the masonry alone). The building was also carefully insulated by spraying rock wool into the ceiling cavities between floors and placing wool in the attic and crawlspace.[2] An efficient central hydronic heating system (using two 94 percent efficient warm-water boilers) was chosen. The two 60-gallon units also provide domestic hot water. There is no air-conditioning as units rely on ceiling fans for air circulation, and a reflective coating applied to the roof reduces interior temperatures on the top floor during hot summer months. The building's ventilation system focuses on the rooms that create the most moisture, the kitchen and the bathrooms. Kitchen exhaust fans are vented to the outside instead of using recirculating hoods and bathrooms also have a direct-vented fan.

The 2.4 kW photovoltaic system installed on the roof provides a portion of the power for common-area lighting and laundry facilities (which are in the basement). This system includes four modules, each containing eight 75-

PROJECT DETAILS

Project Size:	Phase I: 10 units in one 11,694 sq ft building on 0.25 acres
	Phase II: 12 for-sale condos (in two buildings) across the back alley
	Phase III: Will include a common house and additional for-sale units (utilizing a "limited equity cooperative" model to retain affordability in perpetuity) on lot adjacent to Greenway Park Cohousing
Construction Cost:	$791,822 or $67.71/sq ft
Cost/Unit:	$79,182
Total Development Cost:	$1,203,765
Completion Date:	February 2000; originally built in 1916

Project Team

Developer/Owner:	Woodlawn Development Associates
Architect:	Sam Marts Architects and Planners
General Contractor:	South Chicago Workforce
MEP Engineer:	Domus PLUS
Financial Consultant:	Pusateri Development
Energy Consultant:	Domus PLUS
Landscape Architect:	Chicago Botanic Gardens (postoccupancy grant)

Note: All details pertain to Phase I, the affordable cohousing project, only.

SUMMARY OF GREEN FEATURES

Site

- Permeable parking lot created by removing former cement slab garage and laying permeable product that allows grass to grow and snow to melt
- Grassy community open space created between back of building and parking area
- Community gardens funded and designed with resident input and participation by Chicago Botanic Gardens

Water

- Water-conserving showerheads (2.5 gpm)
- Low-flow aerated faucets in kitchens and bathrooms

Energy

- Two warm-water boilers supply space heating, each with an output rating of 105,000 Btu and a seasonal efficiency of 87.3%
- A 2.4 kW rooftop grid-tied photovoltaic system offsets lighting and other common-area loads
- Domestic water heating provided by two water heaters, each with a seasonal efficiency of 94%
- All windows replaced with double-glazed, low-e single-hung windows
- Blower-door tests conducted to ensure tight construction
- Airtight drywall approach (ADA) used to achieve air sealing.
- No mechanical cooling system
- ceiling fans provided for circulation
- CFLs used for all common-area lighting. Twenty-four 27-watt fluorescent fixtures in stairwell and hallways remain on constantly for safety. Seven exterior 27-watt fixtures remain on at night for security
- ENERGY STAR® refrigerators

Materials and Resources

- Interior of masonry walls framed with engineered wood studs
- Rock wool insulation used to improve thermal efficiency of exterior walls by a factor of almost 8. Total R-value is 18.6. (Masonry wall alone has R-value of 2.4.)
- Damage-resistant FibeRock drywall made from recycled newsprint and gypsum installed in high-use areas such as hallways
- Glass tiles containing 70% recycled glass (in bathrooms and front entry)
- Carpeting made from recycled PET (polyethylene terephthalate) plastic
- Rear porch decking and handicap ramp made of recycled plastic lumber

Health and Comfort

- Formaldehyde-free Medex used in place of conventional medium-density fiberboard for interior windowsills, staircase and entryway baseboards, and kitchen countertop bases and substrates
- Nontoxic water-based interior caulk and low-VOC primer
- Water-based urethane floor finish
- Recyled felt carpet padding made of waste fibers without chemical additives
- Carpet secured with tack strips rather than glued down to avoid VOC offgassing
- Reflective roof coating used to reduce interior temperature of top floor units during hot months
- Individually controlled thermostats installed in each unit

watt panels. Two inverters are located in the basement electrical room to convert the power generated by the PV system from DC to AC. When electricity is generated, it feeds into the common-area circuitry instead of using power from the electric utility. When excess power is generated, it feeds back into the utility's system. In order to keep costs down, battery storage was not included.

Pat Wilcoxen of WDA says that the package of energy-efficient measures "has made a noticeable difference [in the building's performance], especially since heating costs have increased. It keeps cooler than other buildings, too."

PROJECT FINANCING

This major rehabilitation project cost $791,822, or $67.71 per square foot, in construction costs, with another $281,178 in soft costs, including land acquisition.

WDA paid $96,600 to purchase the building and land. WDA also paid an additional $37,000 to buy the lot next door. In a demonstration of local grassroots confidence, WDA raised the funds for site acquisition via thirty unsecured loans from friends and families, ranging from $500 to $20,000. These loans were paid back once permanent financing was secured. Predevelopment costs were financed by a $75,000 loan from the Chicago Community Loan Foundation. A $49,000 grant from the Federal Home Loan Bank, conditioned on income and disability requirements, was used as owner's equity. Additional owner's equity came from private donor gifts of $10,414.

Construction was financed by conventional mortgages from three lenders that insisted the contractor be bonded. However, the contractor selected, South Chicago Workforce (a nonprofit organization that trains minorities in the building trades), hadn't been in business long enough to be eligible for bonding. Getting around this requirement necessitated a letter of credit for $40,000, which the contractor did not have. To meet the letter-of-credit terms, WDA applied $20,000 from its earlier predevelopment loan from CCLF (while paying back the rest before construction began) and obtained unsecured loans for $20,000.

The cost of green features was covered by three separate grants from DCCA. DCCA's Illinois Energy Efficient Affordable Housing Program (EEAH) granted $20,000 to subsidize the package of energy efficiency measures that added $2,000 per unit. (Because these measures were integrated into the project—rather than add-ons—these funds were factored into the original lending package.) This grant also included technical assistance and post-occupancy performance evaluation. After closing, DCCA provided additional grant monies directly to the contractor to cover the cost of the 2.4 kW photovoltaic system ($29,720) as well as to subsidize green materials ($25,632) that cost more than conventional building materials.

Savings and Additional Costs: Annual heating costs for the building run around $2,300 (5.0 Btu/ft^{2}F, assuming $0.60/therm) or $230 per unit. Without the energy-efficient building practices, annual space heating costs would have been about $570 per unit, for a total of $5,700. This is an annual savings of $3,400, or $340 per unit. In winter 2005–2006, when the price of natural gas dramatical-

PROJECT FINANCING

FUNDING SOURCES	AMOUNT
Equity and Grants	
Grant from Federal Home Loan Bank (to use as owner's equity)	$49,000
Grant from Illinois Department of Commerce and Community Affairs (for integrated energy efficiency measures; PV, green materials)	$75,352
Private Donations	$10,414
Debt	
Chicago Community Loan Foundation	$75,000
Lasalle Bank (1st mortgage, 30-yr adjustable rate)	$194,000
Illinois Housing Development Authority (2nd mortgage, 0% interest)	$500,000
Illinois Department of Housing Joint Lenders Program (3rd mortgage, 0% interest)	$299,999
Total Sources	**$1,203,765**

ly increased, utility bills were much lower than at comparable buildings in the neighborhood without energy features.

Using green materials at Greenway Park added approximately 3 percent, or $23,755, to the cost of construction, as compared with conventional practices. Applying just the average utility cost savings of $3,400 per year to this upcharge results in a seven-year payback period.

LESSONS LEARNED

Working Together: Green Building and Cohousing
Green building advocates frequently encourage involving all stakeholders early in the planning and design process. Although this effort often focuses on the project team, resident input is also important as is the input of those who will be operating and maintaining a building. Thus the goals of cohousing and green building mesh well, as the early integral involvement of residents is an important facet of cohousing. A cadre of interested potential residents was identified to help shape the plans for Greenway Park. For example, collaboration between the residents and the architect resulted in

an unanticipated floor plan that better satisfied the residents' needs—a combined kitchen/dining room/living room rather than the more traditional living room in the front and kitchen in the back, with bedrooms in between.

In looking toward the design and programming of the building(s) to be developed next door to Greenway Park

---

"Superinsulation has made a noticeable difference [in the building's performance], especially since heating costs have increased. It keeps cooler than other buildings, too."

PAT WILCOXEN
WDA

Cohousing, WDA is again encouraging resident participation, believing the earlier process to have worked well. Says Wilcoxen, "We'll go through this process again by having the residents involved from the outset." Several residents have expressed interest in moving to the new, limited-equity cooperative building once it is finished, while others are also providing input as future users of the common house.

Resource-Efficient Materials: Much has changed since Greenway Park was built in 2000. Many green building materials once considered exotic are now mainstream (e.g., cork or bamboo flooring, materials with recycled content, recycled plastic lumber decking). Numerous new green materials have entered the marketplace, and costs for green projects continue to go down. But at the time Greenway Park was built, applying green materials to low-income housing was a novel idea. Although the architect and contractor were eager to pursue the green agenda, it was the contractor's first experience with many of the materials. Their experiences with and comments about specific materials and products are well documented in a *Home*

Energy article authored by the project's energy consultant Paul Knight.[3] Looking back recently, Knight noted that were this project to be built now, rather than in 2000, the project team would likely specify less toxic, no- or low-volatile-organic-compound finishes, and other materials that contribute to healthy indoor air quality.

In general, WDA and the design/development team were happy with the new resource-efficient materials used. Says architect Marts, "This project confirmed what we felt about green products. From the users' perspective, [the project] was successful because it removed hesitancy in trying new things."

Most of the green products were well received by the contractor, and the team felt their additional cost (if any) could be justified by their benefits. However, opinions differed on the recycled-glass bathroom tiles. According to Marts, "Everyone liked the tile with recycled glass. It lent a little sparkle, and was slip-resistant. We didn't use much, because it was concentrated in the bathroom floor. It came with a quality level that was immediately apparent." However, the contractor found that the Terra Traffic tiles were "more difficult to set, and installation costs were greater."[4] Knight notes that they probably wouldn't use the recycled-glass tiles again because the total incremental cost was steep ($3,200, or almost $3.50 more per tile).

Looking ahead to the next stage of the community's development, Marts says, "There will be green products without even really trying. I imagine the residents will want green materials, because it is part of their mandate."

Approvals and Codes: As is typical with unique projects, at times local codes stood in the way of achieving the project exactly as it was envisioned. During the first year of occupancy, WDA kept the smallest apartment vacant for use as a temporary common space for community meetings and potlucks. However, during an annual review, one of their lenders concluded that the vacant apartment also needed to be rented to meet lending requirements—within sixty days. Since then, the tenants have been holding community meetings and other events in the basement, which works fine, but the space is not as conducive for creating community.

Because of the energy efficiency measures, only one small furnace was needed, but city code officials simply could not believe the low energy use projections. Thus, the basement houses two small, efficient furnaces, but the second is fairly redundant and really functions as a backup furnace. City codes at the time also did not permit the cellulose insulation that DCCA was funding as part of the green materials package. The architect and contractor both tried to get an exception but were ultimately not successful. This led to the substitution of rock wool insulation, which has performed well and has been enthusiastically recommended by the contractor for future projects.

Photovoltaic Panels in Affordable Housing: Greenway Park's rooftop PV system was the first time that the city had issued a permit for a rooftop PV system as part of a "regular" residential building, rather than as a demonstration project. However, it hasn't been completely smooth sailing. One inverter needs replacement, and the residents, who fund the maintenance and repair budget through their collective rents, have not yet identified funds to repair it. Although the utility buys back excess power, the monthly check Greenway Park residents receive is but a pittance, totaling about $100 annually. Despite these realities, Wilcoxen says that WDA would include PV again because, "I think it's only by people doing it and having the experience that things will improve."

Creating Community / Looking Ahead: The aim of cohousing is to create a community in which everyone participates in decision making as well as in maintaining the community. Architect Marts observes that "part of creating community is creating identity as well." The green aspects were "helpful in creating an identity for the community—

not everyone has a solar panel on their roof. [The residents can think], 'My house is special.'" In an article that appeared in the *University of Chicago Chronicle*, university employee and local resident Jim Nitti said, "Since I've known about the Greenway Park project, I've seen a remarkable improvement in the area immediately surrounding it. It's as if the sense of community that the residents of Greenway Park feel and their connection to each other is contagious."

Currently, WDA is focusing on developing a plan for designing and building the common house, as well as some adjacent units. This poses a challenge in a mixed-income community in which renters with lower incomes can't bear much of the cost burden, but the expense somehow needs to be equitable. The new residents should not bear the entire burden if these neighbors in cohousing are also using the common house. One potential solution under consideration is a sweat equity program through which cohousing residents could contribute labor in place of monetary funds. Developing a site plan for the new building is made more challenging by the existence of cherished community gardens currently planted on the vacant lot.

CONTACTS

Developer: Woodlawn Development Associates
Pat Wilcoxen, treasurer and housing chair: 773-643-7495

Architect: Sam Marts Architects and Planners
Sam Marts: 773-862-0123; SMArchPlan@aol.com

Energy consultant: Domus PLUS
Paul Knight, principal: 708-386-0345

SOURCES

"Airtight Drywall Approach," Energy Fact Sheet 24, developed by Southface Energy Institute with funding from the GA Environmental Facilities Authority, USDOE, USEPA, March 2002, www.southface.org/web/resources

&services/publications/factsheets/24ada_drywal.pdf. More information on the airtight drywall approach, as well as on the related strategy of simple caulk and seal, can be found at www.eere.energy.gov/consumer/your _home/insulation_airsealing/index.cfm/mytopic=11310 and www.healthgoods.com/education/healthy_home _information/Building_Design_and_Construction /airtight_drywall.htm.

"Building for Sustainability: Creating Energy-Efficient and Environmentally Friendly Affordable Housing in Chicago," a publication of the Chicago Community Loan Fund, 2001 (includes case study on Greenway Park, pp. 16–21), www.cclfchicago.org/pdf/green-guide.pdf.

Cohousing Association of the United States: http://www.cohousing.org/default.aspx.

"Encouraging Photovoltaic System Installations in 'Green' Affordable Multifamily Housing," a report prepared by Peregrine Energy Group for the Clean Energy States Alliance, April 14, 2005, www.cleanenergystates.org /library/Reports/Peregrine_Multifamily_PV_Scoping _Memo.pdf.

Energy and Environmental Building Association, "Criteria for Energy and Resource Efficient Building," www.eeba.org/technology/criteria.htm#criteria.

Knight, Paul, "Green Products Brighten Multifamily Rehab," *Home Energy Magazine Online,* (November/ December 2000), http://homeenergy.org/archive /hem .dis.anl.gov/eehem/00/001114.html#partners.

"Residents of Woodlawn Seeing Improvements, as a 40-year Rebuilding Effort Starts to Pay Off," *University of Chicago Chronicle,* November 2, 2000, http://chronicle.uchicago.edu/001102/cohousing.shtml.

NOTES

1. According to the Cohousing Association of the United States, cohousing communities share six defining characteristics: (1) *participatory process:* future residents participate in the design of the community so that it meets their needs, and participate in regular community meetings; (2) *neighborhood design:* the physical layout and orientation of the buildings encourages a sense of community; (3) *common facilities:* common facilities are designed for daily use, are an integral part of the community, and are always supplemental to the private residences; (4) *resident management;* (5) *nonhierarchical structure and decision making;* and (6) *no shared community economy.*

2. For in-depth technical detail on this project, please refer to energy consultant Paul Knight's *Home Energy* article "Green Products Brighten Multifamily Rehab," *Home Energy Magazine Online* (November/December 2000), http://homeenergy.org/archive/hem.dis.anl.gov/eehem/00 /001114.html#partners.

3. Ibid.

4. Ibid.

High Point

Delridge Neighborhood, Seattle, Washington

HOPE VI PROJECT / NATURAL STORMWATER MANAGEMENT / LARGE-SCALE COMMUNITY PLANNING AND DESIGN REDEVELOPMENT

Longfellow Creek is a 3-mile, year-round urban creek in West Seattle's Delridge neighborhood that once teemed with salmon. A comprehensive community effort is now under way to restore the creek as a vital fish habitat.

Almost 10 percent of the stormwater that ends up in Longfellow Creek falls on the ground of High Point, originally a 716-unit affordable housing project built during World War II. Run down and decaying, the project was ripe for redevelopment. With over $37 million in federal HOPE VI funds, the Seattle Housing Authority (SHA), an independent public corporation that functions as both a property manager and a nonprofit developer, began plans to redevelop the entire site into a mixed-income

Sidewalks, narrow streets and wide planting strips (swales) encourage biking, walking, and getting out and about around High Point.
Photo courtesy of Seattle Housing Authority.

community. Concurrently, the city of Seattle expressed interest in integrating a natural stormwater drainage system into the redevelopment project to treat the stormwater runoff in an ecologically sensitive way and improve salmon habitat.

SHA spent time in initial planning determining how it could integrate a natural stormwater management system and identifying the specific permits needed. After deliberation, it agreed to integrate a natural drainage system into the project if the city granted several concessions. These included permitting narrower streets (25 feet wide, with parking on both sides) that would reduce impervious surfaces; assisting in the city permitting process; and supporting an approach that integrates the drainage system into a traditional-looking neighborhood. The city agreed to support these concepts, as well as to provide $2.7 million to cover the difference between a typical new-construction stormwater system and the natrual system proposed by SHA.

The desire to improve the water quality of Longfellow Creek became a linchpin in the overall plan to connect the mixed-income community with the surrounding environment and the larger West Seattle neighborhood. Rather than continuing to use an internally focused street circulation plan, the neighborhood street pattern was reinstated. Numerous environmentally responsive strategies protect the watershed and provide an attractive and diverse neighborhood through the natural drainage system, which is the largest in the country.

PROJECT DETAILS

Note: Except where specified, all details pertain to Phase I affordable housing and site design only.

Project Size: 34 city blocks on 120 acres comprising 1,600 units (half affordable housing, half market-rate), community facilities, a 10-acre greenbelt along Longfellow Creek, and 21 acres of total green space; replaces 716 worn-out public housing units built in the 1940s

> Phase I: 60 acres with 344 affordable units built by SHA; 75 senior affordable units built by the Sisters of Providence; 268 market-rate homeowner units; 160 market-rate senior rentals; an estimated 100 market-rate rentals or condos atop a neighborhood-serving retail center situated along the busy 35th Avenue SW arterial; and a new branch library, medical and dental clinic, and neighborhood center

> Phase II: 60 acres with 256 affordable units and 397 market-rate homeowner units

Breakdown of Housing Types (Phase I and Phase II):[1]

> Affordable housing: 796 total units for people earning from below 30% up to 80% of area median income (AMI)

> Market-rate housing: 804 total units

Phase I Construction Costs for the 344 Units Built by SHA:

> Hard costs: $43 million

> Soft costs (builder profit, taxes, etc.): $6 million

Phase I Architectural and Engineering Costs:

> Housing design: $4 million

> Overall site design: $7 million

Total Phase I Development Costs: $102 million

Completion Date:

> Phase I finished in 2006

> Phase II forecast to be completed in 2009

Project Team

Developer/Owner:	Seattle Housing Authority
Architect:	Mithun
General Contractor:	Absher Construction (Phase I)
Infrastructure Contractor:	Gary Merlino Construction Company (Phase I)
Civil Engineer and Right-of-Way Landscape Architect:	SvR Design
Landscape Architect:	Nakano Associates
Traffic Engineering:	Gary Struthers Associates
Community Center Design:	Environmental Works
Geotechnical:	Shannon & Wilson
Builders:	Absher Construction; Devland; the Dwelling Company; Habitat for Humanity; Holiday Retirement Corp.; Lyle Homes; Polygon Northwest; Saltaire Homes; Sisters of Providence

Awards

Recipient of the City of Seattle 2005 Built Green Community Design Award.

One of eight recipients of the American Institute of Architecture's 2006 Show You're Green Awards, given to projects selected for excellence in green affordable housing. High Point is a Built Green three-star-certified community and a Built Green three-star-certified multifamily project—the highest possible rating in both categories

High Point is the first ENERGY STAR®–certified multifamily community in the nation

[1] Breakdown of housing types at High Point: *Affordable housing:* 796 total units for people earning 80 percent or less of area median income (AMI), including 350 rental units for very low-income residents making 30 percent or below AMI; 116 independent living rental units for very low-income seniors at 30 percent or below AMI; 250 tax credit rental units for working families making up to 60 percent of AMI; and 80 units to be sold at reduced rates to low-income families earning up to 80 percent of AMI. The total also includes 35 units for low-income tenants suffering from asthma. *Market-rate housing:* 804 total units, including 160 rental units of market-rate, independent, and assisted senior housing and 644 for-sale homes in a mix of detached single-family homes, carriage units, townhomes, and condominiums.

First, SHA re-built the infrastructure for the entire 120-acre site. This included demolishing most structures (some were deconstructed for reuse) and all streets and utilities, and realigning the street grid so it connected to the larger West Seattle neighborhood. With the basic groundwork in place, the team was able to proceed with the design and construction of a completely reinvented High Point, including a new street grid; over 21 acres of open space, parks, and playgrounds; the natural drainage system; and a number of community facilities.

Upon buildout, High Point will house approximately 4,000 residents in 1,600 units of various types of housing. About half of the units are designated as affordable at various income levels, including senior housing, housing for large families, and 8 homes built with sweat equity by Habitat for Humanity.[1] The rest are a variety of single-family homes, carriage homes, and townhomes, offered for sale at market prices. As of fall 2006, 344 affordable units built by SHA and 75 affordable senior units built by the Sisters of Providence were completed, as well as key community facilities, such as a new library and a neighborhood clinic. Some market-rate homes had been completed and sold, and builders were focusing on completing the rest. Phase II of the project is expected to wrap up by 2009.

GREEN ACHIEVEMENTS

Numerous aspects of High Point's site design address resource conservation and environmental responsiveness. By combining the natural drainage system with traditional neighborhood design, the design team was able to capture synergies stemming from traditional, narrow streets and wide landscaped medians and parkways. Other green aspects are featured in the design and construction of each unit.

Site Design: In developing the master plan the project's architect, Seattle-based Mithun, used many principles espoused by New Urbanism. Narrower streets (now often termed "traditional streets") with short blocks promote a pedestrian-friendly atmosphere that encourages social interaction and decreases the impact and importance of cars. Approximately 2,500 trees were added to the site, and over 100 large trees worth $1.5 million were preserved during the construction process. Twenty-one acres of open space include parks and green spaces of all types, from a large central park that acts as the heart of the community to small pocket parks and trails.

The natural drainage system adds to the quality of the green spaces throughout High Point. One of the drainage system's most important elements is 4 miles of swales, which replace conventional street curbs and gutters with vegetated drainage channels designed to collect, channel, and filter stormwater. The swales line one side of each

The large central pond adds beauty while also functioning as a stormwater detention pond, an integral part of the natural stormwater management system.
Photo courtesy of Seattle Housing Authority.

street and resemble the landscaped parkways that sit between the street and sidewalk in many traditional neighborhoods. Planted with grass, trees, and shrubs, the swales filter rainwater and offer additional play areas. The swales are made possible by reducing the paved area which also reduces the amount of pollutants, such as oil, that enter the system via runoff. The central feature of this system is a pond that, in addition to providing a scenic view and a local gathering place, plays a crucial role in absorbing and filtering stormwater before finally channeling it into Longfellow Creek.

Healthy and Efficient Housing: All housing at High Point is required to meet or exceed a three-star rating by Seattle's Built Green program, a residential green building program and rating system developed by the Master Builders Association of King and Snohomish counties in partnership with the city of Seattle. The three-star rating is the highest achievable in the "Community" and "Multifamily" categories. All of the townhome-style rental units were also built to meet ENERGY STAR® standards. Other green aspects include the use of low-emission paint and construction materials in all rental units. The homes

SUMMARY OF GREEN FEATURES

Site

- Over 100 mature trees protected (assessed at over $1.5 million by professional arborist)
- Approximately 2,500 new trees planted along streets and park, tripling number of previously existing trees.
- Natural drainage system integrated with community, also providing open and play spaces
- 21 acres designated for parks, open spaces, and playgrounds.
- Four-acre central park created at heart of community
- New community facilities built, including branch library, medical-dental clinic, neighborhood center, on-site retail
- Traditional narrow streets, with planting strips wider than standard in Seattle
- Special techniques used to handle stormwater runoff, including network of vegetated and grass-lined swales combined with amended soil that helps handle excess rainfall. Excess water channeled by underground pipes into stormwater pond
- Reduced grading
- All homes built to meet Built Green three-star standards

Water

- Natural stormwater management program
- Water-conserving fixtures
- Front-loading water-saving washers
- Drought-resistant plants

Energy

- Gas-fired, tankless water heaters supply wall-mounted radiators, allowing residents to heat only the rooms they are using, and also provide on-demand warm water to faucets
- ENERGY STAR® washers and efficient dryers
- Whole-house fans
- Low-e, argon-filled windows (0.33 U-value) that exceed state code (0.4 U-value)
- Installed insulation with improved R-values (R-38 for ceiling roof lines, R-19 for walls)

Materials and Resources

- 22 old homes deconstructed; lumber, plywood, plumbing fixtures salvaged for sale or reuse
- Old paving reused as backfill in trenches
- Wood-saving advanced framing techniques used

Health and Comfort

- Ultra-low-sulfur biodiesel fuel (350,000 gallons' worth) used during infrastructure construction to protect air quality
- 35 Breathe Easy homes constructed for asthma prevention and reduced allergy problems
- Natural stormwater management system reduces water contamination in adjacent Longfellow Creek
- Low-allergen, drought-tolerant plants installed
- Indoor environmental quality improved by using no- or low-VOC paint, adhesives, cabinetry, etc., and installing moisture-resistant drywall

Durability and Ease of Maintenance

- Linoleum floors used instead of carpet
- Interiors in rentals painted with same color
- Front yards of rentals considered common areas for easy maintenance

also include appliances and fixtures that go beyond code requirements to save energy and water. Each home features a high-efficiency hydronic heating system. All rental units have ENERGY STAR® dishwashers and front-loading, highly energy-efficient washing machines.

High Point also includes 35 innovative Breathe Easy homes available to low-income families with children suffering from asthma. These homes were designed to create a preventive atmosphere by minimizing exposure to some of the numerous environmental factors that can trigger asthma, including formaldehyde, dust, pollen, and insect remnants. Breathe Easy homes include high-efficiency particulate air (HEPA) filters that remove irritants from the air, no-volatile-organic compound (no-VOC) building materials, and linoleum floors instead of carpet. Construction measures also addressed asthma prevention—for example, smoking was prohibited during and after construction. Residents must also promise to avoid asthma triggers such as smoking or having furry pets. Landscaping outside these homes is comprised of drought-tolerant plants that don't produce pollen, including many plants native to the Pacific Northwest.

Researchers have been tracking the health of the residents of these homes since a year before they moved in, to investigate whether the environment provided by these homes makes a difference to the health of the occupants.

Deconstruction and Reuse: Before the site could be prepared for new construction, the old buildings had to be removed. Twenty-two of the old buildings were deconstructed by hand so that their materials, which included high-quality old-growth fir, could be sold and reused.

Going forward, SHA has mandated that parks and open spaces be maintained using environmentally sensitive approaches. Resident teams of adults and children have conducted environmental outreach, including public education about the value (monetary and environmental) of preserving the large trees.

PROJECT FINANCING

The High Point project will cost approximately $198 million. This price tag includes demolition, deconstruction, and infrastructure development, in addition to building the 344 affordable units in Phase I and preparing the lots to sell to builders for market-rate homes. The construction of the 344 affordable units cost $43 million in hard construction costs, or approximately $125,000 per unit.

Financing was be completed via a complex mix that includes bonds and equity, and $37 million in HUD HOPE VI funds. Selling land to builders funded nearly 30 percent of the overall budget, bringing in almost $59.7 million. Monies allocated specifically for green aspects were $185,000 for the design and construction of the 35 Breathe Easy homes (provided through a $325,000 Healthy Homes Initiative grant from HUD) and $2.7 million from Seattle Public Utilities for the stormwater drainage system.

In total, High Point's green elements cost approximately $1.5 million, approximately 3 percent of the project's $43 million rental housing construction cost. The team was able to find savings in some of its construction strategies,

PROJECT FINANCING

FUNDING SOURCES (Estimate for both Phases I & II)	AMOUNT
Equity	
Proceeds from Land Sales (estimate)	$59,700,000
Low-Income Housing Tax Credit Equity	$52,681,693
Seattle Housing Authority Capital Subsidy	$10,000,000
Deferred Developer Fee	$12,463,736
Interest Income	$235,586
Debt	
Seattle Housing Authority Issued Tax-Exempt Bonds	$18,600,000
Washington State Housing Trust Fund	$4,000,000
Grants	
HUD HOPE VI	$37,462,300
Seattle Public Utilities (for stormwater drainage system)	$2,700,000
HUD/NIH Healthy Homes Grant	$325,000
Total Sources	**$198,168,315**

such as minimizing grading, stockpiling and reusing topsoil, and recycling demolished paving for trench backfill. Narrower streets also cost less to build. Some items incurred no or minimal additional cost, such as low-VOC paints, adhesives, cabinets and other materials; landscaping with native and drought-resistant plants; a framing system that included modified advance framing and panelized walls; and airtight, moisture-resistant drywall.

The additional cost of some green items were offset by rebates from Seattle City Lights for items such as compact fluorescent lights, ENERGY STAR® front-loading washers, efficient dryers, and whole-house fans. Other items did cost more, including a closed-loop hydronic heating system and a flash water heater used in each unit, durable and healthy Marmoleum floor coverings, and windows with higher-than-code R-values. Retaining the 100-plus mature trees incurred an expense, although the trees themselves were valued at $1.5 million. And choosing to deconstruct 22 old units also cost more than bulldozing them all, although some of the cost was re-captured by selling salvaged materials.

SHA was able to negotiate reduced utility allowances based on efficient design, systems, and appliances in the units. This resulted in more rental income accruing to the owner, SHA. Estimated savings in energy use are 20 percent as compared with similar units built by the SHA at its

---

> "The green aspects became an important engine as we went along because they became an important rallying point for people who wanted to help. There was lots of support in the community for making High Point happen."
>
> TOM PHILLIPS
> *project manager, Seattle Housing Authority*

---

built-to-code New Holly project ($371 annually for a three-bedroom unit). Over one-third of the $371 annual savings can be attributed to the tankless hot water heating system ($135 annually), with another 29 percent savings coming from the front-loading washing machines ($106 annually).

LESSONS LEARNED

SHA project manager Tom Phillips, who was called the "driving vision and force" behind the development of High Point, offers a few practices he feels were important in making sure the vision got built:

- Create an open environment.
- Make sure the contractor follows the intent of the plan.
- Don't be afraid to leverage your support.
- Reach out to the community.

Phillips also attributes the success of High Point to "setting sustainable goals very early on. We had a lot of time and a really good schedule to get some of the farther-reaching green items included, like dual-use tankless water heaters. We worked with Seattle City Light to create efficient units by using fluorescent lighting, windows, and high insulation levels for roof lines and walls."

Create an Open Environment: Phillips believes that, especially on such a large project, it is important to create an open environment in which participants feel comfortable asking for information and assistance on new approaches. "The construction industry will be behind on the knowledge curve," he says, "so don't assume that they know how to do something just because it makes sense to a civil engineer."

Make Sure the Contractor Follows the Intent of the Plan: Phillips observes that, in general, the construction process at High Point went smoothly. The biggest lesson learned during construction was that some aspects of this project were breaking new ground and therefore required the contractor to change on-site behavior. For example, the plantings in the swales and around the pond needed to be installed early to achieve their function during the rainy season. Phillips recommends, "Work with contractors really early [in the process]. You just can't educate them enough, and will need to keep educating them about what the system is, and why it is different. It can be a fine line to walk between wearing innovation on our sleeve (which could raise the price of the project) and keeping the guys at the top, in the middle, and in the field educated about what is going on, and why."

Don't Be Afraid to Leverage Your Support: Phillips also found that sometimes, to move the project forward, you need to "call in your chips occasionally." For example, in working to get a building permit from the city, the project team struggled with resistance from some city bureaucrats who just couldn't understand the differences between the High Point system and a traditional stormwater management plan. But because the team already had the support of Seattle's mayor to be innovative, they were able to create some leverage to remove bureaucratic obstacles, including getting a resistant staff person who couldn't let go of the old rules reassigned.

Reach Out to the Community: Phillips and Mithun's lead architect, Brian Sullivan, worked tirelessly to educate and get feedback from various user groups about the proposed plans for High Point, doing "the important work of listening." They focused on bridging differences between various agencies and interest groups, as well as the High Point community, itself a multicultural melting pot in which over ten different language groups are represented. Phillips says that the "hardest work was the first three to four months of the master planning process," which involved plenty of outreach to the city, local neighborhoods, High Point residents, and others. It was "a great example of a good public process speeding up an approvals process, going through it with goodwill instead of ill will. There was only one real change after the foundation was laid." Through a process of outreach and public involvement, Phillips and Sullivan were able to get the residents of the larger West Seattle neighborhood to the west of High Point "on board, so there was not much active opposition to this project, which is the same size as the entire downtown Seattle area."

Phillips explains that "the green aspects became an important engine as we went along because they became an important rallying point for people who wanted to help. There was lots of support in the community for making High Point happen."

CONTACTS

Developer: Seattle Housing Authority
Tom Phillips, project manager: 206-615-3414;
tphillips@seattlehousing.org

Architect: Mithun
Matthew Sullivan, architect: 206-971-3344;
matthews@mithun.com

Civil engineer: SvR Design Company
Peg Staeheli, principal: 206-223-0326;
svr@svrdesign.com

SOURCES

Affordable Housing Design Advisor: www.designadvisor.org. Affordable Housing Design Advisor offers resources and in-depth examples of affordable housing, with a section devoted to projects selected in the annual AIA Show You're Green Awards, including High Point, a 2006 recipient.

City of Seattle, High Point "green home" case study: www.seattle.gov/dpd/stellent/groups/pan/@pan/@sustainableblding/documents/web_informational/dpds_007254.pdf.

Cloward, Brian, and Brian Sullivan, of Mithun, personal interview by Lisa McManigal Delaney, June 21, 2006 followed by email correspondence.

High Point information for potential residents and others: www.thehighpoint.com.

High Point natural drainage system: www.ci.seattle.wa.us/util/About_SPU/Drainage_&_Sewer_System/Natural_Drainage_Systems/High_Point_Project/index.asp.

Nemeth, George, of Seattle Housing Authority, personal interview by Lisa McManigal Delaney, June 15, 2006 followed by email correxpondence.

New Urbanist features of High Point: www.tndwest.com/highpoint.html.

Peirce, Neal, "High Point: Seattle's green community," *Seattle Times*, September 24, http://seattletimes.nwsource.com/html/opinion/2003271360_peirce24.html.

Phillips, Tom, of Settle Housing Authority, personal interview by Lisa McManigal Delaney, August 2006, followed by email and telephone correspondence.

Seattle Housing Authority High Point Redevelopment: www.seattlehousing.org/Development/highpoint /highpoint.html. Contains much information about the project, including the final environmental impact statement, the redevelopment plan, photos, and details on green features.

"A West Seattle Neighborhood Is Being Transformed," *Seattle Post-Intelligencer,* April 12, 2006; http://seattlepi .nwsource.com/local/266373_ncenter12.html.

NOTE

1. Sweat equity: Manual labor and other work performed as non-cash contributions toward home ownership.

Linden Street Apartments

34 Linden Street, Somerville, Massachusetts

**BROWNFIELD REDEVELOPMENT / SMART GRADING /
EXEMPLARY ENERGY SAVINGS**

Located in the urban Union Square neighborhood of Somerville, a city next to Boston, the Linden Street Apartments stand on a former brownfield. The site was previously used as an industrial truck maintenance facility, had no trees, and was completely paved. To prepare the property for residential development, the Somerville Community Corporation hired ECS, Inc., to remediate the site. Hazardous soils were removed, and new topsoil was added. The Massachusetts Brownfields program, run by MassDevelopment, provided funding for the initial site

> Iric Rex believes that the team's green efforts were successful because they were working with "practical design options based on good research."
>
> IRIC REX
> *project architect, Mostue & Associates*

analysis as well as the cleanup. Today the Linden Street Apartments provide 42 units of new, vibrant multifamily rental housing in a series of three-story buildings that blend in with the scale and form of the surrounding neighborhood. The buildings contain one-, two-, and three-bedroom units for low- and very low-income residents. The apartments were developed by the nonprofit Somerville Community Corporation and financed through a variety of public and private funds. Eighteen of the units have Section 8 operating subsidies.

The Linden Street Apartments incorporate a variety of green building strategies, including durable materials, energy-efficient systems, smart site grading, and considerable green space. All apartments are ENERGY STAR®–qualified homes. As a result of its many green achievements, the project received Honorable Mention in the "Places to Live" category of the Northeast Sustainable Energy Association's 2004 Northeast Green Building

View of Linden Street Apartments façade from the street.
Photo courtesy of Greg Premru

PROJECT DETAILS

Project Size:	42 units, 7 buildings, 50,970 sq ft (with 13,100 sq ft footprint) on 1.5 acres
Construction Cost:	$6.79 million
Total Development Cost:	$10 million
Average Cost/Unit:	$214,614
Average Cost/Sq Ft:	$133/sq ft (hard costs)
Completion Date:	January 2003

Project Team

Developer:	Somerville Community Corporation
Architect:	Mostue & Associates
General Contractor:	Landmark Structures Corporation
MEP Engineer:	RW Sullivan
Civil Engineer:	Cygnus Corporation
Structural Engineer:	Ocmulgee Associates
Landscape Architect:	Elena Saporta
Energy Consultant:	Conservation Services Group
Development Consultant:	Paula Herrington

Awards:

Northeast Sustainable Energy Association's 2004 Northeast Green Building Awards (Honorable Mention, "Places to Live" category)

Environmental Design + Construction magazine's 2003 awards (Honorable Mention, "Commercial and Residential—Outstanding Exterior" category)

Awards. The judges wrote that they bestowed the award "for this successful effort to build environmentally conscious, affordable multifamily housing within very strict economic and regulatory limitations. The project fits nicely into its urban setting."

GREEN ACHIEVEMENTS

When architect Iric Rex of Mostue & Associates proposed that green strategies be included in the project, his suggestions met with approval from the Somerville Community Corporation (SCC). Rex says his firm presented an informal life-cycle cost analysis to assure SCC that the green concepts were not too risky and would not result in higher maintenance costs. "I present green options on every job out of a personal inclination," says Rex, and in this case, the client and other team members were receptive. While the team did not write up formal sustainability goals for the project, Rex feels that the team's green efforts were successful because they were working with "practical design options based on good research." But even he was surprised by how successful some of the project's design strategies were and how well the project has performed.

Smart Grading: A carefully developed grading plan resulted in three major benefits. Aesthetically, the architects felt that it enhanced the look of the project to have the buildings placed slightly above the sidewalks. Environmentally, the grading was crafted to manage and control stormwater; the contoured dish shape of the site enables it to hold excess stormwater in the center parking and landscaped areas so the water won't run off the site or flood the homes. And lastly, the grading was done in a way that allows for universal access to all entrances so ramps and railings were not needed. This approach not only reduced materials usage and costs, but the architect feels it also made for a more attractive site and avoided the stigmatizing effect that ramps and railings can have on disabled residents. Rex feels that the multiple benefits—social, aes-

Apartments overlooking the courtyard playground.
Photo courtesy of Greg Premru

SUMMARY OF GREEN FEATURES

Site

- Restoration and cleanup of a former industrial "brownfield" site
- Walking distance to public transportation (5 bus routes through Union Square) and community amenities (e.g., schools, businesses, retail)
- Higher density and clustered buildings allow for more green space (¾ acre) on the site
- Fifty trees of various species planted to provide year-round greenery
- Central community commons and green spaces with children's play areas. Public paths created for neighborhood access
- Exterior lighting carefully placed to avoid overlighting and light pollution around site
- Bike racks installed around site

Water

- Roof rainwater drainage system recharges into groundwater
- Site graded to limit runoff and contain excess stormwater during extreme rainstorms
- Native plant landscaping used to eliminate need for irrigation system
- Low-flow toilets

Energy

- Walls insulated with sprayed-on recycled-content cellulose to achieve R-20
- Roofs insulated with HCFC-free spray-in-place foam to achieve R-40
- Rigid foam insulation used at slab edges and below slabs
- Low-emissivity argon insulating glass windows
- ENERGY STAR® high-efficiency fluorescent lighting (interior and exterior)
- Sealed combustion boilers with indirect-fired hot water

Materials and Resources

- Premanufactured panelized wall framing and roof trusses used to reduce lumber waste
- Site grading eliminated need for ramps and railings

Health and Comfort

- Tall windows for daylight and views of outdoor landscaped areas. Private balcony or patio for each unit
- Buildings oriented and massed to screen residences from views of nearby large retail and commercial buildings and parking lots
- Mechanical ventilation in each unit for automatic exhaust of stale air
- High-efficiency bathroom fans with a timer for measured air changes provide moisture control
- Carpet nailed down rather than glued down with adhesives to avoid volatile organic compounds (VOC) offgassing

Durability and Ease of Maintenance

- Fiber cement siding used, with 15-year paint warranty (compared to 5- to 7-year average life of paint on wood siding) reduces maintenance
- Durable and low-maintenance finishes used, including rubber stairway treads and steel railings

thetic, and environmental—resulted in "a big victory," even though it took extra time for the team to develop such a detail-oriented grading plan.

Comprehensive Energy Savings Approach: The project's rigorous energy efficiency package (which included cellulose and spray foam insulation and low-e windows) allowed for a reduction in the number of boilers installed in the buildings. While reducing boiler redundancy initially met with resistance from the mechanical engineer, it was accepted resulting in a reduction of first costs and operating costs. The team was also able to convince the local building

inspectors to waive the usual requirement to use vapor barriers, given the performance characteristics of cellulose insulation. The project is also designed to reduce lighting costs by not overlighting the site and by using efficient fluorescent lighting throughout. Conservation Services Group conducted ENERGY STAR® energy modeling for the development during the design phase, projecting that natural gas consumption for heat and hot water at the Linden Street Apartments would be 43 percent less than the code baseline.

Indoor/Outdoor Access and Views: The development features many quality-of-life enhancements, to both indoor and outdoor areas. There is an outdoor courtyard and play area, and the balconies, patios, and tall windows in the units allow residents to have physical and visual access to the outdoors. Such access and daylighting is not only psychologically beneficial, it also serves an important safety function by allowing parents to monitor courtyard activity from their homes.

PROJECT FINANCING

The project's total development cost was approximately $13 million, including $1 million for the property acquisition, $6.79 million for construction, and $2.2 million for soft costs. Financial partners included the National Equity Fund,

---

PROJECT FINANCING

FUNDING SOURCES	AMOUNT
Equity	
Low Income Housing Tax Credit Equity	$4,487,513
City of Somerville (capital for property acquisition)	$1,000,000
Somerville Community Corporation (deferred developer fee)	$156,272
Rebates	
ENERGY STAR® standard rebate + low-income upgrade rebate	$100,800
Debt	
Citizen's Bank (permanent and construction financing)	$5,500,000
City of Somerville HOME (permanent/forgivable loan)	$660,000
Massachusetts Department of Housing and Community Development: Massachusetts Affordable Housing Trust Fund (permanent/forgivable loan)	$600,000
Boston Community Capital (construction and permanent)	$500,000
City of Somerville Affordable Housing Trust Fund (construction and permanent)	$210,000
Total Sources	**$13,000,000**

Fannie Mae, City of Somerville, Citizen's Bank, and Massachusetts Department of Housing and Community Development.

Through the Conservation Services Group (CSG), the developer received $100,800 in ENERGY STAR® rebates. Due to the project's use of energy-efficient refrigerators, dishwashers, lighting, and shell features, along with its high HERS (Home Energy Rating System) score, it received a $50,400 standard ENERGY STAR rebate ($1,200 per unit × 42 units). An additional $50,400 low-income upgrade rebate was granted, which helped offset the cost of using cellulose and spray foam insulation instead of fiberglass insulation. Together, the rebates more than offset the increased first cost associated with the project's green measures.

The architect estimates that the added net cost for the project's green strategies was approximately $20,150, which was only 0.3 percent of the construction cost (or the equivalent of less than $0.40/sq ft). This calculation included the addition of green materials such as hydrochlorofluorocarbon (HCFC)-free spray foam insulation, cellulose insulation, and fiber-cement siding. It also took into account the first-cost savings associated with the green strategies, including the ability to use smaller and fewer boiler modules, which helped offset the additional cost of other strategies and materials.

In 2005, New Ecology, Inc., and the Tellus Institute published a report titled *The Costs and Benefits of Green Affordable Housing*. The groups studied a number of housing projects, including the Linden Street Apartments, and conducted a net present value analysis to determine whether the life-cycle benefits of each project's "greening" outweighed the associated life-cycle costs over a thirty-year period. Through their analysis of the Linden Street project, the groups determined that the benefits did indeed outweigh the costs. They estimated that, over a thirty-year period, the green upgrades will create more than $290,000 in operations savings to the project developer and more than $58,000 in savings to each dwelling. These figures were based on higher energy efficiency assumptions than those modeled by CSG, but even if the more conservative energy savings figures are used, the project would still achieve net financial benefits.

LESSONS LEARNED

Wood Framing Materials Efficiency: The first project used premanufactured panelized walls, a first for Mostue & Associates Architects. While using the premanufacturing wood panels did result in less wood waste because of a computerized pre-cutting process at the plant, the architect found that the manufacturers' panels had more studs than were structurally necessary. The use of excess studs in the panels also reduced the space for wall insulation. The architect says that he would try to correct this problem on future projects by reviewing shop drawings and suggesting stud reductions where possible.

Sealed-Combustion Boiler System: By code, ventilation is not required for new sealed-combustion boilers. But the project team discovered that some ventilation was needed to keep the basement boiler rooms from overheating. Commissioning procedures were used to adjust the boiler controls to the correct settings, which also reduced the overheating effect and optimized the efficiency of the systems. Mechanical ventilation was also added after construction in order to cool the boiler rooms.

Thermostat Programming: The building management found that not all tenants knew how to program the thermostats in their units. The lesson learned here is that, if individually programmable thermostats are provided, on-site management staff need to train residents in programming their thermostats correctly for efficiency (as well as comfort), or in some cases, the staff may need to set the thermostats for the tenants.

CONTACTS

Developer: Somerville Community Corporation
Katie Anthony, project manager: 617-776-5931; kanthony@somervillecdc.org

Architect: Mostue & Associates Architects, Inc.
Iric L. Rex, AIA, senior associate: 617-628-5700; irex@mostue.com
Sharon MacNulty, job captain

Energy consultant: Conservation Services Group
Mark Price, outreach manager, ENERGY STAR® Homes Program: 800-628-8413 (x3269); mark.price@csgrp.com

SOURCES

The Costs and Benefits of Green Affordable Housing, a publication of New Ecology, Inc., the Tellus Institute, and the Green CDCs Initiative, 2005, www.fraserinstitute.net/ssg/uploads/resources /affordable%20housing/final_cb_report.pdf.

Interviews and correspondence with Iric Rex of Mostue & Associates Architects (November 2005–August 2006), Mark Price of the Conservation Services Group (March 2006), and Katie Anthony of the Somerville Community Corporation (January 2006–September 2006).

Linden Street Housing, Mostue & Associates Architects website: www.mostue.com/housing1a.html.

The Linden Street Project, the Department of Energy's High Performance Buildings database: www.buildinggreen .com/hpb.

NESEA Building Awards: www.nesea.org/buildings /buildingawards/Linden_submission.doc.

"Post-Industrial Affordability," *Architecture Week,* February 12, 2003, www.architectureweek.com/2003/0212 /environment_1-1.html.

34 Linden Street, National Equity Fund Project Report; www.smt.nefinc.org/uploadProject%5CProject /34linden.pdf.

Maverick Landing

44 Border Street, East Boston, Massachusetts, bounded by New Street, Maverick Street, and Sumner Street

HOPE VI PROJECT / LARGE-SCALE REDEVELOPMENT / RENEWABLE ENERGY

From the rooftop of Maverick Landing, the Boston skyline appears postcard perfect. This new development is not immediately identifiable as affordable housing, nor does it jump out as green building. The transition from the neglected housing project that stood on the site before to Maverick Landing is dramatic.

For over sixty years, several thousand people lived in the Maverick Gardens Housing Project. Owned and operated by the Boston Housing Authority, it was a typical public housing development constructed after World War II, containing 413 public housing units in three-story barracks-style brick buildings. By 2000, the old development was dilapidated and crime-ridden.

Today a new development features 396 mixed-income rental units on both the old Maverick Gardens site and a nearby vacant lot called Carlton Wharf. The sites are in a prime location on the historic waterfront in an active commercial core close to transit and downtown Boston.

Maverick Landing took four and a half years to design and build and was constructed in four phases. Over half of the housing in the project is reserved for people with extremely low incomes, most of which fall in the 30 to 60 percent range of the area median income. Reserving this much housing for extremely low-income residents is unusual among affordable projects. This case study primarily focuses on Phase I, which includes a midrise building with 116 units and four low-rise buildings with 34 units.

Prior to engaging a developer, the Boston Housing Authority (BHA) solicited funds from the Massachusetts Technology Collaborative (MTC). In 2002, BHA received a $453,693 Green Building Design and Construction Grant for the Maverick Landing project from MTC through its Renewable Energy Trust Fund program. BHA also received a large HOPE VI anchor grant from HUD in 2002. The redevelopment of Maverick Landing began

PROJECT SUMMARY

Phase I (On-site) 5 Buildings (1 midrise and 4 low-rise)		Phase II (Carlton Wharf)		Phase III (On-site)		Phase IV (On-site)		Total=21 Buildings
Public Housing/ Low-Income Housing Tax Credit	Market-rate	Public Housing/ Low-Income Housing Tax Credit	Market-rate	Public Housing/ Low-Income Housing Tax Credit	Market-rate	Public Housing/ Low-Income Housing Tax Credit	Market-rate	
116 units	34 units	61 units	19 units	71 units	21 units	57 units	17 units	396 units

with BHA releasing a competitive request for proposals (RFP) that included green building as a desired aspect of the development. In June 2002, Trinity East Boston Development, a partnership of Trinity Financial and East Boston Community Development (Trinity), along with ICON Architecture won the competition. By September 2003 the project was under construction, and by December 2004 Phases I, II, and III were complete and families began moving into their new homes. Phase IV was completed in late 2006.

Maverick Landing's development team focused on conducting a fully integrated design process. This required the team members to meet many times to identify and prioritize green, energy-efficient, and renewable energy investments. The site plan for the development restores the historic neighborhood street pattern, interrupted by the old 1940 development, and reconnects it physically and visually to the surrounding community, park, and waterfront. The plan's siting, scale, and massing of components help the project to act as a transition between the different scales of a low-rise traditional residential area to the east, an industrial area to the north, and a waterfront commercial area to the west.

The Phase I design includes a range of unit types in both midrise and low-rise buildings so that a variety of living situations are accommodated. For example, the ground-floor units in the midrise are two- and three- bedroom apartments with individual entrances, making them more suitable for families. Apartments on the upper floors are one- and two-bedroom, making them more appropriate for singles, couples, and smaller families. Some are barrier-free[1] to allow for greater accessibility. The four low-rise buildings are each three stories with varying architectural details, such as gables and flat roofs, and feature multibedroom flats and three- to four-bedroom townhouses. These units also open onto individual backyards. This mix of unit types, features, and parking options such as on-street parking and a parking garage ensures a family-friendly neighborhood. ICON architect Nancy Ludwig says another goal was to give the neighborhood individual character, so, for example, a resident giving directions to her house could say she lives in "the green house with the bay window on the corner."

GREEN ACHIEVEMENTS

The development team set out with a goal "to identify a reasonable standard for healthy and energy-efficient affordable housing in Boston," according to architect Nancy Ludwig. Her firm worked with developer Trinity to ensure everyone involved in the development process understood the green aspects of the project.

The team focused on the following criteria in order to meet their green goals: Leadership in Energy and Environmental Design (LEED) certification; photovoltaics as a renewable energy source; a high-performance building envelope; resident health and comfort; and an aggressive pursuit of energy savings. The team specifically focused on receiving a LEED NC certification for the Phase I midrise A building. This effort in Phase I informed decisions in subsequent phases. At first, Ludwig says, there was some skepticism about green design, but by the end of the process, Trinity was very proud of the project. Now the developer is focusing more on building green projects.

The cozy family rooms offer the residents comfortable affordable living.
© Peter Vanderwarker Photographs; Courtesy of ICON architecture, inc.

PROJECT DETAILS

Note: This case study primarily focuses on Phase I.

Project Size:

Phase I:	5 buildings with one midrise containing 116 units and 4 low-rise buildings containing a total of 34 units.
Total project:	396 units in the 4 phases; 1.7 acres (21 buildings); 5 new city streets. After initial occupancy, the total target mix of incomes = 29% at 0–10% of AMI; 34% at 11–30% of AMI; 14% at 31–60% of AMI; 23% at market rates.
Cost/Unit:	Phase I: $360,000
Construction Cost:	Phase I: $25,423,227
Development Cost:	Phase I: $54,000,000
Total project:	$121,000,000
Completion Date:	Phase I: December 2004

Whole project: December 2006 final Phase IV completed and occupied (4.5 years for design and final construction)

Project Team

Developer:	Trinity East Boston Development, a partnership of Trinity Financial and East Boston Community Development Corporation
Property Manager:	Winn Properties
Architect:	ICON Architecture
General Contractor:	CWC Builders and Dimes Construction
Legal:	Hale & Dorr
Engineer:	McPhail Associates, Environmental Engineers
Landscape Architect:	Geller DeVellis
Solar Design Consultant:	Solar Design Associates
Energy/Green Consultant:	Massachusetts Technology Collaborative and NE Energy Efficiency Council

Photovoltaics as a Renewable Energy Source: Using the MTC grant to research and implement on-site renewable energy generation, a 37kW photovoltaic (PV) system was selected and mounted on the roof of the midrise building. Along with the PV system, a 75 kW natural gas cogeneration system[2] produces all the power necessary to light the building's common areas, run its elevators, and act as a backup for domestic hot-water heating.

High-Performance Building Envelope: To minimize energy consumption, a tightly sealed, highly efficient building envelope was designed. The envelope's R-value is 20 percent higher than required by the Massachusetts energy code. Additionally, fiberglass windows with double-glazed, low-e glass were specified. Using fiberglass helps control condensation and thermal bridging,[3] thus lowering heating and cooling costs while prolonging the life of the building components. Ludwig notes that this approach helped to "buy down" or reduce the size of the mechanical system.

Resident Health and Comfort: Resident health and comfort was a priority. Fresh outside air is delivered directly into the units, providing ventilation that exceeds code requirements. The LEED requirement toward no-smoking specified high-performance air sealing to eliminate the transfer of smoke from unit to unit. In addition, several apartments, as well as all common areas, are designated nonsmoking.

To reduce the environmental factors that cause asthma, low-volatile-organic-compound (low-VOC) materials and hard surface flooring such as Marmoleum were used. In addition, all wet areas (i.e., kitchens and baths) have smooth and cleanable surfaces that do not trap moisture, thus reducing mold production. To specifically accommodate residents with asthma, 15 units were designated to be carpet-free, and another 15 have a significantly reduced amount of carpet and feature Marmoleum flooring in all bedrooms.

Aggressive Pursuit of Energy Savings: Part of the energy efficiency strategy included seeking incentives and rebates from KeySpan, NSTAR, and ENERGY STAR® for incorporating high-efficiency lighting, ventilation, appliances, and equipment into the building design and operation. Ludwig noted that ENERGY STAR's best-practice program[4] helped guide the design team in the areas of insulation ratings, types, and levels; air-sealing strategies for the building; interior ventilation standards; and suggestions on

SUMMARY OF GREEN FEATURES

Site

- Access to public transportation: Maverick Square, major public transit hub, ¼ mile away
- High density of 88 units per acre
- Water-efficient landscaping; planting species all native to the area and drought-resistant

Energy

- LEED NC used to guide the design (LEED certification pending)
- Window placement and size allows for ample daylighting.
- High-performance fiberglass-composite-frame double-glazed low-e windows
- "Smart" mechanical systems: variable-frequency drives and energy-efficient equipment and motors
- High-efficiency boilers
- Highly efficient gas absorption chiller
- All appliances ENERGY STAR® rated
- Renewable energy: photovoltaic (PV) array and 75 kW cogeneration system

Materials and Resources

- Local materials include structural steel, wall panels, concrete, and granite
- Recycled-content materials such as concrete, steel, and carpeting used throughout
- 50% of construction waste generated from the project recycled

Health and Comfort

- All units conform to Boston Housing Authority's Healthy Homes criteria for floor and wall finishes. Low-VOC paints, adhesives, and materials
- Variety of housing designs creates a living environment of individuality and family friendliness

building wall design. For example, use of a white high-albedo[5] ENERGY STAR®–compliant roof membrane was a key factor in the conservation of energy and was important for controlling heating and cooling costs in the building. Light-colored roofing materials with high reflectance have been shown to reflect up to 85 percent of solar radiation, thus reducing unwanted heat gain when compared with conventional surfaces, which reflect only 20 percent of solar

radiation. In addition, a collaborative design and implementation process with energy raters allowed for review and suggestions on the initial building design, in-process site visits, and final testing of the completed building.

The development team incorporated a commissioning process that verified that fundamental building elements and systems were designed, installed, and calibrated to operate as intended. Ludwig believes this thorough process was instrumental in ensuring the optimal performance of the buildings. She says that the commissioning process[6] enhanced occupant comfort, reduced utility costs, and increased building value. It also resulted in a reduction in costly change orders during construction and helped maintain the project's construction schedule.

PROJECT FINANCING

The $121-million ($54 million in Phase I) Maverick Landing development is unlike most large affordable housing projects. It came in ahead of schedule and under budget, according to Sarah Barnat of the project's developer,

PROJECT FINANCING

FUNDING SOURCES	AMOUNT
Equity	
Trinity East Boston Development	Investment N/A
Low-Income Housing	
Tax Credit Equity (4% and 9%)	$51.4 million
Debt	
MassHousing (permanent loan)	$8.5 million
Grants	
HUD HOPE VI	$35 million
Massachusetts Technology	
(study and construction grant)	$453,693
Boston Housing Authority (capital funds)	$13.5 million
Department of Housing and Community	
Development Affordable Housing	
Programs, City of Boston, and	
other programs	$12.8 million
Total Sources	**$121,653,693**

ENERGY AND WATER USE: TARGET VS. ACTUAL

Phase I - Midrise A Building

END USES	TARGET TOTAL USE	ACTUAL TOTAL USE	PERCENT DIFFERENCE
Gas Heating, AC, Cogeneration	76,390 therms	88,000 therms	15%
Apartment Lights and Appliances	435,400 kWh	350,000 kWh	−20%
Common Area Electricity	216,264 kWh	40,800 kWh	−81%
Domestic Hot Water	10,452 CCF	5,475 CCF	−48%

ENERGY EFFICIENCY COSTS AND SAVINGS

Phase I - Midrise A Building

	ESTIMATED INCREMENTAL DOLLAR COST (COMPARED TO STANDARD) ENERGY EFFICIENCY MEASURES	NET ANNUAL COST SAVINGS
High-Efficiency Gas Absorption Chiller	$84,400	$2,208
75 kW Cogen	$192,500	$11,274
Solar PV	$336,863	$8,142
High-Performance Windows	$35,700	$1,651
ENERGY STAR® Apartment Lights and Appliances	$53,550	$11,125
Air Sealing Controlled Ventilation Upgrades (119 apts)	$35,700	$507
Totals	$738,713	$61,641

Trinity. It is estimated that the project will save $1.5 million as rental income comes into the project sooner than expected and the development's construction loans are retired. (All four phases were completed in 2006.) This savings will be used for long-term services to the residents, including job training and childcare, to be provided by Maverick Landing Community Services.

The Maverick Landing project (Phase I) has achieved significant savings in energy costs through the use of PV panels, on-site power generation, fiberglass windows, and energy-saving lighting and motors. Consumption, for the most part, is dramatically less than targets, due to the team's achievement of its green goals.

The construction cost for the Phase I midrise building was $25 million. Of that total, the cost of renewable energy systems and other energy-efficient features was $738,713, just under 3 percent of the overall construction cost. This incremental cost has a payback period of twelve years. Without the renewables, the cost of energy-saving features was $209,350, or less than 1 percent of the overall construction cost.

The photovoltaic system was designed by Solar Design Associates of Harvard, Massachusetts. The Massachusetts Technology Collaboration website hosts a real-time display of Maverick Landing's energy consumption, savings, and environmental impact. From January through September 2006, the PV monitoring showed that the system produced 28,746 kWh of electrical energy. The display gives very helpful comparisons for understanding the implications of such savings. For example, it illustrates that from January through September 2006, the system offset 38,800 pounds of carbon dioxide emissions, the main cause of global warming.

LESSONS LEARNED

Architect Nancy Ludwig was integrally involved throughout the process and cites a number of lessons learned on the project:

The mix of housing types around the development's courtyards creates a sense of community.
© *Peter Vanderwarker Photographs; Courtesy of ICON architecture, inc.*

- Green buildings do not need to look any different from any other building. From the perspective of a passerby, Maverick Landing looks no different aesthetically than other residential developments.
- Green is not inherently more expensive. A tight envelope reduces the required investment in what would have been a larger mechanical system.
- A tremendous amount of time is needed to discuss the green options. With twenty-six people around the table, a lot of time was needed for discussion, and yet there was also a need to move the discussion forward within the tight time frame of tax credit financing. In the end, the decisions fall upon the design team, and there's

not always a lot of data. For example, Ludwig notes that the energy modeling "happened a bit too late in the process to be helpful." Ideally it should begin early in the design process.
- Teamwork and positive attitudes are needed.

The Phase I midrise A building was submitted for LEED certification, and the team is currently working through interpretation of credits related to air sealing

> ## "Building green is not rocket science. Its common sense and you can get rebates."
>
> NANCY LUDWIG
> *ICON Architecture, Inc.*

because smoking is allowed in parts of the building.

Ludwig says the residents "really like their new homes, but it is very different living. Simple things are noticeably improved, such as mail is now delivered to them and trash is picked up. People learned about the energy efficiency of the building and are happy because with the new development, utility bills are now paid individually. If they reduce their usage, their bills go down."

CONTACTS

Developer: Trinity East Boston Development, LP, a partnership of Trinity Financial & East Boston Community Development
Frank Edwards: 617-720-8400

Architect: ICON architecture, inc.
Nancy Ludwig: 617-451-3333

SOURCES

Anderson, Bendix, "Urban Finalist: Trinity Completes Model HOPE VI," *Affordable Housing Finance,*

www.housingfinance.com/ahf/articles/2006/aug/060
_ahfaug06.htm.

Ibid., "Boston HOPE VI Project Creating Own Power"
*Affordable Housing Finance, Development and
Construction* (November 2003): 40.

Cohn, Jonathan, "Losing Hope" *New Republic* (May 23,
2005), http://www.tnr.com/doc.mhtml?i=20050523
&s=trb052305. Accessed January 2, 2007.

Design Advisor—Maverick Landing:
www.designadvisor.org. Affordable Housing Design
Advisor offers resources and in-depth examples of affordable housing, with a section devoted to projects selected
in the annual AIA Show You're Green Awards, including
Maverick Landing, a 2005 recipient.

ENERGY STAR® best practices program:
www.energystar.gov.

Fulton, Deirdre, "Changing the Environmental Landscape,
One Building at a Time," *From the Ground Up*
(August 12–18, 2005).

Ludwig, Nancy, ICON Architecture, presentation at Build
Boston 2005—"Maverick Landing—One Year Later,"
conference notes.

Ibid., personal interview with Jenifer Seal Cramer, June 14,
2006, and e-mail correspondence 2006.

"Maverick Gardens PV System Real-Time Display":
www.masstech.org/landing/rtd.html.

NOTES

1. Barrier-free design allows people with disabilities to live more independently within their own homes. Barrier-free design assists not only those with disabilities, but also the elderly and even parents with children in strollers.

2. Cogeneration consists of producing electricity and sequentially utilizing useful energy in the form of steam, hot water, or direct-exhaust gases.

3. Thermal bridging is a component, or an assembly, in a building envelope through which heat is transferred at a substantially higher rate than through the surrounding envelope area.

4. In its publication *Fifteen O&M Best Practices for Energy-Efficient Buildings,* EPA offers a proven strategy for superior energy management, with tools and resources to help each step of the way (see www.energystar.gov/ia/business/15best.pdf). Based on the successful practices of ENERGY STAR partners, these guidelines for energy management can assist organizations in improving their energy and financial performance while distinguishing themselves as environmental leaders.

5. Albedo is the measure of a surface's reflectivity.

6. Building commissioning is the systematic process of ensuring that a building's complex array of systems is designed, installed, and tested to perform according to the design intent and the building owner's operational needs. The commissioning of new buildings will be most effective when considered throughout the planning stages and as early as schematic design.

Nageezi House

Nageezi, New Mexico, near Chaco Canyon
in northeast New Mexico
(on the Navajo Reservation)

**LOCALLY SOURCED MATERIALS / CULTURALLY SENSITIVE
DESIGN / PASSIVE HEATING AND COOLING**

A university-initiated design/build process led to the creation of the Nageezi House, a new home for an elderly Navajo couple. The house is located on an isolated, rural site on a windswept mesa in northeast New Mexico, near Chaco Canyon. The Nageezi House replaced the couple's original, conventional home, which had been built over a period of decades and which was dilapidated enough to make renovation impossible. The couple's adult children live on either side, in conventional, HUD-funded homes designed with little regard for the local environment.

The Nageezi House came about when the Stardust Design Center at Arizona State University (ASU) began looking for a project on which to apply its research-based, design/build process. The center wanted to create a replicable model of a culturally appropriate home with a climatically suitable design in an area where most housing is substandard and inefficient. Navajo students in the ASU College of Design with an interest in working in their own community approached the Center. The Navajo Nation provided what the center needed. Indian reservations feature some of the most substandard housing in the United States, up to six times worse than in the general population.[1] The average income in the Navajo Nation is $6,000 a year, making affordability a critical issue.

The Nageezi House was designed to respond to the local high-desert climate (elevation 6,947 feet), in which temperatures can vary 40 to 60 degrees Fahrenheit in one day. Passive heating and cooling provide a comfortable indoor environ-

ment and keep ongoing costs for utilities and maintenance low. The architecture reflects the traditional Navajo culture while addressing today's needs and modern technologies.

The design of the house revolves around two traditional Navajo structures not typically used for modern reservation housing. The first is the *hooghan* (or hogan), the traditional form of Navajo housing, which today is mainly used as a ceremonial structure by Navajo families. The hooghan, a one-room round structure comprised of log, stone, and other natural materials, places a fireplace with a chimney in the center of the main room. Although modernized

The chahash'oh, a shade structure, provides the traditional summer home of the Navajo. Here it serves as part of the passive cooling system, shading the home's south-facing windows.
© *ASU Stardust Center for Affordable Homes and the Family.*

hooghans are beginning to be built in the Navajo Nation, in this case, the house's owners had been living in western-style housing for decades, and did not want to return to a hooghan-style house. In response, the design team "reinterpreted" the hooghan structure into a central courtyard and shade trellis, which, although outside, acts as the heart of the home. Hooghans traditionally utilize a clockwise movement, echoed here in the floor plan, with an entry to the east, and circulation around the central courtyard. The second traditional structure is a shade structure, a *chahash'oh*, the traditional summer home of the Navajo. Here it serves as part of the passive cooling system, shading the home's south-facing windows.

PROJECT DETAILS

Project Size:	One 1,450 sq ft building (original house had been built in the 1960s and added to over four decades)
Construction Cost/Sq Ft:	$90/sq ft
Total Construction Cost:	$130,500
Total Development Cost:	$140,000
Completion Date:	August 2006

Project Team

Developer:	ASU Stardust Center for Affordable Homes and the Family
Owner:	Mary and Kee Augustine
Architect:	ASU Stardust Center for Affordable Homes and the Family/ASU College of Design students
General Contractor:	ASU Stardust Center
Structural Engineer:	Travis Design Associates, PC
Project Director:	Daniel Glenn, Director of Design, ASU Stardust Center
Energy/Solar Consultant:	Ernesto Fonseca, Graduate Research Assistant, ASU Stardust Center
ASU Design/Build Students:	Ernesto Fonseca, Christopher Billey, Peter Crispell, Jason Croxton, Matt Green, Adrian Holiday, Alisa Lertique, Tanya Yellowhair

Several entities within ASU and members of the Navajo Nation collaborated on the Nageezi House. The studio design team, led by the Stardust Center, included graduate and undergraduate students in ASU's College of Design. Construction involved dozens of local tribe members as well as ASU students. Four of the students from ASU's College of Design who participated in the design and/or construction of the project are Navajo. The design reflects their intimate understanding of the culture and their experience growing up in hooghans with their grandmothers. The students also presented design ideas to the local Navajo chapter house and to the Navajo couple in the Navajo language—as one member of the couple does not speak English. Finally, a professor and graduate student in ASU's energy performance and climate-responsive architecture program provided an energy analysis for the project.

This project was accepted as a Leadership in Energy and Environmental Design for Homes (LEED-H) pilot project, and has not yet been certified.

GREEN ACHIEVEMENTS

Historically, culturally responsive design reflected the local environment and climate. This was a natural occurrence in the days before the mass-produced housing development with no regard to solar access, prevailing winds, or other local, natural features. The Nageezi House design reflects both the local climate and culture. The building materials can withstand the harsh climate yet high winds, and require little maintenance. Materials and colors fit within the local context and include native stone pavers in the courtyard and wood beams from nearby forests. The reddish stucco tint echoes the reddish hue of the local soil.

Climatically and Culturally Responsive Design: The building design encourages passive heating and cooling and maximizes natural ventilation and daylighting.

Navajo homes or hooghans traditionally face east, to welcome the sunrise and to protect inhabitants from prevailing western winds. Here, the hooghan-inspired courtyard faces east, as does the main entry. This courtyard design provides cross-ventilation and daylight on two sides of all rooms. Thick, aerated concrete blocks on the building's exterior provide mass and insulation, modulating temperature and reducing the need for mechanical heating and cooling.

Minimal windows on the north and west faces assist passive cooling, while large windows maximize light from the southern exposure and heat capture in the winter. A well-insulated building envelope keeps indoor ambient temperatures stable. Radiant floor heating supplements the passive solar heating.

The building design encourages passive ventilation. Operable and motorized ventilation windows allow for an efficient and controlled air flow throughout the house. A thermostat regulates the clerestory windows to release hot air early on summer evenings and bring in nighttime cooling. A continuous trellis shades south-facing windows, reducing heat gains in the summer months. In the summer, brush also covers the trellis in the local tradition.

Locally Sourced Materials: One of the most interesting aspects of this project is its use of local materials, promoting local economic development and job creation. The design team is most proud of their use of Navajo FlexCrete in the building's interior and exterior concrete walls. FlexCrete is a building product that contains 60 percent reclaimed fly ash, a by-product of coal mining, instead of cement.

The Nageezi House was the first home ever to be built out of Navajo FlexCrete. The designers planned to use straw bale until they learned that the Navajo Nation had recently invested in a new plant that uses fly ash to make concrete blocks. After analyzing various materials, including straw bale, FlexCrete, structural insulated panels, and stick frame, they discovered that FlexCrete performed the best in this climate. The designers valued FlexCrete's combination of mass and significant R-value—as well as the fact that it is a locally sourced material that reuses a waste product while simultaneously supporting economic development on the reservation.

> "Our challenge is to create modern homes that strive to come close to the extraordinary symbiosis of climate and culture that is inherent in indigenous dwellings."
>
> DANIEL GLENN
> *ASU Stardust Center*

Given the particulars of this community, the designers viewed sustainability as an economic issue as well as an environmental one. The Navajo Housing Authority owns and operates the FlexCrete plant, and intends to use its product for housing on the reservation. The Housing Authority also hopes to use it to generate income for the tribe by selling it for use in homes in the greater area.

The Nageezi House also used other locally sourced and recycled products. Doors and windows came from demolished homes in the Phoenix area. The seven large juniper logs that make up the house and the native stone used to pave the hooghan courtyard were gathered locally. The roof's structure is comprised of local timber culled from Arizona forests via local fire prevention programs. Too small in diameter to use as conventional lumber, millers consider these timbers a waste material, and typically use them for compost. The designers used these 8-inch round timbers spaced on 4-foot centers, supporting a composite roof comprised of two layers of oriented strand board (OSB), with 5 inches of rigid insulation in between and metal roofing on top.

SUMMARY OF GREEN FEATURES

Site

- Building oriented to take advantage of passive cooling and heating strategies and to protect it from prevailing winds

Water

- Roof collects rainwater through inverted-shed design. Hand pump used to provide water for plants and animals
- Minimal landscaping uses traditional gravel skirt to transition from surrounding non-landscaped area

Energy

- Energy-10 and DOE II modeling
- Electricity use greatly decreased through daylighting strategies
- Passive solar heating supplemented with radiant floor heating
- Passive cooling achieved with the use of natural cross-ventilation and night-time cooling of thermal mass
- 12-inch-thick aerated concrete exterior walls and 8-inch-thick interior walls provide both mass and insulation to reduce the need for heating and cooling (R-value of 35)
- Double-paned windows
- Reinforced concrete floors offer good thermal storage
- Rigid insulation roof with an insulation value of R-38
- All appliances are ENERGY STAR® rated

Materials and Resources

- Interior and exterior walls utilize aerated fly ash concrete walls (60% reclaimed fly ash content)

- "Waste timber" (from Arizona forests, too small to use for conventional lumber) used for roof framing
- Existing slab from previous home reused
- All reusable lumber from demolition utilized on-site or given away to locals
- During construction, cut blocks were stacked and reused whenever possible for the project, and all remaining blocks and cut blocks of usable size were retained on-site for use by the owner and their sons for future construction efforts

Health and Comfort

- Offgassing from paint was eliminated by using no interior paint. Exterior color comes from the stucco's integral colors, and interior concrete floors are stained
- Airflow maximized through use of operable windows; motorized, thermostat-controlled ventilation windows; and cross-ventilation design
- Solid aerated concrete block walls used to eliminate wall cavities where moisture can penetrate; each block is sealed from the outside with a water-based latex-base stucco to prevent moisture penetration

Durability and Ease of Maintenance

- Concrete walls and floors are durable and can easily be maintained at little cost

---

The builders reused materials wherever possible on this project, starting with the original house. Once dismantled, its usable lumber became the new home's decking and trellis, as well as the framing for doors and windows. The new house went up over the existing slab.

Energy Performance: Energy performance was simulated using both ENERGY-10 and eQUEST software. For a year after completion of the home, the designers monitored its actual performance around the clock, comparing it to a computer model containing the same characteristics via twenty "thermal couple sensors" placed throughout the house. Every thirty minutes, the sensors measured interior and exterior temperatures, heat flow through the walls, outside wind speeds, and solar radiation.

Energy performance during the first winter. Winter energy use performed close to the model's predictions. In January 2006, the Nageezi House used an average of 182,000 Btu/day, compared to nearly 400,000 Btu/day for heating a conventional home of the same size—a 52 percent reduction in a month that featured temperature lows of 4 degrees Fahrenheit.

Initially, the designers predicted that heat loss during the night would trigger the need for the radiant heating sys-

The home's roof design collects rainwater through inverted shed design, and it is then stored in a buried water tank.

© ASU Stardust Center for Affordable Homes and the Family.

tem to heat the house during the morning. However, it turned out that the thermal mass of the concrete floor played a role in keeping the indoor temperature stable throughout the night, retaining enough energy to continue to passively heat the house for over five hours in the early morning. Then, throughout the day, the glazing on the south façade brought in enough warmth that passive heating alone kept indoor temperatures within the thermal comfort zone. According to eQUEST, passive heating reduced overall mechanical heating by 15 to 20 percent. Reduced gas consumption for space heating saves the residents nearly 50 percent, or $3.50 daily compared with conventional homes.

Energy performance during the first summer. Computer simulations forecast zero cooling need, thanks to the concrete block's mass, as well as nighttime flushing through the automatic thermostat-controlled ventilation windows. On the hottest day of the summer (which reached 96 degrees F), the air temperature inside the home rose two degrees beyond the recommended thermal comfort zone for four and a half hours, reaching 85 degrees F. (ASHRAE

55, the adaptive thermal comfort model calculation, recommended a maximum indoor temperature of 82.76 degrees F.) On the coolest day of the same month, the outdoor temperature dropped to 54 degrees F. However, energy stored in the house's thermal mass helped to maintain a comfortable temperature of 76 degrees F. During this month, the passive solar design of the home kept temperatures within the comfort zone for over 90 percent of the time.

Based on feedback provided by the monitoring, the design team has been able to observe how behavioral changes affect energy performance. For example, they observed that the number of days the house remains within the ASHRAE 55 comfort zone parameters in the summer improves when the homeowners keep their windows open longer during the night.

As of August 2006, the home used 70 percent less electricity than a conventional home—even less than predicted. For example, in July 2006, the model predicted the house would use 1.10 kWh/month, yet it only used 0.601 kWh/month. Gas use was nominal—for cooking and water heating only—and the residents used no gas at all for heating between April and October. It is worth noting that the Navajo couple living here uses fewer resources than their average American counterpart.

PROJECT FINANCING

The Nageezi House, paid for by ASU's Stardust Center, cost approximately $140,000 to design and build. The Stardust Center is a self-supporting entity at ASU that charges fees for its work and solicits donations to cover operational costs. The exact cost of this demonstration project is difficult to determine for several reasons. On the one hand, donated materials saved money. On the other hand, costs went up to cover airfare to fly the design team from ASU to the remote site. Working in a remote site also increased costs as outside materials and equipment had to be transported from larger communities an hour or more away from the construction site.

The home was built primarily with paid labor so as to contribute to the local economy. The team is proud of the fact that they hired and trained several dozen local unskilled Navajo workers for the project, paying $10 an hour. Once the workers were trained, the Navajo Housing Authority helped build the team's next house—the Guadalupe House—and also donated the FlexCrete for that project, making it the first home off the reservation to use Navajo FlexCrete.

LESSONS LEARNED

According to architect Ernesto Fonseca, who analyzed the project as part of his graduate thesis work at ASU and who was a member of the design/build team, the following lessons can be derived from the Nageezi House:

- High desert temperature swings are the ideal impetus to use thermal mass in the design.
- Passive heating can mean the difference between a high and a low energy bill, and between comfortable and uncomfortable indoor ambient temperatures.
- Passive strategies should be the first alternative implemented, followed by the optimization of mechanical systems.
- Good design does not necessarily have to increase the price of housing units.
- Sustainability targets long-term affordability.

Computer simulations run before the occupants moved into the house did not take into account some of the realities of life on the Navajo Reservation in a multigenerational setting. Before a washer and dryer were donated as part of the Nageezi House project, this family used solar power to dry clothes after driving a great distance to wash them at a laundromat. So, while the in-home washer and dryer added to their quality of life (and saved much gasoline), it also boosted energy usage above the predictions, and above that used in the previous home with no washer and dryer. Because the client's children live on either side of them,

PROJECT FINANCING

FUNDING SOURCES	AMOUNT
Grants/Donations	
ASU Stardust Center	$110,000
Navajo Housing Authority/Navajo FlexCrete (in-kind donation: materials/labor)	$25,000
Stardust Building Supplies (in-kind donation: doors/windows)	$5,000
Total Development Cost	**$140,000**

and no other family members have a washer and dryer, or even a hot shower, more people are using the home than the model accounted for.

Daniel Glenn, the Stardust Center design director who led the project's design, says the clients anticipated that a "new, green home may cost less, but you can't compete in low energy costs with a home where they heat one room with wood and cluster around it, and nobody is using a washer and dryer or taking a hot shower." Even with an efficient new home, in parts of the first year the occupants spent more on electricity because of the technological improvements and the fact that teenage grandchildren came to live with them for some months. The design team is working with the family to help them realize that while their living standard is now higher, their energy bills are also moderately higher because of the new amenities, a larger space requiring heating or cooling, and additional family members.

Passive Ventilation: Technology Versus Human Actions: The ventilation strategy depends in part on small, motorized windows that automatically open to allow additional cooling when needed. In the first months of occupancy, these windows did not work as intended. They had been improperly installed by someone other than a certified electrician due to budgetary constraints. Glenn sees the window mechanics as "good in theory, but a little worrisome in practice. Anything mechanical can break—will the occupants be able to afford to replace?" He thinks a backup manual system might help if it could include an easy way to access the windows, which are located high up in the walls.

The longer learning curve required for the radiant floor heating system proved challenging in realizing the anticipated energy performance. The occupants had previously heated their home exclusively with wood. In the winter, they would huddle around the wood stove while the other rooms remained cold, or put out the fire when it got too hot inside. Radiant heating, however, works on the premise that it gets cold in November and stays cold until May. The occupants began to shut it off when it got too warm, causing the slab to cool down, which then required a great deal of energy to heat it back up. Needless to say, initial performance was below expectation for the first couple of months until the homeowner learned how to properly operate the system. A highly efficient wood stove may have provided better heat in this case, although the family requested that it be omitted in favor of a fire pit, which was built in the hooghan patio and is used a great deal.

The long-distance monitoring system allowed the design team to provide feedback quickly. For example, when the house got too warm, the team was able to call the client's next-door son and ask him to open his parents' window.

Looking Forward: What's Next: The team is already applying what it learned from this project to several others. The Stardust Center recently signed a contract with Indigenous Community Enterprises (ICE), a nonprofit on the reservation that builds housing, to reproduce the working drawings based on the Nageezi home into two-, three- and four-bedroom models. ICE hopes to take the best of the Nageezi House and simplify the design where possible. For example, creating a hooghan-shaped courtyard using a material like FlexCrete is challenging, because it requires skilled carpenters to interlock the blocks at 45 degrees. The designers are investigating the idea of pouring corners and inserting straight blocks between them to make the construction less complex.

Lessons from the Nageezi have also been applied to a second house using the same materials in a different climate. The Guadalupe House is being built in the small, century-old community of Guadalupe, Arizona, near Tempe. Like the Nageezi House, this home design also focuses on sustainable, culturally responsive housing, this time addressing local Mexican American and Yaqui Indian culture. (The community of Guadalupe was founded by Yaqui Indians from Mexico.) The Guadalupe House also uses locally sourced Navajo FlexCrete blocks and small-diameter timbers from the Navajo Reservation in northern Arizona. A small Navajo-owned start-up, Southwest Traditional Homes, provided logs that would have otherwise been mulched or burned as a waste product.

The Stardust Center used a workshop process to generate the design, gathering input from locals familiar with the culture and from community representatives who provided input about their needs. For example, adult children and their families often live in their parents' home, so multigenerational homes are desirable. The process also reacquainted the participants with traditional native building approaches still common south of the border in Mexico. "In both projects," says Glenn, "the effort has been to create homes that are responsive to the regional climate as well as to the specific culture for which we are designing. We have learned from these projects that these two aspects of culture and climate are integrally related. Our challenge is to create modern homes that strive to come close to the extraordinary symbiosis of climate and culture that is inherent in indigenous dwellings."

ASU student Adrian Holiday comes from Kayenta, Arizona, and was an integral member of the student design/build team for the Nageezi House. About the project, he said, "It was quite an experience learning about my culture. We forecast that other students will follow us. To express our culture in these structures, it's beautiful."[2]

CONTACTS

Architect/developer: Arizona State University Stardust Center for Affordable Homes and the Family

Daniel Glenn, design director: 480-727-5453; daniel.glenn@asu.edu

Ernesto Fonseca, staff architect, energy/climate specialist: 480-727-5452; Ernestofonseca@asu.edu

SOURCES

Fonseca, Ernesto, "Design and Evaluation of Passive Heating and Cooling Strategies Implemented in a New Construction House in a Desert Climate," PowerPoint presentation, 2006.

Ibid., personal correspondence with Lisa McManigal Delaney, 2006.

Glenn, Daniel, personal interview by Lisa McManigal Delaney, with phone and e-mail followup, 2006.

Guadalupe House: www.asu.edu/stardust/design/Guadalupe.pdf.

Indigenous Community Enterprises (builds housing for Navajo elders): www.cba.nau.edu/ice/index.htm.

Nageezi House: www.asu.edu/stardust/design/Nageezi.pdf.

Navajo FlexCrete: www.hooghan.org/flexcrete/default.htm.

NOTES

1. Fonseca, Ernesto, "Design and Evaluation of Passive Heating and Cooling Strategies Implemented in a New Construction House in a Desert Climate," PowerPoint presentation, 2006.
2. Navajo Nation press release, August 14, 2005.

Orchard Gardens

Home Harvest Loop, Missoula, Montana

**INTEGRATED DESIGN / LOCALLY SOURCED AND
ENVIRONMENTALLY RESPONSIBLE MATERIALS /
REDUCED CARBON FOOTPRINT / FOOD SECURITY**

The work of Montana-based nonprofit developer homeWORD is guided by a vision to develop innovative yet replicable housing that achieves affordability through sustainable, holistic methods. Over ten years, each of homeWORD's eight completed projects (a total of 94 rental units and 14 homes) has continued to build on experience gained in past projects. HomeWORD's projects demonstrate a growing understanding of the connections between affordability, community revitalization, and reducing long-term environmental costs through green building strategies such as smart land use, resource and energy efficiency, waste reduction, and community sensitive design. HomeWORD aims to help transform its local housing market by modeling replicable solutions for the construction industry.

Orchard Gardens is homeWORD's most ambitious green project to date. Finished in 2005, Orchard Gardens is located in the rapidly growing west side of Missoula, Montana. The area is rooted in an agricultural tradition and is still home to orchards and small farms. The Orchard Gardens community includes 35 units of one-, two- and three-bedroom apartments for households that earn 50 percent or less of the area median income. The property consists of a straw-bale community barn and four colorful residential buildings, all clustered around a common area that includes a public art display. An underground parking garage is discreetly located below one of the residential buildings, and a bike trail connects to Missoula's trail system. Just under half of the 4.5-acre site has been preserved as open space that includes an organic orchard and community gardens operated by a local nonprofit, Garden City Harvest, and a bike/pedestrian path.

For this project, homeWORD and its project team made each design choice based on homeWORD's goal of creating affordable housing for Missoula that encourages a sense of community and belonging through quality building materials, comfortable living spaces, and environmentally friendly processes. The following green items were priorities for the team:

By placing some of Orchard Gardens' parking in an underground structure, the site plan was able to devote almost half of the site to open space that includes an orchard and gardens.
© Don MacArthur.

- Minimizing the environmental impacts of the project, including reducing the project's carbon footprint[1]
- Preserving open space and the rural character of the existing neighborhood

PROJECT DETAILS

Project Size:	4.54 acres, including 2.4 acres of open space and 35 residential units (31,735 sq ft of finished interior space in 5 buildings, including 1,535 sq ft community barn)
Construction Cost:	$4,586,731 for the 4 residential buildings and all site development and improvements (the community barn cost an additional $231,500)
Construction Cost/Sq Ft:	$122/sq ft for usable finished space
Cost/Unit:	$131,000
Total Project Cost:	$6,779,148 (includes land, site work, new construction costs, professional fees, construction interim costs, financing fees and expenses, soft costs, syndication costs, developer fees, and project reserves)
Completion Date:	January 31, 2006

Project Team

Owner/Developer:	homeWORD
Architect:	MacArthur, Means and Wells Architects
MEP Engineer:	Associated Construction Engineering
Civil Engineer:	Professional Consultants
Structural Engineer:	Beaudette Consulting Engineers
Landscape Architect:	Wonder Land
General Contractor:	Sirius Construction (residential GC); McMahon Construction (community barn)
Green Building Consultant:	Design Balance
Energy Consultant:	Resource Engineering Group
Solar Consultant:	Solar Plexus
Commissioning Agent:	EMC Engineers

Awards

Home Depot Foundation's second annual Award of Excellence for Affordable Housing Built Responsibly, rental housing category, October 2006

Honorable Mention, Charles L. Edson Tax Credit Excellence Awards, rural housing category, February 2006

- Protecting the health of the project's occupants
- Encouraging local economic growth
- Encouraging alternative energy generation
- Evaluating green priorities through modeling
- Establishing tracking systems to maximize the operating efficiency of Orchard Gardens and to help inform other developers
- Encouraging local food security

In October 2006, Orchard Gardens received the Home Depot Foundation's second annual Award of Excellence for Affordable Housing Built Responsibly, in the rental housing category.

GREEN ACHIEVEMENTS

By using an integrated design process, homeWORD was able not just to provide green affordable housing for 35 families, but also to contribute to the local economy through the use of locally sourced materials, partnerships with other local organizations, and by preserving a portion of the site for agricultural use.

Synergy Through Up-Front Design and Planning: By establishing performance goals early and planning carefully, the project team succeeded in reducing the project's carbon footprint, often through strategies that addressed other priorities, too. For example, two other project goals were to preserve open space by reducing the amount of land used for buildings, and to reduce the amount of impermeable surfaces on the land. An elegant solution addressed all three of these green priorities. Since Missoula County does not permit the use of pervious materials for parking surfaces, the team included an underground parking garage in the program. The decision to move a portion of the parking underground preserved the open space needed for the community gardens and orchard. Replacing pavement with gardens also encourages "food security" by producing food on-site.[2] The orchard's trees help reduce car-

SUMMARY OF GREEN FEATURES

Site

- Passive solar access maximized though building orientation and window placement
- Developed land reduced by clustering housing
- Existing cottonwood trees preserved
- Organic farm and community gardens
- Impervious surfaces and asphalt reduced by placing parking underground beneath main building
- Located near major road arterials, public transportation, and a bike/trail system
- Free resident bus pass program available (bus stop is ¼ mile away)

Water

- Landscaping includes native and climate-appropriate plants. Drip irrigation that will be phased out once plants are established
- Bioswales created to channel stormwater for on-site filtration
- Worked directly with plumbing contractor to select low-flow fixtures, including showerheads and faucets, and dual-flush toilets

Energy

- Passive solar shading techniques appropriate for the local climate
- Energy modeling used to select energy-efficient heating and cooling systems
- Buildings commissioned to evaluate energy performance.
- Ground source heat pump for heating and cooling buildings utilizes Missoula aquifer
- Solar heat used to preheat domestic hot water
- On-demand, tankless hot-water heaters
- Photovoltaic system ties into grid (no on-site storage required) and provides part of general electrical needs.
- Double-paned, low-e, argon-filled double-hung windows
- Air-to-air heat exchangers provide continuous ventilation and recover heating/cooling energy from exhaust air
- Sealants and foam insulation create airtight barrier at the building envelope
- High R-value insulation
- ENERGY STAR® appliances chosen for refrigerators and washing machines
- CFL lighting fixtures and motion sensors installed where appropriate (parking garage, hallways, outside)
- Structural insulated panels used in roof structure of row houses

Materials and Resources

- Rapidly renewable materials, including small-diameter log fencing and wheatboard cabinetry
- Recycled-content products, including carpeting, metal roofing, recycled glass for road base, soundboard
- Natural linoleum flooring
- Locally sourced materials used, including sustainably harvested lumber, salvaged wood for barn doors, straw-bale walls in community barn
- Fly ash (a by-product of coal mining) used instead of cement in all concrete work (35% fly ash in four building foundations, and a 100% fly ash foundation for community barn)
- Fifty-two percent of construction waste diverted from landfills through on-site waste management
- PVC-free plumbing system

Health and Comfort

- Formaldehyde-free/ CFC-free polyurethane spray foam used for insulation
- No-smoking policy mandated during construction; reinforced during weekly visits by homeWORD staff and reminders to contractor
- No- and low-volatile organic compound (VOC) paints, sealants, adhesives, carpet.
- Bathroom fans ensure that humid air is removed, thus reducing opportunity for mold growth

Durability and Ease of Maintenance

- Resident manual includes instructions and tips for efficient operations
- Buildings designed with durability in mind through materials selection (such as heavy-gauge commercial-quality roofing) and construction techniques
- Direct digital control system installed to monitor and document trends in energy use from a distance; data provided also aid with maintenance and feedback to residents

bon dioxide created by the buildings, which in turn supports the goal of reducing the carbon footprint.

Encouraging a relationship between materials and job creation fostered yet more synergy. By selecting materials that are not only sustainable (i.e., made with rapidly renewing resources or with recycled content) but also locally sourced, Orchard Gardens was able to support the local economy as well as to conserve resources. Using heat recovery ventilators, which save energy while supplying fresh air in tight buildings, addresses connections between superior energy efficiency and indoor environmental quality.

The Planning Process: The multiple benefits that derive from creating such connections are best achieved by establishing closer coordination and communication among the various building professionals. After homeWORD defined the basic program for this project, they held two design

---

> "This discipline of thought is not applied, but rather, integral to the whole design process from beginning to end . . . it's holistic."
>
> DON MACARTHUR
> *MacArthur, Means & Wells, Architects*

---

charrettes.[3] First came a neighborhood charrette, intended to solicit neighbor input for an inclusionary design process. This charrette addressed issues of density, parking, open space preservation, and options for design vernacular.

Next came an "ecocharrette" that established ambitious green building goals and involved the project's design professionals, including a sustainable building and energy modeling consultants. During the ecocharrette, homeWORD and the design team established sustainable goals and brainstormed creative solutions. For example, homeWORD worked with the civil engineering and design professionals to set water conservation goals early in the charrette and then collaborated to develop a landscaping plan based on a natural approach to stormwater management. For guidance, the team used the U.S. Green Building Council's Leadership in Energy and Environmental Design (LEED) ratings system (using

LEED's *Application Guide for Lodging* because USBGC had not released criteria for residential projects at the time of the charrette).

The architectural firm MacArthur, Means, and Wells (MMW) created a schematic design based on the concepts that emerged from the charrettes. One question MMW kept asking was how local history could be reflected in the project. This led to a decision to preserve and re-create the garden concept of the original subdivision, which consisted of 5-acre plots with homes and gardens. Using the vernacular of local farm buildings as a starting point, the project's front face to the street became a deeply set-back, traditional-looking yellow farmhouse with a wrap-around porch.

Superior Energy Efficiency: Once the basic program had been determined, creating an energy model was the first step in selecting the project's heating, ventilating, and air-conditioning (HVAC) systems and energy-saving measures. This energy model showed the operating cost benefits of various measures and helped the design team to select a ground source heat pump, on-demand hot-water heaters, solar hot water, high-efficiency lighting, and improved insulation. The model predicted energy savings of 43 percent as compared to a conventionally designed project.

Early plans provided specific details about energy-efficient systems, advanced framing systems, insulation, and other options for saving energy. The team used this information in their fundraising efforts with a variety of private foundations to seek support for the sustainable aspects of the design.

Creating Innovative Partnerships to Reach Goals: HomeWORD created several partnerships that supported the local economy by investing in locally sourced materials and reducing construction waste.

Reducing materials and construction waste. HomeWORD required the general contractor to reduce the waste produced on-site by developing an aggressive construction waste management program. The contractor diverted 52

A ground source heat pump, utilizing the local Missoula aquifer, provides the heating and cooling needs for Orchard Gardens. Each unit has individual controls for heating and cooling. © *Mark Fritch*.

percent of the construction waste. Waste disposal savings accrued to the contractor to support exploration of this method. One strategy the contractors implemented was to organize all lumber on-site. By holding to a high standard for keeping the site clean and organized, the workers were able to utilize longer pieces of scrap lumber and reduce waste. For example, during the framing process, they used fewer full sticks of lumber for blocking because they knew where to go to source scrap lumber. The general contractor discovered that implementing these systems for waste reduction reduced the cost of transporting the waste to the

dump as well as tipping fees. He now plans to implement such processes into all his projects.

HomeWORD helped the contractor by creating partnerships to reuse materials with local organizations that support job training and creation. For example, homeWORD collaborated with Home Resource, a nonprofit organization that collects and sells reusable materials, to reuse wood scraps longer than 16 inches. After collecting the wood scrap, Home Resource then partnered with Opportunity Resource, a nonprofit that supports individuals with disabilities, to make shingles from the wood scraps. These shingles are sold through Home Resource to homeowners looking for moderately priced materials for home improvement.

Locally sourced materials. In its quest for locally sourced materials to use at Orchard Gardens, home-WORD developed partnerships that helped create markets for several locally sourced materials. One success story involves the wood used in the buildings. Montana is home to much timber production, and homeWORD felt it could promote the use of sustainably harvested timber while also supporting a fledgling local industry. By purchasing local products, homeWORD knew it could reduce the carbon footprint associated with transportation and support good-wage jobs in the community.

Rather than purchase wood certified by the Forest Stewardship Council (FSC) and trucked in from another state (with its associated cost premium and transportation impacts), homeWORD partnered with Wildland Conservation Services, an organization that encourages local forest stewardship by monitoring and sustainably logging local forests. Wildland Conservation Services sourced the timber from a nearby forest that was logged using sustainable practices. This practice cut out the middle men, sending timber straight to Orchard Gardens from the mill. Says project architect Don MacArthur, "At the end of the day, the product's cost was within pennies per linear foot of the cost of nonsustainably harvested timber. The logging practices that put primacy on forest health and regeneration of the ecosystem were supported by this project."

Since May 2006, this product, now called Good Wood, has been available to the larger community through Home Resource, a not-for-profit, sustainable building product store based in Missoula. (Good Wood is a partnership between Home Resource and Wildland Conservation Resources.) The successful use of Good Wood at Orchard Gardens demonstrated that there was a market for it, and Home Resource is now selling it just as fast as they can get it. As a nonprofit, they aren't interested in a markup, but rather in keeping it as affordable as possible for the local community.

The design team also incorporated fly ash into the concrete at Orchard Gardens. Fly ash is a by-product of coal combustion and replaces portland cement, a virgin product that is high in embodied energy. Fly ash is frequently used to replace up to 20 percent of the portland cement in concrete, but at Orchard Gardens, 35 percent fly ash content was used. In the community barn's foundation, 100 percent fly ash was used, eliminating the portland cement content completely. Requiring fly ash in the concrete at Orchard Gardens created a local market for it, and fly ash is now cheaper in Missoula than portland cement. There are two concrete plants in Missoula, and neither one used fly ash, so homeWORD used a concrete plant in Hamilton. The structural engineer for Orchard Gardens wrote a letter to the two Missoula plants, explaining that they needed to reevaluate their policy on fly ash, and the Missoula plants have now made fly ash readily available.

Straw-Bale Community Barn: The team dreamed of including a barn on-site to store tools for the orchard and gardens, as well as to offer a community space for gatherings. After original plans to salvage and rebuild a nearby historic barn fell through, the team decided to build a structural straw-bale barn to demonstrate the feasibility of build-

ing a load-bearing straw-bale barn instead of a typical post-and-beam barn. Betsy Hands, homeWORD's program manager, says, "This straw-bale barn is an incredible success. It features many of the ideals in green building—energy efficiency, rapidly renewable materials, salvaged materials, and a nontoxic environment"—not to mention the fact that the community helped to construct the barn by stacking the straw-bale walls and helping to apply the stucco finish on the walls. In addition, the large barn doors are made from salvaged wood and open up onto the courtyard with a public art project financed through a "1 percent for art" program (in which a portion of the construction budget is earmarked for an art installation that adds interest to the central community space).

PVC-Free Plumbing Systems: Another unique aspect of this project was the team's commitment to avoiding the use of polyvinyl chloride, or PVC, in the plumbing systems. The production of PVC creates dioxin and other toxic by-products. PVC also contains harmful additives such as lead and phthalate plasticizers, which leach out during use. Committing to reduce the usage of PVC was an unusual step and required replacing PVC with copper, cast iron, and PEX (cross-linked high-density polyethylene) piping. Despite the design team's efforts, many building products contain PVC that could not be eliminated, such as in the insulation of electrical wiring. The general contractor submitted a base bid that included standard PVC products, and an alternate bid that included no PVC in the plumbing system. The team's choice to accept the alternate bid added 1 percent to the project's construction cost. However, homeWORD feels strongly about addressing this issue and, with future projects, plans to continue to research ways to further eliminate PVC.

Food Security: HomeWORD believes that food security is an important component of affordability for families on a limited budget. Food security measures contribute to sustainability by encouraging local self-sufficiency and reducing the cost of transporting food over long distances. After creating a rooftop community garden in a previous project, homeWORD wanted to expand the use of food security strategies at Orchard Gardens. A local nonprofit will manage the gardens and ensure a consistent income stream to support the garden. In addition to the working farm, residents have been given plots to do their own gardening. Some food will go to a local food shelf, some to a community-supported agriculture organization (known as a CSA), and some to volunteers.

PROJECT FINANCING

Orchard Gardens cost $4,818,231 to build. The total project cost of $6,779,148 included land acquisition costs of $373,000, design fees of $406,409 and miscellaneous expenditures for fees, permitting, feasibility studies, insurance, and interest. Solar panels cost an additional $100,000 and were paid for by private funding.

HomeWORD says that integrating green and sustainable features into housing construction is not yet common in the state of Montana, which made funding challenging. Without support from national foundations such as the Home Depot Foundation, the Enterprise Foundation, and an anonymous donor, homeWORD simply would not have been able to incorporate green features.

Driven by its mission to build models for affordable housing and the construction industry, homeWORD asks its staff to seek additional funding and find new sources of support from both private and community foundations. One unique aspect of the project is that an anonymous donor found its own goals and values closely matched those of the project and therefore contributed over half a million dollars to support the green features of Orchards Gardens.

The green features integrated into Orchard Gardens did result in costs over and above those of standard practice in affordable housing, although

PROJECT FINANCING

FUNDING SOURCES	AMOUNT
Equity	
Low-Income Housing Tax Credit Equity	$4,256,737
General Partner Capital	$123,676
Deferred Developer Fee	$291,389
Debt	
First Security Bank (permanent loan)	$530,109
Grants and Donations	
Capital Campaign (multiple sources)	$883,537
Montana Department of Commerce HOME funds	$500,000
City of Missoula CDBG	$193,700
Total Sources	**$6,779,148**

homeWORD has not been able to identify the exact percentage of increase. Although the ground source heat pumps cost more than HVAC systems typically used in affordable housing, the system was chosen early in the planning process on the basis of the energy modeling results, and its cost was not compared with that of alternative possibilities. Because homeWORD has a mission to help move the local housing market toward more sustainable projects, the additional cost was seen as part of achieving this larger vision. Architect Don MacArthur states that, currently, building green affordable housing "takes so much energy and passion and persistence," but as more begin to do it, it will start to infiltrate the awareness of regulatory and financial institutions. He notes that requirements for Montana's low-income tax credits are being rewritten to provide incentives for sustainable measures. When others see that the funding exists, they also may be willing to try green building, and it will become more widespread.

The project team found that while some green building techniques and products were more expensive than typical construction, others cost the same or even less. Replacing portland cement with locally produced fly ash was actually cheaper in the Missoula area. The sustainably harvested wood cost almost exactly the same as typical wood, as did the community barn doors of reclaimed timber, which otherwise would have been purchased as new custom doors, given their size. Many features did not incur additional costs, such as the low–volatile organic compound (low-VOC) sealants and adhesives, because of the economies of scale enjoyed by a 35-unit project.

LESSONS LEARNED

Because homeWORD has made a long-term commitment to addressing sustainability issues in an integrated way in its projects, it is very interested in deriving lessons learned from each project, and in documenting such lessons for the future. Although lessons are always learned in the building design and construction process, the team's clarity and focus supported them in meeting the goals established early in the process.

The project utilized several methods to obtain feedback on the buildings' energy performance. For example, homeWORD and MMW Architects worked with the Montana Department of Environmental Quality to perform infrared camera testing and blower door testing on the building envelopes. This testing led to the discovery of cold spots around the windows and at the base of walls. These problem areas then received additional caulking to eliminate air infiltration and improve the project's energy efficiency. The project also utilized commissioning[4] to help ensure the HVAC systems were functioning properly.

Systems to Monitor Ongoing Performance: A direct digital control system was installed that monitors and documents trends in energy use from a remote location. This system allows homeWORD to monitor each unit's energy usage and identify areas with poor energy performance. These areas can then be addressed quickly and efficiently by homeWORD's maintenance staff. The data provided by the digital control system also aid with maintenance. For example, if a resident complains that his or her unit is too hot, the building's management staff can check the system to see what might be happening and offer suggestions from a distance, providing immediate feedback while saving time and money by not having to go out to the site.

Getting the Project Approved: Some neighbors opposed affordable housing in their neighborhood, as well as the proposed density, which increased the allowable density from six dwelling units per acre to eight. A coalition was created to fight the project. In response, says homeWORD's program manager Betsy Hands, "We organized more neighborhood meetings, talked with the neighbors who worked with us during the initial design charrette, knocked on the doors of the entire neighborhood to educate the people about the goals of the project, and listened to their concerns. During construction we were able to respond to some of the neighbor concerns about the color of a few buildings. I think our ability to listen and respond to individuals about their concerns has helped build strong support and appreciation of the Orchard Gardens housing development."

Including the Right People: Throughout the project, homeWORD was careful to include the right people on the design team, including a green building consultant who helped identify appropriate products to meet indoor air quality goals; an energy consultant who helped model the project's energy performance; and engineers who designed structural, mechanical, electrical, and site systems to meet the sustainability goals established in the charrette. Throughout the project, MMW Architects worked to create a holistic design process to achieve homeWORD's goal of developing a model of sustainable, affordable housing.

When asked what he was most proud of on this project, MacArthur answered, "We have used a discipline of thought . . . at answering the questions before us from the perspective of sustainability. This discipline is not applied, but rather, integral to the whole design process from beginning to end . . . it's holistic."

CONTACTS

Developer: homeWORD

Betsy Hands, project manager: 406-332-4663;
betsy@homeword.org

Architect: MacArthur, Means & Wells Architects

Don MacArthur, architect: 406-543-5800;
don@mmwarchitects.com

SOURCES

"Green Building Techniques: Use of Materials," *Rural Voices* (fall 2005), www.ruralhome.org/manager/uploads/VoicesFall2005.pdf.

Hands, Betsy, homeWORD, personal interview with Lisa McManigal Delaney, followed up with e-mail and phone correspondence, 2006.

"Home Resource Introduces Cedar Saver Shingles," *Re-use News* (Spring 2006): 6; www.homeresource.org/news/HR_Newsletter.pdf. Information on cedar shingles reused after construction at Orchard Gardens.

"Home Resource to Offer Sustainably Harvested 'Good Wood' to Customers," press release, April 27, 2006, www.homeresource.org/news/GoodWood.pdf. Information on sustainably harvested lumber similar to that used at Orchard Gardens.

homeWORD, "Final Report for the Green Communities Initiative" (December 8, 2005).

Ibid. Application to the Home Depot Foundation's Awards of Excellence for Affordable Housing Built Responsibly (2006).

homeWORD, www.homeWORD.org.

Macarthur, Don, of MacArthur, Means and Wells, personal interview with Lisa McManigal Delaney, followed up with e-mail and phone correspondence, 2006.

Nord, Mark, Margaret Andrews, and Steven Carlson, *Household Food Security in the United States, 2001,* Food Assistance and Nutrition Research Report No. 29 (U.S. Department of Agriculture, Economic Research Service, Food and Rural Economics Division, 2002; www.ers.usda.gov/publications/fanrr29/fanrr29.pdf.

NOTES

1. A carbon footprint is a measure of the amount of carbon dioxide (CO_2) emitted through the combustion of fossil fuels. A carbon footprint is often expressed as tons of carbon dioxide or tons of carbon emitted, usually on a yearly basis. Building-related activities that affect the carbon footprint of a building include electricity use, if provided by nonrenewable resources; home heating use; and the amount of food bought from nonlocal sources. (Source: Wikipedia.)

2. Food security can be defined as "access by all people at all times to enough food for an active, healthy life. Food security includes at a minimum: (1) ready availability of nutritionally adequate and safe foods, and (2) an assured ability to acquire acceptable foods in socially acceptable ways" (source: USDA, http://www.ers.usda.gov/Publications/fanrr35/).

3. A charrette is an intensive workshop that involves all team members, lasts from three to fours hours to a day or more, and aims to create a clear vision for how the project will be developed, including how the green building elements will be incorporated.

4. The process of ensuring that systems are designed, installed, functionally tested, and capable of being operated and maintained to perform in conformity with the owner's project requirements (source: LEED NC version 2.2 reference guide). Commissioning assists in the delivery of a project that provides a safe and healthful facility; improves energy performance; optimizes energy use; reduces operating costs; ensures adequate O&M staff orientation and training; and improves installed building systems documentation. A new guideline, Guideline 0-2005, *The Commissioning Process*, from the American Society of Heating, Refrigerating and Air-Conditioning Engineers (ASHRAE) describes how to verify that a facility and its systems meet the owner's project requirements. Those requirements also define sustainable development goals and how the building will function before designers begin the design process. To keep costs at a minimum, the design team must understand what they are tasked with accomplishing, which is provided by the requirements (source: http://www.wbdg.org/project/buildingcomm.php).

The Plaza Apartments

Northeast Corner of Sixth and
Howard Streets, San Francisco, California

**SUPPORTIVE HOUSING FOR FORMERLY HOMELESS / HEALTHY INDOOR
ENVIRONMENT / SAN FRANCISCO REDEVELOPMENT AGENCY PILOT
PROJECT / ENTERPRISE GREEN COMMUNITIES PROJECT**

The Plaza Apartments exemplify how to create a humane, healthy, noninstitutional environment for extremely low-income residents. A colorful, urban high-rise building, this newly constructed project provides studio apartment housing and on-site supportive services for formerly homeless residents. Each of the building's 106 residential units includes a full bathroom and kitchenette and averages approximately 300 square feet. This mixed-use building also includes ground-floor retail (approximately 2,200 square feet) anchoring the corner of Howard and Sixth Streets, a 99-seat community theater (still to be built out), and community spaces comprising a kitchen, a courtyard, and laundry facilities. Located in San Francisco's South of Market area, the project is part of broader efforts to revitalize its gritty Sixth Street neighborhood.

In 2005, San Francisco became the first city in the United States to adopt green building principles for all new affordable housing projects. The Plaza Apartments are San Francisco's first "Green Communities" project, built to the standards of Enterprise's Green Communities criteria. In 2002, the Public Initiatives Development Corporation (PIDC) was created as a nonprofit subsidiary of the San Francisco Redevelopment Agency (SFRA) to develop affordable housing and, specifically, this project. The Plaza Apartments were chosen to serve as a model in creating sustainable design for other developers to follow. The project was done in partnership with several other entities. Global Green USA acted as a catalyst, facilitating a green building charrette[1] that clarified the team's green building goals. The Enterprise Green Communities Initiative provided technical assistance and grant funds later in the development process. The city of San Francisco's Department of the Environment provided information on topics such as renewable energy and manufacturers of sustainable flooring.

Project goals included providing a noninstitutional, comfortable, and healthy environment for a population with disabilities and challenged immune systems, lowering operating costs through energy and resource efficiency, and using durable and easily maintained materials and equipment.

The Plaza Apartments are one of eight recipients of the American Institute of Architects' 2006 Show You're Green

This new, urban high-rise building has added color and character to its surrounding San Francisco locale.
© *Tim Griffith Photography.*

PROJECT DETAILS

Project Size:	One 65,000 sq ft building (9 stories plus basement) with 106 residential units, ground-floor retail, support services, and community theater; replaced a 2-story, 38-unit single-room-occupancy building with ground-floor retail and theater
Construction Cost:	$16.5 million; $255/sq ft
Total Project Cost:	$22.8 million
Construction Cost/Unit:	$150,000
Completion Date:	December 2005

Project Team

Owner/Developer:	Public Initiatives Development Corporation (PIDC), a wholly owned subsidiary of the San Francisco Redevelopment Agency
Architect:	Leddy Maytum Stacy Architects and Paulett Taggart Architects, in association
Mechanical/Plumbing Engineer:	C&B Consulting Engineers
Electrical Engineer:	POLA, C&B Consulting Engineers
Civil Engineer:	Telamon Engineering Consultants
Structural Engineer:	OLMM Consulting Engineers
Landscape Architect:	Gary Leonard Strang Landscape/Architecture
General Contractor:	Nibbi Brothers
Construction Manager:	Armando Vasquez Architecture and Construction
Green Building Consultant:	Global Green USA: charrette, LEED documentation/coordination done in-house
Commissioning Engineers:	LMS Architects, Timmons Design Associates

Awards, presented to projects that provide "outstanding housing that is both affordable and green." The project is also on track for a Leadership in Energy and Environmental Design (LEED) silver rating.

GREEN ACHIEVEMENTS

The program for the project was to redevelop a dilapidated single-room-occupancy building with 38 inferior 100-square-foot units and only 1.5 bathrooms for the building as a whole, no kitchen, and no open or common spaces. The project team wanted to deconstruct the existing building and recycle construction waste, setting a goal of diverting at least 75 percent of construction waste from landfills. The team surpassed this goal with a diversion rate of 94 percent. Another crucial goal was to provide a healthy and comfortable indoor environment for tenants that was aesthetically attractive and avoided an institutional feeling. The team also wanted to provide building systems and materials that would be efficient to operate, durable, and easy to maintain over the long term.

Healthy Indoor Environment: Among the most unique aspects of this project are the synergies between the needs of the target population—formerly homeless individuals—and sustainable design. This is one of the first green projects to be built for such low-income residents, many of whom suffer from addictions, mental health problems, physical disabilities, and challenged immune systems from years of living on the street. The healthy features of this building go beyond improved indoor air quality and energy efficiency and address less tangible human needs by providing plenty of natural light and ventilation, attractive views, and a warm, noninstitutional feeling.

Good indoor air quality is critical in such a building because many residents are frail or have complicated medical and psychological problems. Offgassing materials were avoided wherever possible when specifying cabinetry, paints, carpet, and other finishes.

Design That Reinforces the Green Goals: The building was designed to bring plenty of daylight into all residential spaces and corridors, as well as to most public and support spaces. Standard double-loaded corridors are avoided through a pinwheel floor plan that offers windows and views from all vantage points in the short corridors, allowing residents to orient themselves to the outside cityscape.[2] All units have windows that provide plenty of

A storefront design provides ample daylight.
© *Tim Griffith Photography.*

light and views, including floor-to-ceiling "aluminum storefront" windows that have smaller, operable windows embedded within them. Each unit has ample glazing opposite its entry door, which reflects light off the walls and brings it back to the kitchen area.

The building's entire concrete structure is exposed, and is used as part of the finish on both exterior and interior, reducing the need and associated cost for other materials. The building façade features Parklex panels, which consist of a core made of recycled kraft paper core infused with nontoxic resin, and a hardwood veneer that is durable and weather-resistant. Parklex wood veneers are from sustainably harvested forests, and are certified by the Pan-European Forest Certification Organization [PEFC]. Although Parklex has been used widely in Europe for the past decade, it is just beginning to be used in various applications in the United States.

Energy Efficiency: Energy efficiency provides clear, direct benefits to affordable housing projects, as energy cost savings increase the budgets of the owners or residents who pay utility bills. As PIDC project manager Erin Carson notes, "Affordable housing is so difficult to manage on a shoestring budget that if you can control energy costs, you

have done a lot. Most strategies are easily replicable, and you can do fairly simple things to improve energy efficiency without a lot of cost." The exterior design includes a rainscreen, which is a second skin that involves an exterior wall with an exterior layer of insulation, then an air gap, and then the exterior cladding (Parklex). This combination creates air flow in the cavity, which equalizes pressure and temperature, helping with interior heat gain.[3] The rainscreen also helps prevent moisture from entering the building.

The heating system is comprised of a hydronic hot-water system with central boilers, eliminating inefficient electric baseboard heating and providing more even, energy-efficient heat for tenants. The building relies on natural ventilation, supported by a small air-handling unit on the roof that blows in air on each floor near the elevators. This mainly passive system saves energy and also creates better indoor air quality.

Operations, Maintenance, and Durability: All flooring materials were chosen for their durable qualities, as well as for being resource-efficient and/or low emitting. Hallways of the buildings feature carpet tiles, which can be selectively replaced as needed. Originally, the architects also included carpet tiles in the individual units because the project manager was adamant about including carpet in the living spaces to strengthen the noninstitutional feeling. However, the property management team predicted the need to replace an entire unit's carpet whenever there is tenant turnover, which meant that replacing carpet tile would be much more expensive than replacing conventional broadloom carpet. Thus, lower-grade carpeting was installed, and ample sums for carpet replacement were allocated to the operations budget.

To assist with waste separation, recycling collection areas are located on each residential floor, and tenants are provided with trash and recycling receptacles in their units. Enterprise Community Partners commissioned the development of green maintenance manuals for the Plaza Apartments' tenants and property management staff. These

SUMMARY OF GREEN FEATURES

Site

- Transit-oriented development proximate to bus and regional rail. Increased density by redeveloping underutilized urban site
- Neighborhood appearance improved through creative design utilizing colorful façade with numerous windows
- Impact to city stormwater system minimized by water filtration directly to soil for entire courtyard and east façade runoff through deck areas

Water

- 1.5 gpm low-flow showerheads and 1.6 gpm low-flow toilets
- Irrigation control system with drip irrigation combined with bubblers

Energy

- Exceeds California Title 24 Energy Code by 22.2%.
- Tight building envelope includes a rainscreen with additional continuous rigid insulation to minimize heat gain and loss
- 26 kW photovoltaic system on roof provides approximately 12% of electrical design house electrical loads
- Hydronic heat used (95% efficiency central boiler with radiant heating in units)
- ENERGY STAR® appliances
- Insulated windows with lightly tinted glass to minimize heat gain
- Insulation with increased R-value on exterior walls and roof.
- Efficient light fixtures
- Lighting controls and occupancy sensors installed in public spaces

Materials and Resources

- 94% diversion of demolition and construction waste
- Concrete structure used as part of exterior and interior finish, reducing amount of additional finish materials required.

- Fly ash used in concrete as replacement for 50% in foundation and 20% on suspended slabs
- Steel framing and rebar minimum 20% recycled
- Forest Stewardship Council–certified wood products used for concrete formwork and other temporary construction elements
- Fiberglass rigid insulation with 35% recycled content from glass bottles
- Expanded polystyrene board roof insulation with 30% postindustrial recycled content
- Carpet and Rug Institute Green Label carpeting with minimum 45% recycled content, 100% recyclable
- Sustainable flooring includes recycled-rubber flooring in residential bathrooms and laundry room, bamboo in common areas, and linoleum in kitchenettes

Health and Comfort

- No-/low-volatile organic compound (VOC) paint, adhesives, and sealants
- Low-emitting CRI Green Label–compliant carpet (tiles and broadloom material)
- Formaldehyde-free wheatboard cabinetry
- Direct daylighting and views in all units and corridors
- Operable windows in units and most public areas
- Individually controlled airflow, temperature, and lighting

Durability and Ease of Maintenance

- Durable slate tile flooring used in elevator lobbies and ground-floor main entry path
- Green maintenance manuals provided for residents and building management
- Carpet tiles in hallways can be selectively replaced
- Linoleum flooring used in kitchenettes (lasts up to 3 times longer than vinyl flooring)
- Exterior façade comprised of Parklex, a durable and easily maintained material

---

manuals are meant to serve as models for other San Francisco/Enterprise Green Communities affordable housing developments. The building owner is also developing a "green rider" to the retail space lease, which stipulates that retail tenant improvements and maintenance meet sustainable criteria consistent with the rest of the building.

PROJECT FINANCING

The Plaza Apartments cost a total of $22,888,498, including hard costs of approximately $16.5 million. Soft costs totaled approximately $6 million, including $1.25 million in design fees, as well as furnishings and equipment, the developer fee, permits, and a prefunded operating reserve. The land is leased from the city for approximately $30,000 per year.

The project team has not been able to pinpoint any specific additional costs for green products and systems due to ongoing uncertainty over what constitutes a baseline, or "standard" building, in California. In order to be competitive in California's tax credit allocation process, affordable housing projects must already target a base level of green building, such as exceeding California's Title 24 energy efficiency standards by 10 percent.[4]

Construction of the Plaza Apartments cost $255 per square foot, which is approximately 3 percent higher than the norm for San Francisco affordable housing projects.[5] It is difficult to attach the increased cost to any specific green measure, in part because the nature of integrated design means that some areas will cost more, while others will accrue savings. For example, the pinwheel building design increased natural ventilation in the corridors, requiring less in the way of mechanical ventilation and lighting loads.[6] On the other hand, the hydronic heating system had higher first costs, although they will be recovered over time. The building's rainscreen was more expensive than a typical building, while at the same time the exposed concrete structure saved money through avoiding the use of the lathe, concrete, and plaster inherent in conventional exterior skin.

Energy Savings: Based on energy modeling results, the Plaza Apartments project is expected to use at least 22.2 percent less energy than the Title 24 baseline. This performance would lead to an annual savings in electricity use of $8,790 (58,860 kWh/yr) and a saving in natural gas use of $6,800 annually (8,085 therms/yr). See "Energy Performance Comparison" chart for data on expected energy performance as compared with the energy usage of a "standard building" in California (defined as a building that meets but does not exceed California's Title 24 requirements).

Project architect Roberto Sheinberg notes that "one of

PROJECT FINANCING

FUNDING SOURCES	AMOUNT
Equity	
San Francisco Redevelopment Agency	$11,200,518
Low Income Housing Tax Credit Equity	$11,409,000
Accrued SFRA Construction Loan Interest	$124,980
General Partner Capital	$100
Grants and Rebates	
Enterprise Green Communities Initiative Grant	$50,000
State of CA rebate for Renewable Program	$88,000
PG&E ENERGY STAR® Homes Program	$15,900
Total	**$22,888,498**

the often overlooked benefits of electricity reduction is the associated emissions reduction that accompanies it. Most California power plants are natural gas fired, which generate 1.32 lbs of CO_2 per kWh generated. (Electricity produced from coal generates 2.37 lbs of CO_2 for every kWh generated, while electricity produced from oil generates 2.14 lbs of CO_2/kWh). Since most California power plants are natural gas fired, our project is expected to eliminate approximately 77,700-lbs of CO_2 annually." He also noted that one gallon of unleaded gasoline produces approximately 20 pounds of CO_2. Assuming an average vehicle efficiency of 25 miles per gallon, a vehicle would need to

ENERGY PERFORMANCE COMPARISON

Standard Building

Electric energy usage:	581,860 kWh/yr
Natural gas usage:	39,085 therms/yr
Electricity usage cost:	$86,930/yr
Natural gas cost:	$32,870/yr

Plaza Apartments (Projected)

Electric energy usage:	523,000 kWh/yr
Natural gas usage:	31,000 therms/yr
Electricity usage cost:	$78,140/yr
Natural gas cost:	$26,070/yr

drive 97,000 miles "to generate the CO_2 the Plaza Apartments avoid generating in one year."[7]

LESSONS LEARNED

Integrated Design: An integrated design process is critical to the success of a comprehensive green building. Sheinberg attributes the success of this building in part to "very smart decisions made the first day." He observed that "the biggest benefits are going to come from the basic design concept, not later" in the process. For example, the pinwheel floor plan layout was determined early on, and addresses sustainability, IAQ, character, and functional design issues.

While the project team already planned to create a green building, the charrette conducted by Global Green USA played an early catalytic role in creating consensus and enthusiasm among the design and development teams on strategies to be researched and incorporated. Ultimately, the charrette assisted in setting the direction for the building's systems, materials, and appliances. The commitment of the owner, combined with knowledgeable and dedicated architects, was also crucial. "I think the fact this project is pushing the envelope in terms of green and sustainable design has meant that the project team has responded with greater passion and commitment to the entire process. . . . Without that higher expectation, it would have been just another project. I didn't expect this benefit. Everyone involved truly seems to love this project," said Carson. Project manager Carson and architect Sheinberg both were willing to be involved in the nitty-gritty details, putting in numerous hours to ensure that subcontractors met the building's intent—for example, ensuring that they used the low-toxic caulks that were specified and did not smoke on the job site.

Early Involvement of the General Contractor: The nature of a public bid process raised several issues and concerns. Since the Plaza Apartments was a hard bid project, relying on a competitive bidding process at the end of design development (rather than the more typical negotiated bid

process where a general contractor [GC] joins the project team early on and provides costing assistance to the team during the design process), the GC could not be involved until the construction phase. Not having the GC on board at the charrette stage meant that there was no opportunity to get input from the person most likely to have intimate knowledge of current market conditions for building products and hands-on experience with the materials. Although the architect did much of the research and legwork early on, he experienced difficulty in determining the best way to document the green requirements, as it was as yet unknown what kind of experience and commitment the GC would possess in terms of green materials and processes, knowledge of LEED requirements, and other necessary details.

To address such constraints, Carson and Sheinberg believe that involving the GC as early as possible, including in a charrette, contributes the contractor perspective to the process and will ensure continuity. If a public bid process or other constraint precludes early GC involvement, they suggest hiring a GC to participate in the charrette, and if that isn't possible, making sure a construction manager or owner's representative attends the charrette and meetings to ensure that the green goals are carried through from design into construction.

Sourcing Green Materials: The constraints of a hard-bid project also raised the issue of identifying enough suppliers to competitively bid green products. In San Francisco's hard-bid projects, three suppliers typically need to be identified. However, it was difficult to find three suppliers for several low-emitting products. For example, formaldehyde-free cabinetry was specified, but the GC's bid included standard manufactured cabinetry. It turned out that the GC could not secure formaldehyde-free manufactured cabinetry from typical sources so instead planned to purchase wheatboard cabinetry from a custom cabinet shop—at three times the cost of standard cabinets. Since the GC had to absorb this cost, the owner and design team agreed to modify the design specs from wood veneer to plastic laminate (p-lam) veneers to reduce the overall cost impact to the GC.

Fortunately, the cost of many green products continues to decrease, making them competitive with standard products. For example, several additional formaldehyde-free particleboard and wheatboard products are now available, which will provide cabinet manufacturers with the ability to source materials to produce green products. Says Carson, "Once this market change occurs, we can do the right thing without killing ourselves or our budget."

Looking back, Carson states that greening the Plaza Apartments has been "worth the struggle. Affordable housing developers already know how important it is on so many levels. We are getting to the point where it won't be as hard. Manufacturers are getting on board, prices are coming down, and products are becoming more readily available. . . . It is finally becoming easier to accomplish."

CONTACTS

Owner/developer: San Francisco Redevelopment Agency
Erin Carson, senior project manager: 415-749-2535; erin.carson@sfgov.org

Architect: Leddy Maytum Stacy Architects
Roberto Sheinberg, senior associate: 415-495-1700; rsheinberg@lmsarch.com

Architect: Paulett Taggart Architects, AIA
Paulett Taggart, architect: 415-956-1116; pt@ptarch.com

SOURCES

Carson, Erin, of PIDC, personal interview by Lisa McManigal Delaney and e-mail and telephone correspondence, November 2005–September 2006.

Green Communities, Plaza Apartments case study: www.greencommunitiesonline.org/documents /PlazaApts-2006.pdf.

Green Affordable Housing Coalition, Bay Area Case Studies/Plaza Apartments: www.frontierassoc.net /greenaffordablehousing/CaseStudies/BayArea.shtml.

King, John, "It's All Good at the New Plaza: Supportive Housing Provides Green Oasis on Gritty Sixth Street," *San Francisco Chronicle*, March 3, 2006, www.sfgate.com/cgi-bin/article.cgi?f=/c/a/2006/03/03 /BAGFQHHP8H1.DTL.

Leddy Maytum Stacy Architects: www.lmsarch.com.

Maynard, Nigel F., "Exterior Products Review: Alternative Cladding," www.ebuild.com/guide/resources /product-news.asp?ID=134261&catCode=14.

Lelchuk, Ilene, "Mayor Touts 'Green' Goal in Affordable Housing: Recycled Wood, Solar Panels Used at Apartments for Poor," *San Francisco Chronicle*, August 3, 2005, www.sfgate.com/cgi-bin/article.cgi?f=/c/a/2005 /08/03/BAGD7E1SEJ1.DTL.

Parklex information: www.fcpcusa.com/parklex1000.htm.

Paulett Taggart Architects: www.ptarc.com.

"San Francisco Adopts Green Building Standards," *American Chronicle*, August 2, 2005, www.american chronicle.com/articles/viewArticle.asp?articleID=1572.

Sheinberg, Roberto, of Leddy Maytum Stacy Architects, personal interview by Lisa McManigal Delaney, project documents, and telephone and e-mail correspondence, November 2005–September 2006.

Title 24 Energy Efficiency Standards: www.energy.ca.gov /title24.

NOTES

1. A charrette is an intensive workshop that involves all team members, lasts from three to fours hours to a day or more, and aims to create a clear vision for how the project will be developed, including how the green building elements will be incorporated.
2. A pinwheel design groups services such as elevators and stairs in the structure's central core, with short, easily navigable corridors emanating outward in a pinwheel arrangement. In this case, each corridor ends with a

floor-to-ceiling window that provides views, daylight, and natural ventilation.

3. The rainscreen approach, by effectively managing moisture, can enhance the durability of exterior wall systems. Rainscreen systems are exterior claddings that incorporate a designed airspace between the sheathing and the exterior cladding to allow water to flow faster to an exit point. The airspace is created by vertical furring strips (boards), a drainage mat, or some other means to hold the cladding off the wall framing/sheathing and create a gap.

4. Title 24 refers to California's Energy Efficiency Standards for Residential and Nonresidential Buildings. These standards were established in 1978 in an effort to reduce energy consumption in California. A periodical process of updating the standards allows for consideration and possibly incorporation of new energy efficiency technologies and methods. It is estimated that California's Title 24 standards, along with standards for energy-efficient appliances, have saved over $56 billion in electricity and natural gas costs since 1978, and will save an additional $23 billion by 2013; www.energy.ca.gov/title24.

5. Additionally, single-room occupancy projects tend to cost more than other affordable housing projects because they are so densely filled with mechanical, electrical, and plumbing systems. The Plaza Apartments were more intensive because each studio includes a kitchen.

6. The pinwheel design reduced costs for mechanical system and lighting because the shorter corridors, ending in large windows, meant that air and light had shorter distances to travel, thus reducing the length of ductwork and requiring less lighting.

7. The following websites offer CO_2 conversion data: http://yosemite.epa.gov/oar/globalwarming.nsf/content /ResourceCenterToolsCalculatorAssumptions.html; www.conservationfund.org/?article=3142.

Portland Place

2601 Portland Avenue,
Minneapolis, Minnesota

PLACE MAKING AND DEFENSIBLE SPACE / OWNERSHIP /
NEIGHBORHOOD RESURGENCE

The Phillips neighborhood of south Minneapolis is often compared to Ellis Island in New York City. It is the Minneapolis community where most new immigrants reside before relocating to other areas. The 1995 "People of Phillips Neighborhood Action Plan" stated, "Phillips is a microcosm of the larger world population, as we have a broad spectrum of humanity represented within the blocks that comprise Phillips." But this diverse neighborhood has suffered. In the early 1990s, it was considered an urban blight as the poorest and highest-crime area in Minneapolis. The Portland Place project represents a catalyst redevelopment of two city blocks to provide 51 affordable homes. In many ways Portland Place spawned the resurgence of the entire neighborhood.

The site for the project is adjacent to the former Honeywell headquarters (which recently merged with Allied Signal and moved to their headquarters in Morristown, New Jersey). Honeywell had a long-term presence in the community and wanted to help the deteriorating neighborhood that surrounded it. The mayor of the city also pushed Honeywell to get involved. In the mid-1990s, Honeywell bought up two city blocks and donated the land for the project, along with $3 million toward redevelopment. With these donations, the company insisted that the project be structured as an ownership model (versus rented) with a homeowners association established to ensure the long-term viability of the community. The community agreed with this model and also felt strongly about maintaining the scale of the neighborhood.

Around the same time this project was in the early conception stages, the city was also in the process of creating the Minneapolis Neighborhood Revitalization Program, establishing 82 neighborhood groups to essentially function as community development corporations. The program required each neighborhood group to develop a needs assessment and master plan. Later a pool of approximately $60 million was allocated to provide these groups

> "This project caused a resurgence of redevelopment for the area—creating a ripple effect outward of reinvestment."
>
> CHRIS WILSON
> *director of real estate, Project for Pride in Living*

with funds to execute their approved plans, requiring a 50 percent allocation of funds to go to affordable housing. This program helped form the Phillips neighborhood group People of Phillips (POP), which shaped the development of Portland Place.

Honeywell and POP partnered with Project for Pride in Living (PPL), a nonprofit organization founded in 1972 focused on preserving or creating new affordable housing and revitalizing neighborhoods. Its mission is to assist lower-income people and families working toward self-sufficiency by providing housing, jobs, and training throughout the Minneapolis and St. Paul Twin Cities metro area.

PROJECT DETAILS

Project Size:	51 units for direct purchase: 4 renovations and 47 newly constructed homes in a mix of single-family homes, duplexes, and townhomes (24 three-bedroom, 22 four-bedroom, 1 five-bedroom); 6 Habitat for Humanity homes for very low-income buyers (incomes below 30% of AMI) using sweat equity from owners and donated labor from volunteers; 32 of the units sold to families earning below 80% of AMI
Total Development Cost:	$11,892,440
Cost/Unit:	$252,022
Cost/Sq Ft:	$146/sq ft
Start Date:	1995 for site assembly
Completion Date:	2001

Project Team

Developer:	Project for Pride in Living
Architect:	LHB Engineers
General Contractor:	Flannery Construction
MEP Engineer:	LHB Engineers
Green Building Consultant:	Green Institute

Awards

A winner of the 2002 Minneapolis Committee on Urban Environment (CUE) awards.

Fannie Mae Foundation: Affordable Housing Design Finalist Maxwell Awards of Excellence Program.

PPL served the Portland Place project by managing all aspects of the project from inception to completion, as well as assembling the complex financing package.

Project for Pride in Living worked closely with many groups to address concerns and ultimately gain support for the project. Along with local architectural and engineering firm LHB, PPL hosted design charrettes around place making to achieve an appropriate scale, character, and identity, and to develop a new vision for the two-block development.[1] The charrette participants came up with several overarching goals for the project: safety, affordability, comfort, and sustainability. The overall concept was to create a new village with a traditional street pattern and more open space. To accomplish this goal, the originally conceived 100 units were decreased to 51.

The restored neighborhood plan included small lot, single-family and duplex homes with porches combined with townhouses. In collaboration with PPL, Habitat for Humanity built 6 homes for very low-income residents (below 30 percent of area median income). Common space is featured on the interior of each of the two blocks providing a playground and green space. Contextual details of the home designs help blend the new homes into the surrounding neighborhood, including matching setbacks, traditional housing design features, and materials.

Chris Wilson, director of real estate for PPL, says, "This project caused a resurgence of redevelopment for the area, creating a ripple effect outward of reinvestment." Honeywell's leadership in neighborhood revitalization provided a model for another major employer, Abbott Northwestern Hospital, to launch a concentrated eight-block improvement program across the street from Portland Place a year later. This project provided home improvement grants to area residents and offered capital for the acquisition and rehabilitation of some of the most deteriorated rental housing units. The rental rehabilitation portion, coordinated by Joe Selvaggio, capped affordability controls at 40 percent of area median income for these rental units. Ownership of the rehabbed units was consolidated with PPL as the general partner. Wilson noted that these two projects complemented each other, providing a mix of affordable housing types.

GREEN ACHIEVEMENTS

With sustainability identified as a goal during the design charrettes, PPL partnered early in the project with the Green Institute, a local nonprofit that champions environmental responsibility and sustainability. This led to Portland Place accomplishing a number of green achievements, both in the physical buildings and socially.

Materials Reuse: A plan was put into place to salvage and sell reusable materials generated during demolition of the run-down existing homes on the site. A few salvageable homes were offered for free to those who would move them off-site, and a beautiful old Victorian home was rehabilitated and left as the cornerstone of the project. This home was, and still is, owned by an existing homeowner and a neighborhood leader.

Site Design: For the site design, the team worked within the context of the mature trees, landscaping, and topography. Rick Carter, project architect with LHB says, "We oriented buildings for better solar access, adjusting unit types from one side of the street to the other to achieve this. It's a small measure, but it makes a big difference." By clustering units and designing for zero lot lines (versus having side yards), the design retained more open space and allowed for more units than a standard single-family development. Special attention was also paid to creating defensible space as crime was a major concern in the neighborhood.[2] The development team looked closely at illumination levels for outdoor lighting, sight lines, and definitive boundaries, and provided clear circulation paths. Certain architectural design solutions were put into place, such as providing either very low or very tall landscaping materials to eliminate concealed areas. Alleyways can be seen from the townhouses.

Materials: The new homes are designed as low-maintenance, durable buildings that fit in with the aesthetic of existing homes in the larger neighborhood. The architects selected long-lasting materials such as brick, stucco, color-coated sheet metal, and cedar for exterior uses. For the interiors, selections for fixtures, mechanical systems, and windows were based on durability and energy efficiency.

As a strategy to build a larger market for the new homes, potential homeowners were given a list of finish options. This allowed for the individualizing of homes as well as bulk purchase of some green materials.

Healthy interiors of the family room in the Portland Place development ensure good indoor air quality for the residents. © *Don Wong.*

Construction: To simplify construction, floorplans and unit types were repeated, but unique contextual details were added to differentiate the homes. Carter noted that in the design they tried to achieve a "very place-based architecture."

To keep costs down, townhouse units are stacked on top of garages to reduce foundation and roof materials. Bathrooms are also stacked to minimize plumbing runs. Basements were built with quick-assembly prefabricated concrete panels that require no footings. These insulated concrete panels offer energy savings, fire resistance, and superior structural integrity, and eliminate job site construction waste. Structural plans called for floor and roof trusses, eliminating the need for a central bearing wall and making mechanical system installation easier.

Mechanicals: Mechanical exhaust was selected for proper ventilation in the homes. Carter noted that it was important to educate the new owners on some of these special features of the homes, "particularly the air-to-air heat exchangers." Good mechanical ventilation acts as the lungs

SUMMARY OF GREEN FEATURES

Site

- Buildings oriented for better solar access
- Existing mature trees and some of the existing landscape retained
- Existing street lighting reused
- Clustering of units and a zero-lot-line design provided more useable space and allowed for more units than a standard single-family development
- Salvageable historic homes moved off-site
- Served as a catalyst for positive redevelopment of the surrounding neighborhood and job creation

Water

- Low-flow water fixtures
- Existing landscape reused, minimizing watering of new plantings

Energy

- Fixtures, mechanical systems, and windows selected on the basis of efficiency and durability
- Insulated concrete forms (ICFs) selected for energy efficiency
- Non-combustion mechanical exhaust utilized for proper ventilation

Materials and Resources

- Basements built with quick-assembly prefabricated ICFs
- Trusses for the floor and roof structure eliminate need for a central bearing wall
- Townhouse units were stacked on top of garages to reduce amount of foundation and roof material
- Demolition plan included selling off reusable materials for salvage
- Plumbing stacked to minimize length of water and sewer pipe runs
- Bulk purchase of materials made possible by large development

Health and Comfort

- Buyers given the option to select finishes from a list that included green materials
- Neighborhood security created by views of common areas and concealed areas
- Community homeowners association established

Durability and Ease of Maintenance

- Long-lasting materials for exterior finish: brick, stucco, color-coated sheet metal, and cedar

---

for the homes by supplying continuous fresh, filtered air, while exhausting the stale, contaminated air.

PROJECT FINANCING

The total development cost for the project was $11,845,047, with an average cost per unit of $252,022. The design work made up the largest part of predevelopment costs for Portland Place. This work was financed by noninterest loans from two community nonprofits. Home sales funded 37 percent. Additional funding was acquired from private and public sources. Grants were awarded for the security system and playground.

The rising costs of construction were a problem throughout the building of the project. Fortunately, PPL was able to change the unit mix in Phase II to better accommodate these cost increases without a reduction in the number of units. Also, in an effort to defray costs, Habitat for Humanity harnessed the energy of 1,000 volunteers and acquired donations of windows, lumber, and other construction materials for the six homes they constructed.

LESSONS LEARNED

"The two-block redevelopment of Portland Place creates its own market. With this size project (Phase I and II), you can get past the tipping point to transform a neighborhood—turn the neighborhood around," observes Chris Wilson, PPL's director of real estate. The ripple effect resulted in people caring about and improving lots and homes throughout the neighborhood.

Wilson notes that this area has seen the highest property value appreciation in the state while a mix of price controls ensures a diversity of income and demographics in the

PROJECT FINANCING

FUNDING SOURCES	AMOUNT
Equity	
Buyer Equity (down payments)	$213,000
Grants	
Minneapolis Community Development Agency	$2,280,000
HUD EDI Grant and Section 108	$760,000
Minnesota HFA/CRF Grant	$400,000
Metropolitan Council	$250,000
Family Housing Fund	$400,000
Honeywell Grant and TIF Grant	$3,085,940
Fannie Mae Foundation	$75,000
Debt	
Minneapolis Foundation (0% loan, deferred to closing)	$200,000
Greater Minneapolis Metropolitan Housing Corp (0% loan, deferred to closing)	$171,000
40 Mortgages with Conventional Lenders (8.5% 30-year loans)	$4,057,500
Total Sources	**$11,892,440**

community. Wilson says he doesn't worry about gentrification. "Things were so bad here at the time, our development team and Honeywell thought we'd be lucky to just sell the homes in this high-crime area." By the end of 1999, however, 30 units had been built and sold to a wide variety of buyers. Sixty-five percent of the new owners had incomes at or below 80 percent of the area median income, and 80 percent came from Minneapolis neighborhoods. One-third of all buyers were African American; one-third were Caucasian; and one-third included a diverse mix of Hispanic, Native American, Asian, East African, and Middle Eastern, reflective of the neighborhood diversity.

Architect Rick Carter of LHB is very happy with the way the project turned out and about his firm's commitment to green building. "All we do now are green projects and we now use the new LEED [Leadership in Energy and Environmental Design standards] for homes as a guide," Carter remarked. "People come to us now for green design."

CONTACTS

Developer: Project for Pride in Living

Chris Wilson, director of real estate: 612-455-5100

Architect: LHB Engineers, Architects and Engineers

Rick Carter, architect: 612-338-2029

SOURCES

Carter, Rick, architect, LHB Corporation, personal interview with Jenifer Seal Cramer, June 6, 2006.

Fagotto, Elena, and Archon Fung, The Minneapolis Neighborhood Revitalization Program: An Experiment in Empowered Participatory Governance, February 15, 2005, pages 32, 45, 47, 48, and a discussion on the neighborhood on pages 53–54, available at: http://www.ids.ac.uk/logolink/resources/downloads/Recite_Confpapers/NRPFinal.pdf.

Fannie Mae Foundation: "Affordable Housing Design Finalist: Project for Pride in Living, Inc.," Maxwell Awards of Excellence Program, 2000, pp. 46–49, www.fanniemaefoundation.org/grants/ahd_pride.pdf.

McCormick, Barbara, "Private Sector Partnerships: Investing in Housing and Neighborhood Revitalization: Portland Place: A New Vision of Neighborhood Revitalization," *National Housing Conference Affordable Housing Policy Review* 3, no. 2 (June 2004): 25–26.

"People of Phillips Neighborhood Action Plan," October 27, 1995.

Wilson, Chris, director of real estate, Project for Pride in Living, personal interview with Jenifer Seal Cramer, June 16, 2006.

NOTES

1. A charrette is an intensive workshop that involves all team members, lasts from three to fours hours to a day or more, and aims to create a clear vision for how the project will be developed, including how the green building elements will be incorporated; "Placemaking is a term that began to be used beginning in the 1970s by architects and planners to

describe the process of creating more livable towns and cities through the inclusion of such items as squares, plazas, parks, streets, and waterfronts that will attract people because they are pleasurable or interesting. Placemaking is often characterized by a focus on human activities and community involvement, and landscape often plays an important role in the design process." (Adapted from Wikipedia.)

2. Defensible space is the idea that crime and delinquency can be controlled and mitigated through design. For more information, see Oscar Newman, "Defensible Space: A New Planning Tool for Urban Revitalization," *Journal of the American Planning Association* 61, no 2 (Spring 1995).

The Street Where Dreams Come True

Corner of Lakewood and Miller Reed Avenues, Atlanta, Georgia

**SWEAT EQUITY HOUSING / HOMEOWNER EDUCATION /
COST-EFFECTIVENESS / EARTHCRAFT HOUSE CERTIFICATION PROGRAM**

Since Habitat for Humanity was founded in 1976, it has built over 150,000 homes in the United States and more than eighty other countries. Relying principally on volunteers who donate their labor to construct the house, Habitat's "sweat equity" model provides housing for families who commit to contributing hundreds of hours of their own labor into building their homes and the homes of others. Homes are funded by donations of cash and building materials. The residents' zero-interest mortgage payments help build still more Habitat homes. Residents pay their own utilities as part of developing financial management skills.

In early 2002, Habitat for Humanity's Atlanta affiliate created a small green community—The Street Where Dreams Come True—by building 9 single-family, single-story bungalows on an abandoned, overgrown lot. The first seven homes were built in just nine weeks. Two additional homes, whose lots had been used for staging construction of the first seven homes, were built a short time later. Several of the project's goals were to integrate a green homes certification process into Atlanta Habitat's existing building practices, expose a large number of volunteers to green building practices, and provide lessons for application to future projects. Building on the success of The Street Where Dreams Come True, Atlanta Habitat decided in 2004 that all its homes would be certified by Earthcraft, a green building program developed by Southface Energy Institute that is used throughout the Southeast.

Atlanta Habitat is the largest builder of homes for low- and very low-income families in Atlanta. It is not only among the most prolific of Habitat affiliates (900 homes to date), but is one of the furthest along in building green homes. This status is in part attributable to Atlanta Habitat's close working relationship with Southface Energy Institute, an Atlanta-based organization that promotes sustainable, energy-efficient building in the southeastern United States. The EarthCraft House program, founded in 1999 by the Greater Atlanta Home Builders Association and Southface, is a point-based system that provides guidelines for the construction of healthy, comfortable homes that protect the environment and reduce utility bills. Ray Maynard, Atlanta Habitat's director of

Architectural details on each of the homes on "The Street Where Dreams Come True" are designed to fit in with existing homes in the surrounding South Atlanta neighborhood. © *Atlanta Habitat.*

construction, has been working with Southface for twelve years, continuously introducing new green techniques to Habitat Atlanta's building process. For The Street Where Dreams Come True project, Atlanta Habitat partnered with Southface to ensure that Habitat staff would become trained to build EarthCraft-certified homes and to oversee volunteers in doing so. The homes also qualified as ENERGY STAR® homes after meeting strict guidelines for energy efficiency set by the U.S. Environmental Protection Agency.

This project educated all involved on how to build in a greener way. Constituencies included homebuyers who contributed sweat equity by helping to build their homes, as well as Atlanta Habitat staff and volunteers who participated in the process. Instead of building one home at a time, approximately 2,000 volunteers donated thousands of hours over nine weeks to construct the entire community simultaneously. Each home was sponsored by a corporation or other organization. Southface collaborated with the Home Depot to develop the energy-saving design, using off-the-shelf products found at home improvement stores.

The homes were built on a vacant lot in a challenged South Atlanta neighborhood; one of the project's goals was to help revitalize the neighborhood. Atlanta Habitat had committed to building 50 affordable homes in the larger South Atlanta area, including this project. In reflecting on

Each Habitat home is built with the donated labor of numerous volunteers as well as future residents.
© *Atlanta Habitat.*

PROJECT DETAILS

Project Size:	7 single-family homes (avg. 1,150 sq ft) on 9,000 sq ft lot
Construction Cost:	$502,641; $72/sq ft
Construction Cost/Unit:	$71,805
Total Development Cost:	$582,546
Completion Date:	March 2002

Project Team:

Developer/Owner:	Atlanta Habitat for Humanity
Architect:	No Architect. Atlanta Habitat has used same basic floor plan for 10 years, with cosmetic changes such as rooflines and porches, and adjustments for EarthCraft certification process
General Contractor:	Atlanta Habitat for Humanity
Green Building and Energy Consultant:	Southface Energy Institute

Awards

Recipient of EarthCraft House's Nonprofit Builder of the Year Award, 2005

this experience, Maynard explained, "The Street Where Dreams Come True showed us that we could do it . . . that we had the expertise and ability to make green building happen. So when we considered building all EarthCraft-certified homes in 2004, it wasn't a difficult decision. We stepped into it easily based on our accumulated experience, and with encouragement and the full support of Southface Energy Institute."

GREEN ACHIEVEMENTS

Saving Energy Through Incremental Improvements: One of the project's goals was to reduce residents' water, gas, and electricity bills by 30 percent in comparison with standard-construction homes in the area. In order to keep costs as low as possible, Atlanta Habitat pursued many small, volunteer-friendly initiatives that incrementally increased energy performance, rather than focusing on bigger-ticket items that individually save more energy. Improving airtightness, locating ducts in an intelligent

SUMMARY OF GREEN FEATURES

Site

- Crumbling, abandoned road behind homes dug up and replaced with 350 pine seedlings
- Site cleaned up and reused, preventing future neglect.
- All trees outside building footprint saved
- Groundcover kept in place on back half of each building lot to minimize stormwater runoff
- New trees planted to provide shade to homes and HVAC equipment

Water

- Washing machines upgraded to ENERGY STAR®–rated models.
- Stormwater management techniques such as swales and silt fences

Energy

- Airtightness improved by installing a double layer of foam board on house exteriors; joints were staggered so there were no cracks through both layers
- Air sealing system designed by Southface used to seal areas where different building elements meet
- Ductwork located in semiconditioned crawl space instead of in exterior walls
- Insulated box with sealed lid installed above attic pull-down stairs to eliminate draft and heat gain/loss of standard pull-down stairs
- Duct blaster and blower door tests conducted by Southface.
- Photovoltaic sensor on exterior lights installed to turn lights on and off automatically at dusk/dawn
- Fluorescent lighting
- ENERGY STAR appliances (washing machine and refrigerator) and high-efficiency water heater
- Double-glazed, vinyl-frame, double-hung windows with low-e glass and 30-year warranty (U-value <0.56, solar heat gain coefficient <0.4)
- Increased insulation: ceiling R-30, exterior wall sheathing R-5, crawl space walls R-8, walls R-13

Materials and Resources

- Advanced framing techniques used to reduce materials needed: interior studs 24 inches on center; ladder headers in non-load-bearing walls; fewer two-by-fours at corners to allow more insulation in wall; wall blocking at intersecting wall locations rather than standard tee
- Wood waste reduced by using engineered I-joists, OSB, and trusses
- Off-site framing done at centralized location to reduce waste (panels assembled at Habitat's warehouse)
- Construction waste recycled, including cardboard, wood pallets, scrap aluminum flatgoods, scrap steel, and beverage containers
- All "drops" from the building process reused to make small framing components
- Drywall added to ground as soil amendment
- Siding, roof shingles, and concrete block ground up as base for driveway concrete
- Non-pressure-treated wood waste ground into chips for landscape mulch
- Carpet pad with a minimum of 50% recycled materials
- Durable materials such as Hardie cementitious siding selected
- Flashed windows and doors using 30-lb felt paper installed to prevent rainwater leakage

Health and Comfort

- Crawl space insulated to create semi-conditioned air, keeping house at comfortable temperature
- Zero-volatile organic compound (VOC) paint
- Water heater closet sealed and insulated
- Bathroom exhaust fans installed that switch on at the same time as the light to ensure use

way, and working to eliminate drafts aren't necessarily exciting, but get good results at low cost. For example, the living space directly beneath the pull-down attic stairs is often drafty. To minimize the heat gain and loss caused by leakage in this area, an insulated box with a sealed but operable lid was installed over the opening, a simple step that is, however, rarely taken. Air filtration was reduced via numerous actions, including a focus on sealing locations where different elements of the building come in contact with each other, such as oriented strand board (OSB) decking and the bottom wall plate, mud sills and outside bands, and so forth. In addition, every penetration of the building envelope (where wires or pipes pass through it) was sealed with caulk or expandable foam.

Greening the Site: The site design was constrained by the fact that the land had already been platted, so the design could not fully take into account solar access, shading, or natural lighting. However, homes were built far enough apart to allow access to sunlight, and all existing trees outside the building footprints were preserved to provide shading for the houses and their heating, ventilating, and air-conditioning (HVAC) equipment. During construction, each tree was protected by fencing installed around its drip lines. To help minimize stormwater runoff, ground cover on the back part of each lot was preserved during construction, and silt fences were installed around the perimeter of each lot.

The back of the site is adjacent to a recycling company. To create a buffer between the two uses, Atlanta Habitat dug up a crumbling, abandoned road (formerly owned by the recycling company) and planted 350 seedlings to create a 17,000-square-foot long-term natural visual buffer. Houses were sited as close to the front of the site as the code permitted, to provide the largest possible backyard.

Recycling Construction Materials: Significant efforts were made to conserve and recycle construction materials. A tub grinder was used to recycle various building materials on-site. Ground-up shingles, fiber-cement siding, and concrete blocks provided a base for the newly poured concrete driveways. Wood grindings were used for landscaping mulch, and drywall was added to yard dirt. Wood scraps longer than 4 feet were returned to the warehouse to make components such as spacer blocks for framing, mailbox posts, and decorative elements for the front porches. In addition, all steel and aluminum scraps and cardboard packaging were recycled.

PROJECT FINANCING

The project's total development cost was $582,546, including $76,651 to acquire the property and $502,000 for construction. As with most Habitat projects, up-front

PROJECT FINANCING

FUNDING SOURCES	AMOUNT
Corporate House Sponsors	$455,000
Grants	$39,157
Donations	$46,682
Other Income (bequests, in-kind, homeowner payments, etc.)	$39,412
Special Events	$1,786
Product Sales	$510
TOTAL	**$582,546**

hard costs for building the houses are covered, in part, by sponsorship funding, grants, and donations. Volunteer labor saved thousands of dollars, reducing the purchase price for homebuyers. For this pilot project, Atlanta Habitat partnered with a number of corporations, including Black & Decker, GE, Turner Broadcasting System, the Home Depot, and local celebrity/consumer advocate Clark Howard. The bulk of the cost was covered by the sponsors, each of whom sponsored one or two homes. The future owners also provided sweat equity.

LESSONS LEARNED

Cost: The most important lesson the developers learned through this project was that they could build their homes to EarthCraft certification standards without spending an enormous amount of money. If Atlanta Habitat, with its tight budgets and reliance on volunteer labor, could do it, anyone could. Achieving EarthCraft certification cost an additional $2,180 per house. (Thanks to donations and sponsor support, the Atlanta Habitat affiliate paid only $1,603 of the $2,180 additional cost per house.) Southface has calculated that homeowners on this street save an average of $217 annually in heating, cooling, and water heating expenses. Over the life of a thirty-year mortgage, this will amount to a savings of $6,510—all for a cost of $2,180.

When subsequent homes were built in 2004, the added

EarthCraft certification cost decreased to only $310 per house. The difference was partially due to the fact that Atlanta Habitat and Southface had agreed to certain upgrades for the pilot partnership that were not included in subsequent homes. Georgia's energy code has also improved, now requiring more energy-efficient windows (identical to those required by EarthCraft standards) and a higher seasonal and energy efficiency rating (SEER) for air conditioners.

The Street Where Dreams Come True pilot project allowed Habitat Atlanta to determine which materials and techniques offered the highest return in terms of sustainability, energy conservation, and durability. Strategies and materials that cost more but only slightly improved energy efficiency, health, or resource conservation were eliminated. For example, Atlanta Habitat would have liked to purchase air-conditioning equipment with a higher SEER (a SEER of 12 was used), but to have done so would have been cost-prohibitive. Instead, they focused on smaller actions able to be carried out by volunteers, such as using more caulking to accomplish air sealing, and installing a sill seal, a vapor barrier in the crawl space, and expandable foam around all doors and windows. They would also have liked to have added radiant barrier decking on the roof, but this, too, was cost-prohibitive.

Materials: Since the EarthCraft certification program focused somewhat more on reducing energy use than on sustainably sourced or recycled materials, energy efficiency measures received the most attention. The project team did investigate using sustainably certified lumber, but found it to be prohibitively expensive because it was not available from a local supplier at that time. As more green or sustainable materials have appeared on the market, the EarthCraft criteria have ratcheted up over the years to reflect additional choices. Additionally, Southface is working with the U.S. Green Building Council's new Leadership in Energy and Environmental Design (LEED) for Homes rating system to ensure a good interface between the programs.[1]

Education of Volunteers and Subcontractors: Education is a strong component of Atlanta Habitat's program, as the organization depends on a labor force comprised mainly of volunteers and homebuyers. Because Atlanta Habitat set a goal of building 100-percent EarthCraft-certified homes two years after this pilot project, it was important that requirements for certification can be implemented using volunteer labor. According to Ray Maynard, Atlanta Habitat discovered that "it was easy to teach our volunteer labor force how to do many of the tasks required to gain certification." Many volunteers were interested in learning about the different materials and methods required for an EarthCraft home, and many reported plans to use EarthCraft criteria in the future when purchasing or renovating their own homes.

One area that required constant education and monitor-

> "The Street Where Dreams Come True showed us that we could do it . . . that we had the expertise and ability to make green building happen."
>
> RAY MAYNARD
> *director of construction, Atlanta Habitat for Humanity*

ing was grinding construction waste on site. Initially it proved challenging to get staff, subcontractors, and volunteers to consistently separate materials. However, Maynard says that "it was well worth it for the amount we saved in trucking and landfill charges. We particularly wanted all the wood waste to be ground for mulching. You can imagine how unsatisfactory it would be to have concrete blocks ground at the same time as the wood." Another issue was persuading subcontractors to try new products or techniques to meet EarthCraft criteria. They were sometimes reluctant to do so, and at times Atlanta Habitat staff simply had to insist that they meet the guidelines. In particular, the

HVAC subcontractors had to be repeatedly reminded to correctly air-seal the joints in their ductwork. This requirement was reinforced by the fact that subcontractors would not receive final payment for their work if a house did not pass its ductwork exam (required as part of certification) as the cost of each test would be deducted from their payment. Maynard also notes that it was important to do sealing during the framing stage because it would be too difficult to find leaks later, once drywall was already up. (Southface now tests for leaks before insulation is installed.)

Education of Residents: During construction, homeowners learned firsthand about the green materials and techniques that would make their homes more efficient to operate. Each new homeowner participated in a one-and-a-half-hour walkthrough to review maintenance and energy efficiency issues, including insulation, the HVAC system, the water heater, and the importance of cleaning the filters for the furnace and dryer. Habitat homeowners are required to take an additional home maintenance class in which these features are reviewed, and tips are provided on items such as thermostat controls, fluorescent lightbulbs, water conservation, and appropriate water heater settings. Atlanta Habitat staff has found that encouraging habitual behaviors to improve energy efficiency requires a process of continuous education. For example, the filters in the HVAC unit must be changed regularly, or else the equipment could be damaged. Including regular reminders in homebuyer publications ensures that such regular maintenance is more likely to happen.

In addition to providing manuals on home maintenance, Atlanta Habitat recently developed a handout highlighting the features that earned EarthCraft certification, including tips for conserving energy and money in the home.

Another resident education issue pertained to the trees—both those that had been newly planted and those that had been carefully preserved on-site. Atlanta Habitat staff found that homeowners often preferred a home site without trees, because they feared the trees would fall on the house. This issue has required education on the benefits of trees in terms of natural shading and cooling, as well as monitoring to ensure that trees are not cut down. Owners are also encouraged to periodically check for and remove dead branches for safety reasons.

Participation and EarthCraft Certification: Atlanta Habitat learned that the tasks necessary to achieve certification were actually not difficult to carry out with a volunteer labor force. One exciting aspect of this project was that because Habitat projects rely on volunteer labor, numerous people besides future homeowners learned about EarthCraft certification and green building techniques.

Maynard reported that "volunteers tell us that they enjoy learning what it takes to make homes more energy-efficient. They can then use the techniques learned at Atlanta Habitat on their own homes. So the EarthCraft partnership works well for both our homebuyers and volunteers. Homebuyers benefit not only from learning energy-efficient construction techniques, but also from lower monthly utility bills."

Looking Forward: Even though the cost differential for green materials is decreasing steadily, Atlanta Habitat has not been able to include a number of green building measures in homes built after the Street Where Dreams Come True pilot project. A remaining concern is ensuring that each extra dollar to improve one home's sustainability is a dollar that is not diverted from creating a home for another deserving family. Another challenge is that many materials are donated by corporations or local suppliers, which creates a vast cost differential between the donated standard material and a more sustainable choice. For example, paint is typically donated, which has precluded the affiliate from continuing to use zero-volatile-organic-compounds (zero-VOC) paint. Compact fluorescent lights (CFLs) were donated by GE, keeping this upgrade off the balance sheet of the project. However, the replacement cost of CFLs has kept Atlanta Habitat from using them in subsequent projects.

Habitat for Humanity has a decentralized, affiliate-focused structure, which makes it difficult to institute an across-the-board transition to green building. Since the majority of fundraising for home construction is done locally, the decision to go green is the role and responsibility of the individual affiliates. In addition to Atlanta Habitat, numerous other motivated Habitat affiliates around the country are incorporating green measures that are location- and project-specific. The New York City affiliate has been building to ENERGY STAR® standards for several years and its forthcoming 41-unit project in Brooklyn is designed to gain certification in the LEED for Homes pilot. The Denver Metro affiliate builds energy-efficient homes that use passive solar heating techniques and low-VOC paints, and some homes include photovoltaic panel or solar hot-water heating systems. Other affiliates, such as Tucson Habitat, have built homes that incorporate rammed earth and other green building strategies. Additionally, over fifty Habitat affiliates in the United States and Canada sell donated building materials through retail outlets called "Restores." Sales of such materials support the work of each store's sponsoring affiliate while reducing, reusing, and recycling building materials.

Habitat for Humanity International has also formed a donation partnership with Whirlpool Corporation to make ENERGY STAR appliances available to all affiliates and is exploring additional partnerships to help make the use of energy-efficient and green products standard practice in all homes built through the Habitat organization.

CONTACTS

Developer: Atlanta Habitat for Humanity

Ray Maynard, director of construction: 404-223-5180, ext. 138; ray.maynard@atlantahabitat.org

Partner/consultant: Southface Energy and Environmental Resource Center

Sean Blething, EarthCraft House program manager: 404-391-5103; sean@earthcrafthouse.org

SOURCES

Atlanta Habitat's application for the Home Depot Foundation's award program, 2005.

"Building Green: Energy Efficiency Takes Root at Habitat for Humanity," emagazine.com (January/February 2005).

EarthCraft House program: www.atlantahabitat.org/about_history.asp; www.atlanta-habitat.org/programs_earthcraft.asp; www.southface.org/web/earthcraft_house/ech_main/ech_index.htm.

"Habitat for Humanity Goes Green!" Motherearthnews.com (no. 197, April/May 2003).

Personal interviews with Amy Macklin of Atlanta Habitat by Lisa McManigal Delaney, including e-mail and telephone correspondence, 2006.

Personal interviews with Ray Maynard of Atlanta Habitat by Lisa McManigal Delaney, including e-mail and telephone correspondence, 2006.

NOTE

1. Southface Institute Winter 2005 Journal: Green Building Partnerships, http://www.southface.org/web/resources &services/publications/journal/sfjv405/sfjv405greenbuilding -partnerships.htm.

CHAPTER 4

Green Operations and Maintenance

An affordable housing project designed and built with green strategies, materials, and systems can be truly green only if it is also operated and maintained with green products and procedures. Energy and water efficiency, indoor air quality, durability, and resource efficiency are determined as much by postoccupancy operations and maintenance (O&M) as by design. O&M practices have significant impacts on the health, safety, and comfort of a building's residents, the overall long-term environmental benefits, and on financial performance, as the cost of operating and maintaining a building over its lifetime usually far exceeds the initial construction cost.

Preventive maintenance to keep a building's systems and materials optimized and in good condition is the most essential, effective, and economic way to keep a building environment healthy and resource-efficient, prevent the need for premature replacement or repairs, and reduce disruption to building residents and staff. While most green materials and components require the same maintenance as conventional products, others do require special maintenance procedures or products.

This chapter provides practical recommendations for green building operations and maintenance procedures in the areas of groundskeeping, building systems, waste reduction and recycling, indoor air quality management, pest prevention and control, and healthy housekeeping.[1]

GREEN O&M MANUAL

Every development should have a green operations and maintenance manual prepared specifically for the project and used by the property management and maintenance staff. If the property management company has its own O&M manual, it is advisable to integrate the green concepts into that manual, rather than create a separate document that could be forgotten or ignored.

The O&M manual should cover the applicable topics presented in this chapter and provide a list of the green materials (exterior and interior), finishes and furnishings, systems, and equipment used in the project. If the project features green components that are not yet commonly used in most buildings (e.g., bamboo flooring, photovoltaics, etc.), or that property management maintenance staff are not familiar with, these components should be described in greater detail on specific product summary sheets within the manual. The sheets should list the products' green attributes, manufacturer and supplier information, care and maintenance guidelines, disposal or recycling suggestions, and installation or replacement guidance.

The manual should also include reference documents that provide more in-depth information on technical topics or local services. These reference documents should include green cleaning standards, a list of third-party-certified cleaning products, a project-specific mechanical filter replacement schedule, a project-specific lighting maintenance and lamp schedule, an integrated pest management guide, local recycling pick-up and hazardous waste drop-off options, and public transit information and maps. The manual should be accompanied by the manufacturer's product information—compiled and provided by the general contractor—including owner's and operating manuals, product specifications, and warranty information, schedules for routine pre- and postwarranty maintenance, and as-built drawings.

CREATING A GREEN O&M PROGRAM

In conjunction with the manual, the owner/developer and the property management company should develop a comprehensive green O&M plan and program, with assistance from maintenance staff and green consultants. The program should address the suggested best practices described below and incorporate those that are appropriate to the specific project. A member of the on-site management staff should be designated as the point person in charge of coordinating and monitoring all of the development's green O&M activities.

Green Groundskeeping

Groundskeeping practices that can be conducted in a more environmentally responsible way include: irrigation, landscape plantings, pest management, exterior lighting, parking/garage maintenance, and stormwater filtration.

Irrigation

Check the irrigation system regularly to prevent leaks, overspray, and watering the plantings just before, during, or immediately following rainy days. Even on dry days, make sure the system is not overwatering the plants, oversaturating the soil. Reprogram the irrigation system seasonally and adjust it to water in either the early morning or late evening to reduce water loss through evaporation. If the irrigation system needs to be replaced, install high-efficiency bubblers, microspray, and other efficient irrigation heads. For a comprehensive assessment of the irrigation system, hire a specialist to do an irrigation audit.

Plantings

Use compost and mulch to keep soil healthy and to eliminate or minimize the use of chemical fertilizers. When plantings need to be replaced, select native or adapted drought-tolerant and climate-appropriate plantings. When major landscape maintenance work is done, property management or the landscape contractor should ensure that all tree and plant clippings are composted or mulched. Some cities will issue a recycling bin to the building for collecting landscape trimmings or "green waste."

Pest Management

Pests can be animals such as mice, rats, and squirrels, or insects such as ants, roaches, fleas, and bedbugs. In controlling pests, avoid the use of chemical pesticides, and insecticides to the greatest extent possible, as these can be hazardous to humans, pets, and other animals. The most comprehensive way to prevent and control pests without using toxic chemicals is to implement an integrated pest management (IPM) program, which uses physical barriers, traps, biological controls, and other nontoxic forms of pest control.

If a pesticide must be used, use it sparingly and select a product with the lowest toxicity possible. The building management should notify residents and staff at least 72 hours before it is applied (or for emergency applications, at least 24 hours before) and should require or encourage occupants to stay away during the application if possible.

If any pesticides are stored at the building, store them in a locked and ventilated (preferably outdoor) room. Do not stockpile large quantities on-site, and always keep products in their original containers. Keep in mind that exposure to pesticides is not limited to the outside, as chemicals can be tracked into the building on people's shoes.

Exterior Lighting

Check that exterior lights are not on during daylight hours, motion sensors are working properly, and daylight sensors, controls, or time clocks are adjusted as necessary throughout the year as daylight hours change. Select energy-efficient and long-life bulbs (as well as low-mercury options for any fluorescent or metal halide bulbs) for bulb replacement. To minimize glare and light pollution of the night sky, make sure that exterior light fixtures are pointed down and are not emitting more light than needed for safety and security purposes. Extremely bright lights can create glare and shadows that reduce visibility and compromise security. If new fixtures are added, select full cutoff or downlit luminaires.

Parking Lot and Garage Maintenance

For indoor or below-grade garages, check the mechanical ventilation systems regularly to ensure that carbon monoxide and other exhaust fumes are removed and ample fresh air is provided. Promptly clean up any fuel, oil, or antifreeze spills to protect groundwater and air quality and to prevent toxic or corrosive substances from being tracked into the building.

Stormwater Filtration

If the project has a stormwater filtration, drainage, or catchment system, check the filters and mechanical components periodically to make sure that they are working and are not clogged by debris. Clean any trash out of swales, and prune overgrown plants that may cause unwanted ponding of water.

Building Systems

The U.S. Department of Energy's Federal Energy Management Program (FEMP) defines O&M as "the activities related to the performance of routine, preventive, predictive, scheduled, and unscheduled actions aimed at preventing equipment failure or decline with the goal of increasing efficiency, reliability, and safety."

Proper maintenance practices can lead to substantial energy savings and increase the equipment's life span and maintain occupant comfort. Using straightforward O&M best practices can "save an estimated 5 to 20 percent on energy bills without a significant capital investment."[2]

Mechanical Equipment

Keeping mechanical systems operating efficiently involves the vigilant maintenance of ducts and filters, fans, pumps, hot-water heaters or boilers, and cooling and heating systems. It is essential to include a mechanical filter schedule in the building's green O&M manual, with recommended filter change-out rates. All mechanical equipment documentation and records (including system testing, cleaning, and complaint records) should be easily accessed by building managers and maintenance staff, and ideally they should be stored and updated on a centralized computer system.

Electrical Equipment

Electrical equipment, such as lighting, various sensors, and photovoltaic, systems, requires regular monitoring and maintenance. For projects with photovoltaic systems, the property management and maintenance staff should receive documentation and training from the manufacturer or installer on how to clean and maintain the panels and their wiring.

GENERAL ENERGY EFFICIENCY TIPS

- Schedule contractual maintenance services in advance so that all building systems and equipment are serviced at the intervals called for by the manufacturer's warranty agreement.
- Make sure that the building temperature settings is not set too high or too low. Thermostats in common areas should be programmed for "night setbacks" to provide less heating (or cooling) at night. Also make sure that the building's domestic water temperature is not set higher than 120 degrees.
- Educate the residents on how to set the thermostats properly in their units, and make sure that they are not overheating their units or leaving heat on when their windows are open.
- Clean refrigerator coils yearly, and check that older refrigerators are not running long after they are closed or turning on or off too frequently. If a unit is not operating properly and cannot be repaired, it should be replaced.
- Clean out dryer lint filters, ducts, and vents periodically; accumulated lint not only reduces efficiency, it also poses a fire hazard. Make sure that the exhaust vent is working and closes tightly.
- When systems/equipment and appliances must be replaced or are added, select products with ENERGY STAR® ratings.[1] Even better, select one of the *most* energy-efficient appliances, as identified by the American Council for an Energy-Efficient Economy.[2]
- For major retrofits, consider an energy performance contract. (See Chapter 5 for more information on the energy service company, or ESCO, process.)

1. U.S. Environmental Protection Agency, ENERGY STAR product list, www.energystar.gov/products (accessed January 10, 2007).
2. American Council for an Energy-Efficient Economy, *Consumer Guide to Home Energy Savings: Condensed Online Version*, www.aceee.org/consumerguide/index.htm (accessed January 17, 2007).

LAMP REPLACEMENT AND MAINTENANCE

- When purchasing lamps/bulbs, look for products that are both ENERGY STAR® labeled, long-life, and—for fluorescent and metal halide bulbs—also low mercury.
- Select lamps with a minimum color-rendering index (CRI) of 80 to provide high-quality light.
- Whenever replacing a lamp, inspect the lamp ballast and clean the fixture and lens with a clean, moist cotton cloth (to prevent static). A dirty lens can reduce a fixture's light output by up to 50 percent.[1]
- Inspect occupancy sensors regularly to make sure they are working properly.
- Dispose of all mercury-containing lamps properly. Both fluorescent and metal halide high-intensity discharge (HID) lamps contain mercury and are considered "universal" hazardous waste. Exit signs that contain compact fluorescents and neon signs also contain mercury.

1. Commonwealth of Pennsylvania, the Department of General Services' Property Management, and Green Seal, *The Pennsylvania Green Building Operations and Maintenance Manual* 58: www.dgs.state.pa.us/dgs/cwp/view.asp?Q=118184&A=363.

Water Efficiency

In addition to some of the obvious water conservation strategies that everyone can employ—not running faucets longer than is necessary and running dishwashers and clothes washers only when full—property managers and maintenance staff can take a number of steps to reduce water use from building operations, both indoors and outdoors.

Water conservation tips:[3]

- Check regularly for leaks. A leaking toilet can waste more than 50 gallons of water each day, and a dripping faucet or showerhead can waste up to 1,000 gallons per week.
- Install low-flow faucet aerators, which are low-cost, simple to install, and reduce water consumption by up to 50 percent.
- Adjust boiler and cooling tower blow-down rates to maintain total dissolved solids (TDS) at levels recommended by manufacturers' specifications.
- Minimize the use of water to clean paved areas. Sweep instead of hosing down entrances, sidewalks, parking lots, and loading docks.

Waste Reduction and Recycling

Reduce waste by participating in municipal recycling programs or recycling programs administered by the building operator or contracted waste hauler, recycling waste from building maintenance and rehabilitation projects, and providing for hazardous waste disposal.

Recycling Programs

For a recycling program to be successful, it must be easy for occupants to participate. A recycling bin should be issued for each residential unit (for very small units, a bin in a common trash room is an alternative) and placed in all common areas (such as laundry rooms and community kitchens), as well as janitors' closets. An easily accessible bin also should be placed in the parking area. All recycling bins in the building should be washed out often to remove sticky residues that might attract pests.

Property management should educate both maintenance staff and residents about the building's recycling program and specific procedures—which types of materials are and are not accepted by the local recycling program, and which materials need to be rinsed and separated. This information should be posted in trash or recycling areas and on recycling bins, and should be provided in the resident manual. If staff or residents are not participating in the recycling program or are recycling improperly, the owner or

---

WASTE PREVENTION TIPS

- Avoid purchasing disposable materials when possible. For example, use reusable cloths rather than paper towels.
- Select and request items with less packaging, or purchase items in bulk quantities or in concentrate. Avoid products with unnecessary packaging, such as individually wrapped items.
- Select products with recycled content (e.g., paper and office products, furniture, etc.).
- Select products that are recyclable, such as carpet made of nylon 6, whenever possible.
- Order from suppliers that will take back surplus materials.

Many major carpet manufacturers now have carpet take-back programs. Some, including Collins & Aikman/C&A Floor coverings, will take any manufacturer's carpet back and recycle it into new carpet. There is often a fee associated with having carpet recycled, though it could be less than what it would cost to dump the material in a landfill. According to the Carpet America Recovery Effort (CARE), the cost is often 5 cents to 25 cents per pound of old carpet (carpet typically weighs about 4 to 5 pounds per square yard). The cost is partly determined by the proximity of the carpet to recycling facilities, and by the type of fiber.

building manager should consider creating an incentive program to reward individuals who recycle properly and regularly.

Some municipalities distribute bins for compost (food waste) or yard waste and offer curbside pickup for those materials. If this service is available in the project area, consider instituting a program to collect these materials as well. Even if the property manager feels it would be difficult to get residents to collect their food waste or that doing so would be problematic from a pest control perspective, it is relatively easy to collect landscape trimmings and compostable food waste from a common kitchen area.

Building Renovation Waste Management

Scrap and debris from construction and demolition (C&D) work—including maintenance and rehabilitation projects—makes up approximately 30 percent of the waste stream that is dumped into landfills. The majority of construction waste is recyclable, including cardboard, drywall, paint, carpet, scrap metal, wood and pallets, plate glass, landscape trimmings, asphalt and concrete, rocks and dirt, bricks and tiles, rubber scrap, roofing, appliances, and electronics. Many types of building materials are also accepted by salvage yards. Examples of reusable building materials include furniture, flooring, electrical equipment, ducts, plumbing fixtures, light fixtures, doors, and windows. Some areas also have materials exchange programs; these sometimes feature online databases where you can post items or find items for free. Diverting this waste through salvage, donation, or recycling programs saves tipping fees and landfill space and provides feedstock for industries that are creating recycled-content materials.

Hazardous Waste Disposal

Hazardous waste materials must be dropped off at appropriate facilities for safe disposal or recycling so they do not contaminate the community's air, water, and soil. Contact the city or county disposal facility to find out what types of hazardous materials can be dropped off or picked up in your area.

Indoor Air Quality Management

It is much easier to prevent indoor air quality (IAQ) problems through good maintenance practices than it is to try to correct them after they have developed. The following are basic strategies for safeguarding indoor air quality:

- Regularly clean the entryways and entryway mats or grates to keep particulates from being tracked into the building.
- Prohibit smoking inside the building, or outside near the building's entryways, windows, or air intakes or enforce the no-smoking policy.
- Control and remove moisture (from humidity, condensation, or water leaks/intrusions) through preventative ventilation and maintenance to prevent mold. If the mold problem could be serious, hire mold remediation specialists to assess and remediate the problem.
- Keep carpeting clean and dry.
- Perform routine maintenance of the heating, ventilating, and air-conditioning (HVAC) system, including regular filter replacement and duct cleaning.
- Select low-toxic materials and products, including building materials (see Chapter 3) as well as low-toxic cleaning products, pest control products, and landscaping fertilizers and herbicides.
- Monitor and maintain the building's ventilation system to make sure it is working properly and meeting airflow specifications to deliver enough outside air to all areas of the building.
- Store any toxic products and chemical supplies (including paints) in a room that has negative pressure and that is vented directly to the outside. Providing such a space requires coordination in the design of the building and mechanical system.
- Open windows for natural ventilation, when appropriate, to get outside air flow-

COMMON HAZARDOUS WASTE MATERIALS

- Paint, paint thinners, primers, and stains
- Glues and adhesives
- Chemical cleaning supplies (cleaners, disinfectants, graffiti removers, polish, deodorizers, etc.)
- Fluorescent lamps/lightbulbs
- Switches or thermostats that contain mercury
- Pesticides, herbicides, chemical fertilizers
- Computers, TVs, printers, and other electronic equipment
- Printer or copier ink/toner
- Batteries (all types)
- Medical/biohazard waste (including needles and mercury thermometers)
- Used motor oil

ing through the rooms, particularly when doing repairs, cleaning, or installations that might involve any noxious or offgassing chemicals (including painting, gluing, or applying finishes) or when bringing new furniture into the building.

- When preparing to do any rehab work or major cleaning, maintenance, or repair projects inside the building, refer to SMACNA's (Sheet Metal and Air Conditioning Contractors' National Association) IAQ Guidelines for Occupied Buildings Under Construction, Chapter 3, for instructions on protecting ducts, containing dust, and mitigating other IAQ risks. If possible, isolate the part of the HVAC system serving the work area zones from the rest of the system. Inform building occupants about any work that may affect their health or comfort, and provide respiratory equipment, if needed. Carpet removal, among other rehab activities, can release a lot of dust, mold, and allergens into the air.
- If residents or building staff develop unexplained and similar health problems, including chronic respiratory symptoms, bring in an IAQ specialist to do a thorough investigation and building assessment.

Pest Prevention and Control

There are many ways to prevent and control pests—indoors and outdoors—without using toxic chemical pesticides or insecticides. Integrated pest management (IPM) programs emphasize the use of physical barriers, biological controls, and other natural forms of pest control to minimize the use of pesticides to the greatest possible degree. IPM can be used to deal with a variety of pests, including cockroaches, ants, rodents, flies, fruit flies, fleas, pigeons, and so forth. Studies have linked some pesticides to cancer, birth defects, neurological disorders, and immune system disorders, as well as allergies. If a pesticide must be used, select one from a list of low-toxic pesticides, such as the San Francisco Reduced-Risk Pesticide List.

PEST PREVENTION TIPS ————————————————————————————————

- Clean up any unsealed food, crumbs, and liquid/spills from all floors and surfaces.
- Sweep floors and vacuum regularly, with a high-efficiency particulate air (HEPA) filter vacuum if possible.
- Rinse bottles, cans, and containers before putting them in the recycling bins.
- Clean out the recycling bins periodically to remove sticky residues.
- Seal all door cracks or other openings in trash rooms.
- Minimize clutter, paper files, and storage supplies that can provide hiding places for pests.
- Make sure that penetrations around kitchen cabinets, plumbing, and electrical lines are fully sealed.
- Repair all water leaks and dry any moisture-damaged materials.
- Do not overwater indoor plants, as wet soil and standing water in overflow dishes provide drinking areas.

Green and Healthy Housekeeping

The building management entity should have a policy that requires the use of healthy cleaning procedures and techniques. Custodial staff should be trained in the building's green housekeeping and low-toxic cleaning practices. If it's an option, have product supplier representatives come in to give trainings on the safe use of their products. Get feedback from custodial staff on their experience with using new products (or techniques) and adjust products or practices as necessary.

Informational sessions and a guide to green and healthy cleaning practices should also be provided for residents, to encourage the use of such practices in their homes as well. The *Healthy Home Guide for Residents of the Plaza Apartments*, published by Enterprise Community Partners, provides one example of a green O&M guide for residents.

Cleaning Procedures and Equipment

The O&M manual and related trainings should address specific cleaning strategies and techniques, including the proper dilution and mixing procedures for concentrated cleaning products, the use of safety gear, provision of adequate ventilation, and strategies for reducing the cleaning-related waste of energy, water, or supplies. Maintenance staff should also be educated about how and where to properly store and dispose of cleaning products.

Procurement criteria for janitorial supplies should promote the use of reusable supplies (e.g., microfiber cloths) in lieu of disposal products, and should call for a high recycled content for all paper goods, trash bags, and other commonly used products.

Specifications for selecting housekeeping equipment should include particulate removal, low-noise, low-vibration, and water-conserving criteria. The Leadership in Energy and Environmental Design for Existing Buildings (LEED-EB) rating system has useful guidelines on healthy and efficient housekeeping equipment within its indoor environmental quality section. For example, vacuums with high-efficiency particulate air (HEPA) filters should be selected. In rental properties, the owner or property management should consider purchasing a number of high-quality HEPA vacuums that tenants can borrow from the main office. Dust, animal hair, and other common indoor pollutants are asthma triggers. Frequent vacuuming reduces exposure to these pollutants and the related risk of asthma attacks.

Low-Toxic Cleaning Products

While cleaning products help remove harmful contaminants such as mold, bacteria, and particulates, exposure to many conventional cleaning products can also create health problems, particularly for individuals who have preexisting health conditions such as asthma or allergies, or who have chemical sensitivities or a compromised immune system. Some cleaning products can cause headaches, dizziness, skin irritation, respiratory irritation, eye irrita-

The number of nontoxic (or low-toxic) cleaning products on the market is increasing, and many of these products are just as effective as their more conventional counterparts. When selecting cleaning products, look for those that are labeled "nontoxic," "low VOC" (low volatile organic compounds) or "zero VOC," and "biodegradable," and that have the following attributes:

- Water-based and/or plant-based (rather than petroleum-based solvents)
- Neutral or mild pH (close to 7), to avoid high acidity or alkalinity
- Less than 10 percent VOC concentration (by weight) when diluted (or less than 1 percent by weight for general purpose cleaners, per Green Seal); or less than 25 grams of VOC per liter of cleaning solvent (per California's South Coast Air Quality Management District—SCAQMD)
- Concentrated (for less packaging)
- Can be diluted in cold water
- Readily biodegradable (60 to 70 percent biodegradable within 28 days)
- Unscented (some people are allergic to certain fragrances)
- Recycled-content containers and/or minimal packaging
- Recyclable packaging or reusable, returnable, or refillable container

---

tion, while others contain cancer-causing substances, reproductive toxins, central nervous system toxins, and endocrine system/hormone disruptors. A study in the January 2001 *American Journal of Industrial Medicine* found that California janitorial workers experience the highest rates of occupational asthma—more than twice the rate for any other occupation. Cleaning product toxicity affects the greater environment as well; some products contain substances that are toxic to aquatic life and others contribute to smog formation. The types of cleaning products that are often highly toxic include disinfectants, graffiti remover, drain cleaner, toilet bowl cleaner, chlorinated scouring powder, carpet and upholstery shampoo, mold and mildew cleaner, furniture and floor polish, and oven cleaner.

The project's O&M manual and trainings should provide some criteria for selecting low-toxic cleaning products, a list of products and ingredients to avoid, information on certified green cleaning products, and suggestions on products to use.

As a general rule, avoid products that are labeled "Danger—Poison." Products with "Warning" labels are also dangerous, but less so; products labeled with "Caution" are the least harmful of the three, though they can still be hazardous. Also avoid products that are labeled as "Corrosive," "Severely Irritating," "Highly Flammable," or "Highly Combustible," properties that should appear on the product label and/or the product's material safety data sheet (MSDS). Avoid aerosols, when possible, as they often contain hydrocarbon propellants, which are flammable and can contribute to indoor air quality problems.

Many of a product's ingredients and properties, as well as safety and first aid information, are provided on its MSDS. Building managers should request and review the MSDS for all cleaning and maintenance products used in the building, and make sure

In 2005, Urban Edge, a Massachusetts-based community development corporation, partnered with the Massachusetts Coalition for Occupational Safety and Health (MassCOSH) to implement a green cleaning initiative. Urban Edge wanted to design a program to replace its existing cleaning products with those that would be better for the health of the environment, residents, and custodial staff, using a centralized purchasing system.

First, MassCOSH conducted a baseline survey to assess Urban Edge's current cleaning products and practices. Survey results revealed a need to provide training on product disposal and storage, so MassCOSH held a training for custodial staff and property managers about the results of the survey and discussed the benefits of switching to safer, less toxic alternatives.

Then, Urban Edge solicited proposals from vendors that provide green cleaning products. Potential providers submitted samples of their green products, which were then tested by Urban Edge's custodians, who provided feedback on their satisfaction based on effectiveness, costs, customer service, and training. The majority of the custodians observed that the green products performed better than existing products. When a vendor was selected, it provided training on product use as well as general environment and health safety issues for all janitors.

───

that staff are familiar with the MSDS format and know where the sheets are kept. The U.S. Occupational Safety and Health Administration requires all manufacturers to provide an MSDS with the first shipment of any hazardous chemical product, and requires that users of the product keep a copy on file and available for review by employees.

However, not all ingredients and hazards are disclosed on the MSDS, and chemicals are sometimes known by several different names, so they can be difficult to identify. Furthermore, manufacturers' product claims regarding health and environmental safety can sometimes be misleading or unsubstantiated. Fortunately, there are third-party certifiers who verify specific product claims. The nonprofit organization Green Seal has green standards for industrial and institutional cleaners (GS-37), and industrial and institutional floor care products (GS-40). Many cleaning products have undergone testing using those standards and received Green Seal certification. A list of Green Seal–certified cleaning products is available on the organization's website. GREEN-GUARD Environmental Institute also certifies low-emitting cleaning products, and Scientific Certification Systems certifies biodegradability and other single-attribute claims. In addition, the EPA's Design for Environment (DfE) Formulator program has recognized a number of cleaning products that comply with their standards.

In addition to the less-toxic commercial cleaning products that are available, there are some basic and inexpensive "household" substances that can serve as effective and nontoxic alternatives for most residential cleaning jobs. These substances include baking soda, white vinegar, salt, lemon juice, borax, dishwashing detergent, and hydrogen peroxide. For example, a mixture of baking soda, hot water, and vinegar can clear drains

Nueva Vista Apartments (Santa Cruz, California)
Mercy Housing California

Nueva Vista, a 48-unit urban infill project in Santa Cruz, California, first opened in December 2003. The project includes a childcare facility and a community center that residents and people in the surrounding neighborhood can utilize. The project protects the health of residents by using a variety of nontoxic finishes and lowers operating costs by incorporating a solar photovoltaic system and energy efficiency measures. Upon opening, the green features of the project presented a new set of challenges for Mercy Housing's property management staff. The management team was faced with maintaining systems, green finishes, and materials that were unfamiliar to them. Nueva Vista has now been in operation for over three years, providing some valuable insight into the operations and maintenance of a green affordable housing project. The project sees a savings of $5,000 per year in maintenance costs in comparison with similarly sized properties.[1]

According to property management staff, the green finishes, which include natural linoleum and low–volatile organic compound (low-VOC) paint, have held up well over the years. No significant portions of the linoleum have had to be replaced thus far. Mercy Housing staff make an effort to educate residents about the green materials, their environmental benefits, and how they improve the health of indoor areas. Due to the increased first cost of the linoleum, Mercy Housing includes an addendum to each tenant's lease that requires residents to properly care for the flooring. The addendum also places the cost of repairing or replacing the linoleum onto residents who do not take proper care of the flooring. With the lease addendum, Mercy Housing staff also provide information and training on the proper sealing and cleaning of the linoleum. Annually, each resident is provided with enough sealer and cleaner to maintain the linoleum for another year. The on-site property manager also keeps a small supply of sealer and cleaner that is available to residents who want to clean the linoleum more frequently. See Appendix C for the language of Mercy Housing's lease addendum.

1. Interview with Jorge Astacio, property manager, Nueva Vista Apartments, Mercy Housing, Santa Cruz, California, May 11, 2006.

---

and borax or hydrogen peroxide can remove stains and mildew. Building owners or managers should consider purchasing some low-toxic cleaning products in bulk to give or to sell to residents for their use. In the Oleson Woods development in Tigard, Oregon, the developer gives new residents the ingredients for natural cleaning products, and provides recipes for natural cleaning solutions in the resident manual.

IMPLEMENTING THE PROGRAM

Manuals and other documentation must be supplemented by other ongoing strategies, policies, and activities, such as the following:

- *Education* for staff and residents, to ensure that the recommended best practices are understood and carried out. On-site trainings, tours, demonstrations, and instructional videos are all good ways to educate the building occupants and maintenance staff about the expectations put forward in the plan. When there is staff or resident turnover, provide new training sessions.

- *Lease provisions,* for green products or systems that require special maintenance. These requirements should be clearly stated in the lease agreement and discussed before tenants move in.
- *Green procurement/purchasing policies and service contracts,* for maintenance companies and vendors/suppliers. Green selection criteria should be established for cleaning supplies and equipment, paper goods, and fluorescent lamps.
- *Signage,* to provide reminders or clarification about specific green practices, maintenance products to avoid, or special settings for equipment. The signage should be made from green materials—for example, non-PVC recycled-content materials with low-toxic adhesives.
- *Periodic monitoring of all building systems,* to adjust settings and controls, and to ensure that systems are balanced and operating at optimal efficiency.
- *Incentive programs,* to encourage conservation and the proper implementation of best practices by residents.
- *Feedback,* solicited from staff and residents on the conditions of the buildings and any O&M issues or questions they might have.

NOTES

1. Substantial portions of this chapter are excerpted and adapted from the *Green Operations & Maintenance Manual for the Plaza Apartments: Best Practices for a Healthy and High-Performance Building,* (2006) with permission from Enterprise Community Partners. In addition to that manual, which was developed for use by the building's management and maintenance staff, Enterprise has also published a *Healthy Home Guide for Residents of the Plaza Apartments* (2006), as well as customizable templates of both documents. These documents can be downloaded from www.greencommunitiesonline.com/resources.asp (on the Operations and Maintenance link).
2. U.S. Department of Energy, Federal Energy Management Program, *What is O&M?,* available at www.eere.energy.gov/femp/operations_maintenance/ (accessed June 2006).
3. Adapted from Resource Venture's "Water Conservation" webpage: www.resourceventure.org/

CHAPTER 5

Costs and Financing

Financing affordable housing is a challenging and complex undertaking. Even after acquiring a site, navigating neighborhood concerns, and gaining local approvals, a successful affordable housing project requires the nimble assemblage of a financial package that includes contributions from local, state, and federal programs; subsidized loans of all shapes and sizes; and conventional debt. And though the national need for affordable housing grows every day, resources remain scarce. Competition for those resources is intense, leading to ever more creative financing arrangements for affordable housing projects, including those with green building features.

The multiplicity of financing sources for affordable housing is matched only by the multiplicity of benefits, described throughout this book, that green affordable housing delivers to the community. However, it is an axiom of green affordable housing development, and much of green building development in general, that there is a temporal and a categorical mismatch between funds and benefits.

On the timing side, while financing is available for the up-front costs necessary to build an affordable housing project, the benefits are delivered only after the project is completed. And while the sources can all be accurately quantified in dollars and cents, only some of the benefits of green affordable housing, such as utility savings, can be easily quantified. Other direct benefits, such as lower incidence of respiratory illnesses, are harder to measure in dollar terms or are difficult to ascribe solely to a particular affordable housing project. This latter difficulty is particularly acute when considering the regional environmental benefits, such as avoided stormwater runoff or reduced waste going to landfills, of a specific green building project.

In terms of categories, there is often a disconnection between those who invest in green building features and those who ultimately reap the benefits. Affordable housing developers investing in energy-efficient technologies often have little or no ability to recover the investment through higher sale prices or increased rents. This is because rents and sale prices are fixed by government lending or tax credit agencies. As a result, the increased first cost of green features is often seen as taking money from future development projects. This makes many types of green affordable housing financing fundamentally different from market-rate for-sale housing, where the builder can expect to recover extra green investments in the form of increased sales prices or higher rents.

The successful financing of green affordable housing relies on creating a closer alignment between who is making the investment and who is ultimately deriving benefits. This chapter looks at ways affordable housing developers—and those who support them—can seek this realignment of costs and benefits in practical and effective ways by explaining methods of:

- Expanding the definition of cost to include concepts of life-cycle costing, payback, and return on investment
- Determining long-term value—and who derives that value—in order to present a more complete financing picture
- Balancing who benefits from the green features with how they are paid for
- Clarifying how the realignment of costs and benefits can alter the design process
- Conducting a five-step process for assembling a green-friendly financial structure

FINANCING SOURCES FOR AFFORDABLE HOUSING

Figure 5.1 shows the vast array of financing sources for affordable housing. Within these programs—all of which have excess demand for a limited supply of resources—three basic rules stand out for those who want to understand how to pursue green affordable housing.

- *Rule 1:* It is critical to recognize the difference between equity and debt. Many of the programs provide equity to a project. In affordable housing development, equity usually is not "paid back" to the investor but instead comes in the form of tax credits (which are used to generate equity), grants, or rebates. The amount of equity is not dependent on operating costs and is usually combined with some form of long-term debt.

FIGURE 5.1. Affordable housing funding sources chart.

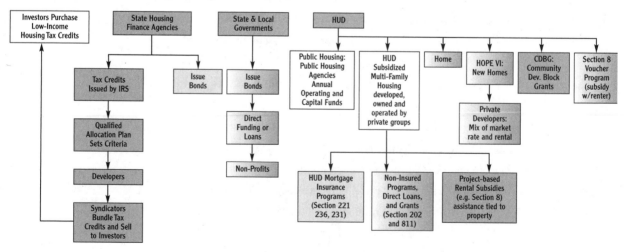

EXPANDING THE DEFINITION OF COST

Costs in a development project can be separated into three basic categories: soft costs; hard costs, and operating costs.

- *Soft costs* are expenditures that take place away from the building site, such as design and engineering consultants, financing and transaction costs, insurance, permit fees, and legal fees.
- *Hard costs* are directly related to the building site and include land, building materials, the labor necessary to install those materials, site and landscape expenditures, contingency costs, furniture, fixtures, and equipment.
- *Operating costs* are those that occur after a building is completed and include utilities, maintenance, replacement costs, vacancy, and insurance.

Within the affordable housing development community, the most talked-about cost (along with the price of land) is hard costs. There is a simple reason for this. With funds for affordable housing development limited, most government housing programs attempt to restrict first costs as much as possible through caps on per-unit construction costs or through considering projects with low construction costs more favorably. The

---

Debt, even if subsidized, must be paid back and is thus very sensitive to a project's expected cash flows and revenue. The greater the revenue, the more debt a project can encumber and the less equity a project needs to seek out. Increasing the amount of debt a project can support, either through lowering maintenance costs or reducing utility bills, is one way to finance the increased costs of green features.

- *Rule 2:* The single largest source of equity in affordable housing is the federal Low-Income-Housing Tax Credit that supports the development of affordable rental projects. Each state gets a per-capita-based allocation of tax credits and sets its own rules about how to distribute them in the qualified allocation plan (QAP). QAPs generally have a point system for allocating tax credits in a competitive manner. Providing additional points for green building measures in a state's QAP is one of the most effective ways of incentivizing green affordable housing practices.

- *Rule 3:* Each debt and equity program has different rules. These differences can lead to conflicting signals about priorities in terms of green building measures, how much attention should be paid to them, and their relative value. Clarifying the technical design and construction requirements across programs early in the development process makes it easier to focus on the implementation of green building.

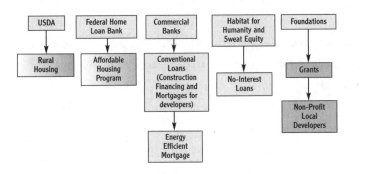

implicit understanding is that a dollar saved on one residential unit is a dollar that can then be spent to help build another residential unit.

When looking at costs, financiers (and therefore developers and the project teams that support them) generally only look at *first cost*—the cost of procuring a material and installing it. While in some instances green building can lower first costs by eliminating or downsizing infrastructure or equipment, most studies of commercial and institutional projects have shown that green building typically adds 2 to 4 percent to the first cost of a project.[1] This general trend holds true of the affordable housing sector. In "The Costs and Benefits of Green Affordable Housing," a report completed in 2005 by New Ecology, Inc., researchers found that out of the sixteen completed green affordable housing projects studied, the median construction cost increase was 3.83 percent. When soft costs and land were included, the median total development cost increase was 2.94 percent, while the average cost increase was 2.42 percent.

In the area of affordable housing, where most projects are owned by the same person or entity for fifteen years or more, first cost may not be the most appropriate way to account for cost. A more effective approach is to use *life-cycle costs*. Life-cycle costing incorporates the expenditures necessary to maintain and replace part of a building by accounting for a material's durability in addition to first costs. A material that is cheaper in first-cost terms may be more expensive from a life-cycle cost perspective.

Resilient flooring offers one example of this dynamic. In first-cost terms, sheet vinyl is one-third the cost of natural linoleum. However, natural linoleum, if properly installed and maintained, lasts six times longer than sheet vinyl. Over a thirty-five-year period, the life-cycle cost of 10,000 square feet of natural linoleum is actually $20,000 less than the sheet vinyl (see Table 5.1).

An affordable housing developer may object to this examination of life-cycle costs as merely theoretical. Because financiers only consider first costs when allocating construction funds, sheet vinyl may seen to be the only viable option. However, developers of affordable rental housing must include replacement reserves for every item in the financial analysis of a project. If those reserves can be reduced because more durable products (backed by warranties) are installed, then the project will have additional cash flow. That cash flow can then in turn support the additional debt needed to cover the higher first cost of the more durable product.

Payback is another way of looking at cost that factors in long-term operating savings and asks the question: How long does it take for the operational savings generated by a particular product or system to pay for the additional first costs? In the commercial real estate industry, acceptable levels of payback are usually between three years or less. In government-owned or publicly financed buildings, a decade or more is a common level of acceptable payback.

TABLE 5.1. LIFE-CYCLE COST OF SHEET VINYL VERSUS LINOLEUM ───────────

SHEET VINYL	LINOLEUM
10,000 sq ft	10,000 sq ft
$2/sq ft installed	$6/sq ft installed
Replace every 7 years	Replace every 40 years
Total 35-yr. cost: $80,000	Total 35-yr. cost: $60,000

Dual-flush toilets provide a simple example of how to calculate payback. A dual-flush toilet can typically cost $150 more than a conventional toilet. That toilet will generate $2.50 worth of water savings every month. Therefore it will take sixty months, or five years, to "pay back" that extra $150 spent on the dual-flush toilet.

Return on investment takes this concept of operational savings and extends it over the useful life of the particular material or technology. Using the dual-flush toilet example, if the toilet were to have only five years of useful life, then the return on investment would be zero. But since that toilet can be expected to last fifteen years, it will return a $2.50 per month savings for ten years *after* the five-year payback period. Thus, over a ten-year period, the toilet will save $300, or twice as much as the initial cost premium. Thus spending the extra $150 up front provides an annual savings of $30 and an annual return on investment of 20 percent.

Return on investment is a helpful metric because it allows for an "apples-to-apples" comparison of different green building measures in terms of their full economic impacts

LIFE-CYCLE COST VERSUS LIFE-CYCLE ASSESSMENT ─────────────────────

Life-cycle cost is a way of accounting for both the initial and the future costs of a particular building material or system, keeping the analysis within the realm of pure economic analysis. *Life-cycle assessment,* on the other hand, takes life-cycle cost and adds an environmental dimension to the calculation, considering the full range of a product's environmental impacts, from resource extraction to manufacture through installation and ultimate disposal. Life-cycle cost is then added in, allowing for comprehensive and multidimensional product comparisons. With flooring, for example, life-cycle assessment compares the resource extraction impacts and durability of hardwoods with the manufacturing impacts, emissions during use, and potential recyclability of carpet. Theoretically, each product can be given an overall life-cycle score, taking into account all the factors shown in Figure 5.2.

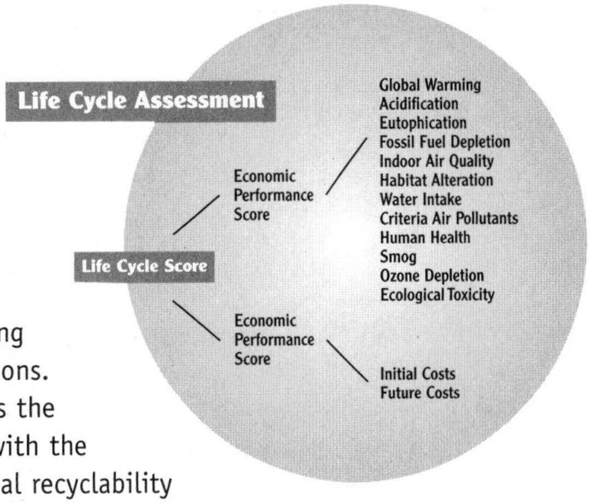

Life Cycle Assessment

Economic Performance Score

Life Cycle Score

Economic Performance Score

Global Warming
Acidification
Eutophication
Fossil Fuel Depletion
Indoor Air Quality
Habitat Alteration
Water Intake
Criteria Air Pollutants
Human Health
Smog
Ozone Depletion
Ecological Toxicity

Initial Costs
Future Costs

FIGURE 5.2. Analysis of life-cycle assessment versus costs.

TABLE 5.2. LONG-TERM VALUE OF GREEN AFFORDABLE HOUSING ——————————

PROJECT	LOCATION	# OF UNITS	TOTAL DEVELOPMENT COST GREEN PREMIUM	DESIGN PREMIUM
20th St	Santa Monica, CA	34	3.17%	0.00%
Arroyo Chico	Santa Fe, NM	17	7.40%	0.00%
Betty Ann	San Jose, CA	76	1.92%	9.64%
Brick Capital	Sanford, NC	5	1.64%	0.00%
CAST	Santa Monica, CA	42	0.62%	0.00%
Colorado Court	Cambridge, MA	44	9.09%	0.00%
Erie Ellington	Emeryville, CA	50	-18.33%	0.00%
Emeryville	Boston, MA	3	2.95%	0.00%
Johnson Creek	Portland, OR	15	7.25%	0.00%
Linden	Somerville, MA	42	0.18%	0.00%
Melrose	Bronx, NY	90	2.51%	0.00%
New Homes	Chicago, IL	25	8.15%	0.00%
Positive Match	San Francisco, CA	7	2.93%	0.00%
Riverwalk	Spokane, WA	52	6.24%	1.22%
Traugott	Seattle, WA	50	4.67%	7.28%
Woodlawn	Chicago, IL	10	5.02%	0.00%
Mean			*2.42%*	*1.13%*
Median			*2.94%*	*0.00%*

1. Bradshaw, William, et al., *The Costs and Benefits of Green Affordable Housing* (Cambridge, MA: New Ecology Inc., 2005), 164–66.

on a project. While economic metrics do not capture all the benefits of green building, they are valuable tools to help developers and designers maintain discipline when evaluating different strategies, making choices, and understanding what trade-offs are needed.

DETERMINING LONG-TERM VALUE

Another economic tool used to determine the value of green building in affordable housing is to look at net present value (NPV). Net present value is a standard method for evaluating competing long-term projects in capital budgeting. It measures the excess or shortfall of cash flows, in present terms, once financing charges are met. As a general rule, projects or green strategies with a positive NPV should be undertaken as long as first costs can be covered.

CONSTRUCTION PREMIUM NPV OF GREEN ITEMS	RESIDENT/HOMEOWNER NPV OF GREEN ITEMS	DEVELOPER/OWNER OF GREEN ITEMS	COMBINED NPV
17.15%	$6,460	$(507)	$5,953
9.70%	$7,820	$-	$7,820
2.56%	$6,919	$789	$7,708
1.76%	$(140)	$-	$(140)
2.12%	$1,962	$1,027	$2,989
11.41%	$-	$5,673	$5,673
-25.00%	$23,451	$34,764	$58,215
4.51%	$11,506	$-	$11,506
38.94%	$9,953	$(1,842)	$8,111
0.30%	$59,861	$8,031	$67,892
3.27%	$36,721	$(306)	$36,415
4.40%	$13,702	$(4,012)	$9,690
4.40%	$1,497	$(9,730)	$(8,233)
8.19%	$15,213	$3,904	$19,117
6.59%	$1,211	$7,829	$9,040
3.10%	$6,064	$(2,015)	$4,049
5.29%	*$12,637*	*$2,725*	*$15,363*
3.83%	*$7,370*	*$-*	*$7,965*

In affordable housing, it is clear that green building measures generate a positive NPV. As seen in Table 5.2, fifteen of the sixteen projects analyzed in the New Ecology, Inc., study showed a positive NPV for their green building measures, with an average NPV per project of $15,363 and a mean of $7,965.

Within this overall positive picture, there is an important nuance to observe. Although fourteen of the projects' green measures were positive (in NPV terms) for the resident or homeowner, only seven recorded a positive NPV to the developer or owner of the property. Six of the projects were negative to the developer or owner, and three were neutral. This categorical mismatch is largely the result of developer investments to increase energy efficiency, investments that result in lower utility bills for tenants but for which the developer cannot realize a financial return.

BALANCING WHO BENEFITS

Under U.S. Department of Housing and Urban Development (HUD) regulations, a housing unit is classified as affordable if the monthly "housing burden" to the resident is no greater than 30 percent of that resident's income. Publicly subsidized housing, regardless of ownership, is restricted to people and families earning a certain percentage below area median income (AMI), usually between 40 and 80 percent of AMI. Thus, the maximum housing burden for an affordable unit restricted to low-income people will be 30 percent of that percentage of AMI. Table 5.3 shows an example of the maximum housing burden of a family earning 40 percent of AMI, where AMI is $50,000.

The crucial issue is that the definition of "housing burden" includes utility costs. Local public housing authorities (PHAs) set utility allowance schedules that take into account whether a home has electric or gas cooking or if air-conditioning is supplied, and are prorated on the basis of the number of bedrooms in a home. In a rental property, a developer must deduct this utility allowance when setting actual rents, or include the utility allowance in the rent and pay for the respective utilities. In a home ownership situation, this utility allowance is deducted from the maximum allowable mortgage payment a potential owner is allowed to incur. Table 5.4 extends the example given in Table 5.3, using a utility allowance of $100 to derive a maximum allowable monthly rent.

The link between the New Ecology, Inc. study's findings and the issue of maximum allowable rent and utility allowances is the fact that utility allowances are set based on a sample of affordable housing units within the PHA territory. Because older, less efficient buildings dominate the sample, utility allowances rarely reflect actual utility costs in newer, energy-efficient buildings, and developers are unable to capture the operating cost savings of up-front investments in energy efficiency. Developers—be they intent on pursuing environmental goals or simply lowering the monthly expenses for low-income tenants—may still choose to make investments in energy efficiency. However, standard utility allowances can be a strong economic disincentive to make significant investments in energy-efficient technologies.

There are, however, several ways to capture the benefits of energy efficiency and on-site energy generation through

TABLE 5.3. MAXIMUM HOUSING BURDEN

Area median income (AMI)	$50,000
40% of AMI restriction	$20,000
Monthly income	$1,666
Maximum housing burden (30% of monthly income)	$500

TABLE 5.4. MAXIMUM RENT

Area median income (AMI)	$50,000
40% of AMI restriction	$20,000
Monthly income	$1,666
Maximum housing burden (30% of monthly income)	$500
Monthly utility allowance	$100
Actual maximum monthly rent	$400

TABLE 5.5. MAXIMUM RENT (WITH REDUCED UTILITY ALLOWANCE)

Area median income (AMI)	$50,000
40% of AMI restriction	$20,000
Monthly income	$1,666
Maximum housing burden (30% of monthly income)	$500
Monthly utility allowance (reduced from $100)	$80
Actual maximum monthly rent	$420

adjustments to the standard utility allowance. First, developers are able to apply for project-specific utility allowances. Energy modeling data and information on the high-efficiency elements of a project—windows, insulation, equipment, appliances—can be submitted as support for a reduced utility allowance based on the lower bills the tenants are expected to receive. The second option is to use an energy-efficient (EEUA) and/or on-site generation (OSUA) utility allowance schedule, if it has been established, or advocate that the local PHA establish these schedules. These schedules can be used by any developer in the PHA territory that meets certain criteria to related energy efficiency (meeting the ENERGY STAR® home standard, for example) or by documenting the expected kilowatt-hour production of an on-site solar or other distributed generation system. The estimated savings are then used to reduce the conventional utility allowance by most but not all of the projected savings. This protects the tenant in the event the savings do not meet projections, while also allowing the owner to increase rents and thus overall operating income. A projected 25 percent energy savings could thus generate a 20 percent reduction of the standard utility allowance, leaving a 5 percent buffer to protect the tenant in the event the savings turn out to be slightly less than projected. Table 5.5 further extends the example given in Tables 5.3 and 5.4 with a 20 percent reduction of the utility allowance from energy savings, thereby increasing the allowable monthly rent.

In home ownership projects, a similar disconnect exists between who makes the initial investment and who benefits, placing similar constraints on the design process. Because of limits on the allowable sale price, the developer may not be able to capture any additional costs related to meeting an energy efficiency or green standard. Utilizing an energy-efficient mortgage (EEM) allows the developer to sell the home for a higher price, and thus recoup the increased costs, while maintaining the same overall housing expense for the owner. Buyers purchasing homes built to the ENERGY STAR home standard are eligible for EEMs, which increase the potential buyer's income slightly to reflect lower expected utility costs. For example, an expected savings of $25 per month would generate approximately $4,000 in additional borrowing power, or roughly the additional first cost associated with reaching the ENERGY STAR standard in most states. By capitalizing the energy savings, the EEM enables developers to incorporate energy efficiency features into their projects without restricting the pool of potential buyers. EEMs can be used in combination with most HUD mortgage guarantee programs for tribal housing (Section 184)[2] and first-time or

FIGURE 5.3. Standard Utility Allowance.

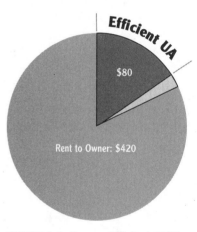

FIGURE 5.4. Energy-Efficient Utility Allowance.

FIGURE 5.5. On-Site Energy Generation Utility Allowance.

low-income homebuyers (Section 203(b)).[3]

IMPACT ON DESIGN

The misalignment in affordable housing between who is making the investment and who is benefiting from that investment can inject an added complexity into design decisions. One area that requires particular attention is the metering of utilities. Central heating or central domestic hot-water systems are often more efficient, and can be lower in first costs, than individual systems. In properties where the owner will be responsible for paying the utility bills, such as special needs or senior projects, there can be a strong push for central systems. In other projects, the impetus for individual metering is strong in order to lower the financial risk to developers. People who pay their own utility bills tend to use less energy. A study by the New York State Energy Research and Development Authority (NYSERDA) showed a reduction of 10–26 percent after master-metered buildings were switched to individually metered.[4] A study of water savings generated by submetering showed a reduction of 15 percent.[5] Because the reduced energy consumption resulting from individual metering may surpass the increased efficiency of a centrally metered energy, determining the best approach can be a difficult balancing act for property managers and design teams—even those experienced in green building.

If already established by the local PHA, using an energy-efficient utility allowance schedule can help push project design teams toward individually metering heat and hot water. But if a project-based utility allowance is required, developers often will not know if the allowance has been approved until well after fundamental design decisions, such as central versus individual metering, must be made, thus creating a barrier to integrated design.

Another design challenge is the misconception that all decisions about building systems and materials must be made at the design development phase. Actually, decisions only need to be made regarding the most substantial or least flexible items, such as the type of structure or major building systems. Final decisions on more flexible items, like finish materials, can be delayed until later in construction by using an "add-alternate" approach. Because affordable housing lenders usually require that a significant contingency fund be set aside for each development, many projects have some contingency funds remaining as construction nears completion. By including green finish materials like flooring, cabinetry, and furniture in the project specifications as add-alternates, green upgrades can be made close to project completion with remaining contingency funds.

This approach is most feasible when the developer is able to work with the same general contractor on several projects, because the general contractor can then ask both subcontractors and suppliers for better pricing based on an increase in both the volume and security of future work.

HOW TO FINANCE GREEN

A dedicated development and design team can accomplish a green project by exploring the full range of funding and financing options outlined in the five-step process described below.

Step 1: Minimize Additional Costs Through Integrated Design

The integrated design process described in Chapter 2 allows for the early consideration of green building practices, thus ensuring that high-value, high-priority items are identified and incorporated from the outset. Integrated design has the potential to reduce costs and—by incorporating the green building features into fundamental aspects of the project, such as location, orientation, site grading, and major building systems—to minimize additional costs to the greatest extent possible.

Step 2: Capitalize Lower Operating Costs

Capitalizing lower operating costs enables developers to fund up-front investments in energy efficiency and durable materials with the increased debt-carrying capacity generated by projected operating savings. The various options for accomplishing this goal should be explored in initial conversations with project lenders and other financial partners.

An energy-efficient, on-site generation, or project-based utility allowance allows the developer to capture a portion of the operating cost savings generated by energy-efficient design and building systems. This approach can be pursued on either a project-based level with the local public housing authority or at a policy level, by encouraging the

THE SPECIAL CASE OF RETROFITS AND ENERGY UPGRADES————————————

Typically offered by energy service companies (ESCOs), energy performance contracting is a funding mechanism for installing energy conservation measures that are paid for by the resulting energy savings. The first costs of the energy improvements are borne by the performance contractor and paid for out of the energy savings. Other advantages include the ability to use a single contractor for the necessary energy audits and retrofits, and the ability to guarantee the energy savings from a selected series of conservation measures.

Energy performance contracts are used in retrofit projects where the payment for new heating equipment, utility services, or energy-related building improvements depends on the energy savings performance of such improvements. Performance is defined by utility consumption, and is guaranteed by an ESCO or contractor to be sufficiently better than the existing equipment or building conditions. Thus the total cost to the owner will be no higher than if no improvements had been made, while, ultimately, total costs will decrease. Energy cost savings achieved by the retrofit project over the contract term must therefore be sufficient to cover all project costs, including debt service and contractor fees for design, maintenance, monitoring, and profit.

housing authority to adopt alternative utility allowance schedules for projects that incorporate energy efficiency and/or on-site power generation. Another approach is to reduce the amount assumed for common-area utility costs to the developer due to energy-efficient systems and lighting, or a common-area photovoltaic system. A third approach is to reduce replacement reserve requirements, based on the specification of more durable flooring, roofing, and other materials.

In home ownership projects, the most commonly used approach for capturing energy savings in project financing is the energy-efficient mortgage (EEM). Check with the commercial bank that will be providing the mortgages to ensure that the lending officer is familiar with EEMs and has the necessary applications.

Step 3: Apply for Available Rebates and Grants

Projects should research and apply for rebates that are linked to energy efficiency standards, renewable energy installations, and water-saving technologies. Most states and many local jurisdictions have rebate programs—often administered through the local electricity, gas, or water utility—that can cover additional first costs. The Federal Energy Policy Act of 2005 established tax credits for energy efficiency and photovoltaic systems. While these incentives typically do not pay for the entire up-front cost of energy- and water-saving technologies, they can cover some of the incremental cost between standard construction and building green.

Step 4: Use Add-Alternates, Contingency Funds, and Combined Bidding

Developers should work with their designers and contractors to incorporate product add-alternates in a systemized way. A number of green building items, particularly finishes and furnishings, can be upgraded late in a project if contingency funds remain. For this method to be successful, early planning is required, as incorporating alternative specifications into general contractor bid packages is a must in order to avoid change orders. Explore bidding several projects together to reduce the costs of green systems and materials.

Step 5: Approach Foundations and Local Government

Finally, project teams should approach foundations and local governments about the possibility of covering any remaining gaps that exists between a project's green building goals and the resources available to pay for them. Because of its unique blend of environmental, economic, and social benefits, green affordable housing is an attractive issue for many philanthropists and local policymakers. Developers can potentially leverage these benefits into commitments for additional funds, especially for aspects of a project that provide a distinct local benefit or that cannot be funded elsewhere. Furthermore, local, regional, and state agencies, such as a city green building program, regional water quality control board, county transit agency, or state energy department, may be interested in including the project as part of a pilot program for solar energy, natural stormwater management, transit oriented development, or environmental education.

SUMMARY

By combining smart decision making in the design process, a long-term view of costs, and clarity in understanding who pays and who benefits, developers can follow the steps listed above to either eliminate, offset, or finance the majority of the green features applicable to affordable housing. Keep in mind that green building is a learning process and that green elements that could not be funded in one project may still be viable for future

TABLE 5.6. RENTAL HOUSING

Number of Units	25
Conventional Project Cost	$3,750,000

GREEN BUILDING COST PREMIUMS

HVAC System	$12,500
Structural Materials	$15,000
Finish Materials	$37,500
PV Panels (for common area)	$90,000
Green Building Consultant	$10,000
Energy Rater	$1,800
Total Premiums	**$166,800**
Percentage Increase	4%

GREEN BUILDING EQUITY SOURCES

Appliance Rebates (local utility)	$2,750
ENERGY STAR Home Rebate (state energy agency)	$2,500
PV Rebate (state energy agency)	$45,000
Green Building Grant (local government or foundation)	$10,000
Additional 9% Tax Credit Equity	$95,895
Business Investment Tax Credit (for PV system)	$27,000
Total Equity Sources	**$183,145**
Net Cost or Savings	$16,345

DEBT SOURCES

Additional Debt from Common Area Utility Adjustment ($10 additional income monthly, 6% interest rate)	$20,000
Total Additional Project Funding	**$36,345**

TABLE 5.7. OWNERSHIP HOUSING ─────────────────────────

Number of Units	1
Conventional Project Cost	$150,000
Monthly Mortgage	$900
Utility Cost	$150
Total Housing Cost	$1,050

GREEN BUILDING COST PREMIUMS

HVAC System	$500
Structural Materials	$1,500
Finish Materials	$1,500
PV Panels (for 50% of demand)	$13,500
Green Building Consultant	$1,000
Energy Rater	$750
Total Premiums	**$18,750**
Percentage Increase (without PV)	4%
Percentage Increase (with PV)	13%

GREEN BUILDING EQUITY SOURCES

Appliance Rebates (local utility)	$110
ENERGY STAR Home Rebate (state energy agency)	$100
PV Rebate (state energy agency)	$4,500
Green Building Grant (local government or foundation)	$500
Federal Tax Credit (for PV system)	$2,000
Total Equity Sources	**$7,210**
Net Cost or Savings	$(11,540)
Green Home Cost	$161,540
Monthly Mortgage	969.24
Utility Costs with PV	$75
Utility Costs without PV	$120
Total Green Housing Cost with PV	1,044.24
Total Green Housing Cost without PV	1,047.20
Net Annual Savings to Buyer (with PV)	$69
Net Annual Savings to Buyer (without PV)	$34

projects. Funding sources also change. A growing number of low-income-housing qualified application plans (QAPs) are incorporating green building points, utility programs
are restructured every two to three years, local governments across the country are starting green building programs, and the philanthropic community is looking for programs
and projects like green affordable housing that bring together environmental and social

equity issues. As the movement toward greening affordable housing gains momentum around the country, more and more programs are being created to support the creation of specific projects or to support developers at the organizational level.

NOTES

1. Lisa Fay Matthiessen and Peter Morris, *Costing Green: A Comprehensive Cost Database and Budgeting Methodology* (Los Angeles: Davis Langdon, 2004); Greg Kats, *The Costs and Financial Benefits of Green Building: A Report to California's Sustainable Building Task Force* (Sacramento: California Sustainable Building Task Force, 2003).
2. Section 184 of the Housing and Community Development Act of 1992, as amended by the Native American Housing Assistance and Self-Determination Act of 1996.
3. Section 203(b), National Housing Act (12 U.S.C. 1709 (b)(i)).
4. New York State Energy Research and Development Authority. *Residential Electrical Submetering Manual.* NYSERDA Contracts #4483-IABR-BR-97, #5037 (Albany, New York: NYSERDA), October 1997, revised 2001.
5. National Multi Housing Council & National Apartment Association Joint Legislative Program, *National Multiple Family Submetering and Allocation Billing Program Study*, National Multi Housing Council & National Apartment Association, Washington, DC, 2004.

CHAPTER 6

Looking Forward: Programs, Partnerships, and Policies

G reening affordable housing is clearly achievable if the right combination of enthusiasm, expertise, creativity, and ambition is brought to a project. Leading developers nationally are starting to embrace the comprehensive, systematic application of green building to all of their projects through the integrated design process and by using LEED, Green Communities, or other standards. For many other designers and developers, the core elements of green building have rapidly become standard practice. ENERGY STAR® appliances; efficient windows, air conditioners, and lighting; low–volatile organic compounds (low-VOC) paint; dedicated kitchen and bath ventilation; low water landscaping; engineered wood products; and construction waste recycling are common.

However, to meet the long-term goal of all affordable housing being built to green standards, there is still much work to be done. Further education and technical assistance is needed for the development community. Additional funding support is needed to accelerate deployment of photovoltaic systems, green roofs, heat recovery ventilation, and other emerging technologies, and to be a catalyst for the next generation of net-zero or climate neutral designs. Perhaps most importantly, more and higher quality data on the costs, monetary savings, and other benefits of green building need to be gathered, analyzed, and provided to policymakers, financial institutions, and operations staff.

Following are examples of programs and organizations that are leading the way toward creating affordable housing that incorporates green comprehensively in design, financing, construction, and operation.

GOVERNMENT PROGRAMS SUPPORTING GREEN AFFORDABLE HOUSING

City or county green building programs frame green building within the context of the local development process and geography, help to identify local resources for green building products and services in the community, and often provide technical assistance, especially to projects that involve public financing. Both Portland and Seattle have developed local guidelines specifically for affordable housing. A handful of cities, such

FIGURE 6.1A. Nuevo Amenecer *(Pajaro, CA)*. *Photo courtesy of South County Housing* **FIGURE 6.1B.** Traugott Terrace *(Seattle, WA)*. *Photo Courtesy of Environmental Works* **FIGURE 6.1C.** Erie Ellington Homes *(Dorcester, MA)*. *Photo courtesy of Bruce M. Hampton, AIA* **FIGURE 6.1D.** Bridgeton Hope VI Revitalization *(Bridgeton, NJ)*. *Photo courtesy of Darren Molnar-Port, NJDCA-NJ Green Homes Office* **FIGURE 6.1E.** New Jersey Zero Energy Home *(Atlantic City, NJ)*. *Photo courtesy of Darren Molnar-Port, NJDCA-NJ Green Homes Office* **FIGURE 6.1F.** SOLARA *(Poway, CA)*. *Photo Courtesy of CTG Energetics*

as San Francisco, have adopted policies that require all city funded housing projects to achieve Green Communities or LEED criteria.

State programs for greening affordable housing often work in concert with the state Qualified Allocation Plan (QAP), state housing bonds, or other housing funds, by providing technical assistance or additional rebates to green projects. The New Jersey Green Homes Office, founded in 1998, administers the New Jersey Affordable Green Program (NJAG). NJAG is a comprehensive affordable green building and energy-efficiency program for developers building projects in coordination with the state's Balanced Housing, HOME funds, Low Income Housing Tax Credits, and HMFA Home Express. The NJAG program is a national model for green affordable housing, having increased the use of innovative green materials and design and building technologies in over 2,400 affordable homeownership and rental units and 37 projects in the state over the past nine years.

The Massachusetts Technology Collaborative, the state's development agency for renewable energy and the innovation economy, provides incentives for affordable housing projects that incorporate energy efficiency, renewable energy, and green building features. Incentives are provided for both the installation of green features and to cover the cost of project planning and green strategy analysis, and to offset some additional construction costs. The Maine State Housing Authority developed green building standards in 2005 for all projects applying for funding from the agency. The intent of the standards is to create healthy, economical, and durable buildings that are efficient to

STATE AND LOCAL GREEN AFFORDABLE HOUSING RESOURCES

- *Seattle SeaGreen (Seattle, Washington):* Local program administered by the Seattle Office of Housing. Provides guidelines for green affordable housing and offers incentives for meeting mainstream green building certification requirements.
- *Portland G-Rated for Affordable Housing (Portland, Oregon):* Local program administered by the Portland Office of Sustainability. Provides guidelines, technical assistance, education, and training. Also establishes threshold requirements for green affordable housing projects seeking funding from the Portland Development Commission.
- *New Jersey Green Home Office (State of New Jersey):* State agency dedicated to increasing the sustainability and affordability of housing built in New Jersey. Provides funding, technical assistance, and guidelines for affordable housing developers to incorporate green building into their projects.
- *New Solar Homes Partnership (State of California):* State program promoting the use of renewable energy in California. A portion of rebate funding has been set aside for the use of renewable energy in affordable housing, with the program application process tailored to the development process in affordable housing.

operate and maintain. Maine Housing also administers the Home Energy Loan Program that has the objective of lowering energy costs to homeowners and reducing energy consumption by 15 to 20 percent annually.

Low-Income-Housing Tax Credits and Qualified Allocation Plans (QAPs)

The federal Low-Income Housing Tax Credit (LIHTC) program is one the main financial drivers of affordable rental housing. Although a federal program, the tax credits are allocated at the state level through the QAP. In many states, the tax credits are a staple in the financial structure of affordable housing. Because of the competitive nature of tax credits in many states, the LIHTC via green criteria in state QAPs is one of the most significant tools for increasing the level of green building that is expected of all tax credit–financed affordable developments. The fifteen-year compliance period of tax credit projects also helps to ensure that the projects, including the green features, are well maintained. For these reasons, the green building criteria in state qualified allocation plans (QAPs) are an integral ingredient in encouraging the development of green affordable housing.

In 2005, Global Green USA released the report *Making Affordable Housing Truly Affordable: Advancing Tax Credit Incentives for Green Building and Healthier Communities*.[1] This analysis of QAPs from fifty states identified that an increasing number of states—including California, Georgia, and New Jersey—are incorporating green criteria in their QAPs, although in differing ways. Some states are focused on smart-growth measures such as promoting infill development or locating projects close to public transportation. Other states have highlighted energy efficiency or established criteria related to locating developments specified distances from factories or other noxious land uses.

FINANCIAL INTERMEDIARIES AND INSTITUTIONS

The support of entities involved in the finance of affordable housing, such as tax credit syndicators, commercial banks, community loan funds, housing trust funds, and other financial institutions is essential, so that the long-term benefits of green building are appropriately considered in financial pro formas, tax credit pricing, and lending decisions. Financial entities currently supporting green building include:

Enterprise Community Partners

In 2004, Enterprise Community Partners, along with a group of partners including Global Green, launched the Green Communities Initiative. A five-year $555-million effort to create over 8,500 units of green affordable housing, this initiative has generated

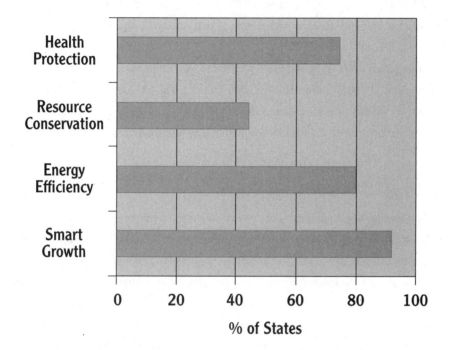

QAPs with Green Criteria Nationally

% of States

FIGURE 6.2. Percentage of states in 2006 that address green building in their qualified application plans (QAPs).

interest among developers nationwide. As part of the Green Communities Initiative, trainings have been held nationally to provide developers, policymakers, architects, and financial institution representatives with detailed information on how to incorporate green practices into their projects.

Enterprise has also developed a rigorous tool for data collection. Each of the projects receiving assistance through Green Communities is expected to provide information on construction costs for the green systems and materials and utility bill information for several years of operation. When significant amounts of this data are collected and analyzed, the true costs and benefits of green affordable housing will be well documented. This type of thorough and consistent data will be essential in furthering public support at the local, state, and federal levels and the private practices of commercial banks to provide greater support for green projects.

Federal Home Loan Bank Affordable Housing Program

The Federal Home Loan Bank, with twelve offices nationally, provides funding to affordable housing through the Affordable Housing Program (AHP). AHP is a competitive program that provides grants twice a year for investment in low- or moderate-income housing. Several offices, including Pittsburgh, Boston, Atlanta, and San Francisco, have incorporated criteria related to green building into the application for AHP funds.

Local Initiatives Support Corporation

Local Initiatives Support Corporation (LISC) operates field offices nationwide, a number of which provide training and technical assistance to support green practices in affordable housing. The San Francisco Bay Area LISC office, for example, is active in promoting energy efficiency and green operations and maintenance practices in the substantial stock of existing affordable housing in the region. The Bay Area LISC has also established a green loan fund, and is developing other resources pursuant to an action plan created by the Bay Area Green Affordable Housing Coalition.

GREEN BUILDING ORGANIZATIONS

As the green building movement has grown so has the number of nonprofit organizations nationally that conduct trainings, develop green building resources, and provide technical assistance. By collaborating with these groups, affordable housing developers can stay abreast of the latest green building strategies, technology, and green building incentives and rebates. Many of these nonprofit groups are able to provide green building technical assistance at low or no cost, through funding from government agencies or foundation grants. At the national level the U.S. Green Building Council established an Affordable Housing Working Group to provide direction in the development of the LEED for Homes rating system. This group provided recommendations during the pilot phase for how to modify or augment the draft LEED for Homes criteria so that the program would be accessible to developers of affordable housing from both a technical and an administrative standpoint. In addition, the USGBC made a concerted effort to include affordable housing projects in the LEED for Home pilot, resulting in more than two dozen projects expected to receive LEED certification.

Other green building organizations that have a focus specifically on the affordable housing sector include:

- Southface Energy Institute, Atlanta, GA
- New Ecology, Inc., Boston, MA
- DC Green Home, Washington, DC
- Global Green USA, Santa Monica, CA, and New Orleans, LA

WHAT'S NEXT?

Innovation is constant in both housing and green building. Housing professionals are preparing for an aging U.S. population by incorporating aspects of universal design into their units. Financial models to provide housing for the extremely low-income, including the formerly homeless, are being developed and implemented in San Francisco and other cities. And strategies to meet the need for affordable workforce housing are being tested in many high-cost urban areas.

On the environmental front, emerging concepts are stretching the definition of green building to include strategies that benefit the broader community by addressing climate change and identifying ways to ensure that economic benefits of green housing flow back to the low-income residents. These include: creating net-zero and carbon-neutral buildings; installing green roof systems, involving communities and affordable housing developers in the trading of carbon reduction credits; developing programs to engage tenants in building operations, through incentive programs that share energy and water savings; and creating not just green housing but entire green communities.

Designers throughout the country are also revisiting the concept of modular housing. A number of approaches are being developed, all with the goal of using manufacturing efficiencies to reduce overall construction costs, improve construction quality, and reduce environmental impacts. Examples include the Eco-Mod home designed by students at the University of Virginia for the Charlottesville Habitat for Humanity affiliate, and a prototype constructed in Gulfport, Mississippi, by Unity Homes (a project of Healthy Building Network) in partnership with the North Gulfport Community Land Trust (NGCLT). If implemented on a large scale, there is the potential to provide factory-built homes for the affordable housing market that cost less than conventional site-built models, with the added benefits of energy efficiency, healthy building materials, and reduced waste.

By following the guidance of this book regarding the integrated design process, recommended practices, financing, and operations, and being inspired by the case studies, housing stakeholders can help build an even more robust portfolio of green developments. These projects, and the lessons learned and shared from them, will be instrumental in accelerating the trend that soon will result in all affordable housing being built to green building standards.

In the years ahead, as knowledge and experience grow in how to best integrate green building practices in affordable housing and as better data regarding the operations and health benefits become available, it is likely that most designers, developers, and policymakers will realize that green building is an essential component of affordable housing, and that, ultimately, we cannot afford to not build green.

NOTES

1. Global Green USA, *Making Affordable Housing Truly Affordable: Advancing Tax Credit Incentives for Green Building and Healthier Communities* (Santa Monica, CA: Global Green USA, 2005).

APPENDIX A

Resources

GREEN AFFORDABLE HOUSING RESOURCES

Global Green USA's Greening Affordable Housing Initiative:
    www.globalgreen.org/greenbuilding/GAHI.html

Affordable Housing Design Advisor: www.designadvisor.org

Green Affordable Housing Coalition: www.greenaffordablehousing.org

Green Communities Initiative: www.greencommunitiesonline.org

National Center for Healthy Housing: www.centerforhealthyhousing.org

New Ecology, Inc: www.newecology.org

AFFORDABLE HOUSING RESOURCES

Affordable Housing Finance magazine: www.housingfinance.com

Building Healthy Communities 101: www.lacity.org/lahd/curriculum/index/html

Enterprise Community Partners–Enterprise Resource Database:
    www.practitionerresources.org

Harvard University's Joint Center for Housing Studies: www.jchs.harvard.edu

HUD Office of Policy Development and Research: www.huduser.org

LISC Community Development Exchange: www.cdexchange.org

National Housing Institute: www.nhi.org

National Low Income Housing Coalition: www.nlihc.org

NeighborWorks America: www.nw.org

GREEN BUILDING RESOURCES

Alameda County Waste Management Authority: www.stopwaste.org

BuildingGreen/*Environmental Building News*: www.buildinggreen.com

California Integrated Waste Management Board's Green Building Design and
    Construction Program: www.ciwmb.ca.gov/GreenBuilding/

Environmental Design & Construction magazine: www.edcmag.com

Global Green USA–Green Building Resource Center: www.globalgreen.org/gbrc

GreenerBuildings: www.greenerbuildings.com

GreenHomeGuide: www.greenhomeguide.com

Healthy Building Network: www.healthybuilding.net

Natural Resources Defense Council, Cities and Green Living: www.nrdc.org/cities

Oikos—green building products and news: www.oikos.com

Rocky Mountain Institute: www.rmi.org

U.S. Green Building Council and the Leadership in Energy & Environmental Design
(LEED) rating systems: www.usgbc.org

Whole Building Design Guide: www.wbdg.org

AFFORDABLE HOUSING FUNDING WITH GREEN BUILDING CRITERIA

Enterprise Community Partners' analysis of tax credit allocation criteria, "An Even Greener
Plan": www.greencommunitiesonline.org/documents/AnEvenGreenerPlan.pdf

Federal Home Loan Bank–Affordable Housing Program, Atlanta: www.flhbatl.com

Federal Home Loan Bank–Affordable Housing Program, Pittsburgh: www.flhb-pgh.com

Federal Home Loan Bank–Affordable Housing Program, San Francisco:
www.fhlbsf.com

Habitat for Humanity International, Construction & Environmental Resources:
www.habitat.org/env

HUD Energy Efficient Mortgages: www.hud.gov/offices/hsg/sfh/eem/energy-r.cfm

ENERGY EFFICIENCY INFORMATION

ENERGY STAR®: www.energystar.gov

Home Energy Saver: www.homeenergysaver.lbl.gov

Public Housing Authority Energy Efficiency Toolbox:
www.globalgreen.org/pha-energytoolbox

U.S. Department of Energy's Energy Efficiency and Renewable Energy/Building
Technologies Program: www.eere.energy.gov/buildings

U.S. Department of Housing and Urban Development's Energy Efficient Rehab
Advisor: www.rehabadvisor.pathnet.org

MATERIALS AND PRODUCT INFORMATION

BEES (Building for Environmental & Economic Sustainability) product life-cycle
assessment software: www.bfrl.nist.gov/oae/software/bees.html

California Integrated Waste Management Board's Recycled-Content Product
Directory: www.ciwmb.ca.gov/rcp

Green Building Products: The GreenSpec Guide to Residential Building Materials; and
the GreenSpec Directory: www.buildinggreen.com/

U.S. Environmental Protection Agency's Environmentally Preferable Purchasing;
www.epa.gov/opptintr/epp

THIRD-PARTY PRODUCT CERTIFICATIONS

Carpet and Rug Institute (CRI) Green Label indoor air quality (IAQ) testing program:
www.carpet-rug.com

ENERGY STAR: www.energystar.gov

Forest Stewardship Council: www.fscus.org

GreenGuard Environmental Institute: www.greenguard.org

Green Seal: www.greenseal.org

Scientific Certification Systems: www.scscertified.com

EPA Watersense: www.epa.gov/watersense/

GREEN BUILDING CASE STUDIES

Affordable Housing Design Advisor: www.designadvisor.org

American Institute of Architects' Top Ten Green Projects: www.aiatopten.org/hpb

California Integrated Waste Management Board's Sustainable Building case studies:
www.ciwmb.ca.gov/greenbuilding/CaseStudies

EarthCraft House: www.earthcrafthouse.com

Global Green USA's Greening Affordable Housing case studies:
www.globalgreen.org/greenbuilding/GAHI_resources.html

Green Affordable Housing Coalition case studies: www.greenaffordablehousing.org

Green Communities Projects: www.greencommunitiesonline.org/projects.asp

Home Depot Foundation's Awards of Excellence for Affordable Housing Built
Responsibly: www.homedepotfoundation.org/awards_housing.html

Smart Communities Network's Green Building Success Stories:
www.smartcommunities.ncat.org/buildings/gbsstoc.shtml

U.S. Department of Energy's High Performance Buildings Database:
www.eere.energy.gov/buildings/database

Glossary

affordable housing – Rents are considered affordable when they are not more than 30 percent of the renter's pre-tax (or gross) income. Mortgages are considered affordable when they are not more than 35 percent of the homebuyer's pre-tax (or gross) income.

AFUE (Annual Fuel Utilization Efficiency) – The measure of seasonal or annual efficiency of a furnace or boiler. Measures the amount of heat actually delivered to the building compared to the amount of fuel supplied to the furnace.

air buoyancy – Forced movement of air upwards due to a difference in indoor-to-outdoor air density resulting from temperature and moisture differences.

area median income (AMI) – The household income for a particular area (city, county, state, etc.) at which 50 percent of households earn a higher income and 50 percent earn less. AMI is calculated annually by the Department of Housing & Urban Development (HUD).

bioswale – A shallow trench planted with trees, shrubs, and groundcover that slows and filters stormwater before allowing it to infiltrate the groundwater system.

Btu (British thermal unit) – A unit of heat used to measure heat output or the embodied energy of a material.

CFCs (chlorofluorocarbons) – Gaseous compounds, often used as propellants, that trap heat in the atmosphere, contributing to global warming.

charrette – An intensive workshop that involves all team members, lasts from three to fours hours to a day or more, and aims to create a clear vision for how the project will be developed, including how the green building elements will be incorporated.

cool roof – Roof system that reflects and emits the sun's heat back to the sky instead of transferring it to the building below.

composting – A waste management system for plant material (e.g., kitchen scraps and garden thinnings) that involves the biological decomposition of organic material into a rich soil amendment.

commissioning – The process of ensuring that systems are designed, installed, functionally tested, and capable of being operated and maintained to perform in conformity with the owner's project requirements.

ecosystem – A complex and interdependent set of natural conditions and elements. Habitat survival depends directly and indirectly on ecosystem health.

embodied energy – A representation of the energy used to grow, harvest, extract, manufacture, transport, and dispose of a material.

equity investor – A person or company that invests money in a development. Equity investors demand a higher rate of return than the typical bank loan interest rate because their funds are not generally secured by collateral (property, buildings, etc.).

extremely low income – A term used to describe individuals or families whose incomes are less than 30 percent of Area Median Income (AMI).

food security – A person's access to readily available, nutritionally adequate, and safe foods, and an ability to acquire foods in socially acceptable ways (that is, without resorting to emergency food supplies, scavenging, stealing, or other coping strategies).

formaldehyde – Urea formaldehyde, a harmful volatile organic compound (VOC), is a binding agent commonly used in composite wood products (oriented strand board, particleboard, etc.). It is a probable carcinogen and poses a range of hazards to human health.

fossil fuels – Nonrenewable resources such as coal, oil, and natural gas, the use of which causes pollution and contributes to global climate change.

gray water – Water that has been used within the home and/or roof runoff. Gray water sources do not include sewage. Gray water can be captured, treated, and used as a nonpotable water source.

greenfield – Previously undeveloped sites which have not been graded that remain in a natural state.

green roof – A roof covered with soil mix and vegetation. Stormwater is absorbed by the soil and vegetation, reducing and detaining stormwater runoff.

HCFCs (hydrochlorofluorocarbons) – Gaseous compounds used instead of chlorofluorocarbons (CFCs), with approximately one-tenth the environmental damage of CFCs.

HOME Investment Partnerships Program – The largest federal block grant program provided by the U.S. Department of Housing and Urban Development (HUD) to state and local governments designed exclusively to create affordable housing for low-income households.

HOPE VI – Federal program provided by HUD that uses public and private development resources to replace distressed public housing with new mixed-income communities.

HOPWA (Housing Opportunities for People with AIDS) – Federal program provided by HUD established to address the specific needs of persons living with HIV/AIDS and their families.

infill development – New development that occurs in centrally located urbanized areas rather than on undeveloped land on the edge of the region.

joint-use – Multipurpose buildings or facilities that share building grounds. Example, a playground that is used as a schoolyard during school hours and is open to the public in other hours.

low-e(missivity) windows – Energy-efficient windows that allow light to pass through but block the flow of heat.

low income – Individuals or families whose incomes are less than 80 percent of Area Median Income (AMI).

microclimate – A unique set of climatic conditions caused by landscape and/or building features. For instance, a paved parking area will absorb and radiate heat to the areas around it. Vegetation can block heavy prevailing winds or funnel them into a concentrated area.

mixed-use – The combination of residential, retail, office, schools, or other uses integrated in the same building or on the same block.

moderate income – Individuals or families whose incomes are between 80 and 120 percent of Area Median Income (AMI).

offgassing – Emission of chemical compounds (e.g., VOCs) into the air from newly installed building materials and finishes.

OVE – (optimum value engineering) – The use of engineering principles and techniques to minimize material usage while also meeting structural performance requirements.

passive solar – Nonmechanical methods of using sunlight to heat the home. Conceptually, sunlight is allowed into the house to heat a thermal mass such as a slab floor, which in turn radiates the heat back into the house when needed at night.

permaculture – A design system that integrates landscape and building issues, permaculture emphasizes low maintenance, edible landscaping, and single design features (including plants) that fulfill more than one function.

PEX – Cross-linked high-density polyethylene that is often used as tubing for hydronic radiant heating systems and plumbing systems.

photovoltaics – Solar power technology that converts energy from the sun into electricity.

phthalates – Class of chemical compounds used to soften polyvinyl chloride (PVC). These compounds are more concentrated in flexible sheet vinyl, for instance, than in vinyl tiles. Phthalates, which are endocrine disruptors and are linked to birth defects, are now being commonly discovered at high levels in tests of humans in the United States.

place making – Creating places that provide a sense of identity and community, such as plazas, squares, parks, streets, and waterfronts.

PVC (polyvinyl chloride) – Form of plastic commonly referred to as vinyl. Commonly used building material chosen for its versatility. Releases toxins during its production and in its usage. Contains toxins such as mercury, dioxins, and phthalates.

pro forma – A financial analysis of the expected costs and income of a proposed development.

public housing – Low-income housing built and operated by a local housing authority using federal funds.

R-value – A unit of thermal resistance measuring resistance to heat flow through a single material. The higher the R-value, the greater the insulating properties.

Section 8 (Housing Choice Voucher Program) – Federal program providing rental payment assistance to qualified low-income recipients in the form of a voucher.

Section 202 – Federal program that provides capital and operating funds to organizations that develop and operate housing for low-income seniors.

Section 811 – Federal program that provides capital and operating funds to organizations that develop and operate housing for persons with disabilities.

SEER (Seasonal Energy Efficiency Rating) – Measures efficiency of a cooling system over an entire cooling season. A higher SEER reflects a more efficient cooling system. SEER is calculated based on the total amount of cooling (in Btu) the system will provide over the entire season divided by the total number of watt-hours it will consume.

smart growth – A more sustainable and holistic model for urban growth that aims to limit low-density development on the urban fringe while creating more livable neighborhoods in urban and suburban areas.

solar heat gain coefficient (SHGC) – The fraction of incident solar radiation admitted through a window, both admitted through a window, both directly transmitted, and absorbed and subsequently released inward. SHGC is expressed as a number between 0 and 1. The lower a window's solar heat gain coefficient, the less solar heat it transmits.

sone – A unit measuring intensity of sound. Select ventilation systems with low sone ratings.

special needs housing – Special needs housing refers to housing for groups with unique needs, such as the disabled, elderly, individuals with physical and mental disabilities, and person with HIV/AIDS.

stick-built – Building that has not been pre-constructed in any way. Is constructed on-site around a "stick frame," piece by piece.

stack effect – The flow of air that results from warm air rising, creating a positive pressure area at the top of a building and a negative pressure area at the bottom of a building. The stack effect can overpower the mechanical system and disrupt ventilation and circulation in a building.

sustainability – Meeting the needs of the present without compromising the ability of future generations to meet their needs.

sweat equity – Involves the homebuyer's participation in the construction of his or her own housing. Their labor helps to offset the price of the home. Construction work can include, but is not limited to, assisting in the painting, carpentry, trim work, drywall, roofing, and siding for the housing.

transit oriented development (TOD) – New pedestrian-friendly, mixed-use developments located near rail and major bus stops. TOD communities allow people to live near transit services and to decrease their dependence on driving.

U-value – A unit of thermal resistance measuring rate of heat flow through a material assembly rather than a single material. For instance, whereas insulation is measured by R-value, the entire wall assembly is measured by U-value. A lower U-value means better insulating properties.

very low income – Individuals or families whose incomes are less than 50 percent of the Area Median Income (AMI).

VOCs (volatile organic compounds) – A class of chemical compounds that can cause short- and long-term health problems. VOCs can be emitted (offgassed) by many building materials and finishes, including particleboard and solvent-based finishes.

watershed – Area of ecosystem(s) bounded by the highest topographic points and focused around where water flows and drains. All water in an area—including the pollutants it carries—flows to the lowest point of the watershed.

workforce housing – Housing aimed at middle-income professionals such as teachers, police officers, firefighters, nurses and medical technicians, who provide essential community services. Workforce families are usually younger, and often include children. The lack of workforce housing is typically of great concern in areas with expensive real estate markets or in resort areas.

xeriscaping – Xeriscaping features water-friendly gardening practices. The name is derived from zero-water landscaping.

Lease Addendum Example

Addendum __
Care of Natural Linoleum Floors
Unit # __

The entryway, kitchen and bathroom floors at _____ are natural linoleum floor covering designed to last many years. In order for the floors to stay clean and in good condition residents must use care when cleaning them. A special cleaner and sealer are required to preserve the floors.

- You will receive instructions for cleaning and sealing the floors at move-in.
- Use the cleaner to remove dirt and stains as needed.
- At least once a year apply a coat of sealer.
- We will provide the cleaner and sealer to you at our cost.

DO NOT USE AMMONIA OR OTHER HARSH CLEANSERS ON THE LINOLEUM FLOORS. ONLY PH NEUTRAL CLEANERS OR THE PROVIDED CLEANER ARE PERMITTED.

If you do not follow the instructions for cleaning and sealing the flooring you will be responsible for the repair or replacement of the flooring.

By signing this Addendum I/We agree to clean and seal the linoleum floors in accordance with manufacturer's instructions and acknowledge that I/We have received a copy of the instructions. I/We also understand that by signing this Addendum we agree to pay for the repair or replacement of the flooring should we not follow the manufacturer's instructions.

_____   _____
Resident   **Date**

_____   _____
Resident   **Date**

_____   _____
for Housing Developer/Manager (Agent)   **Date**

Solar RFP Example

RE: Request for Proposal: Photovoltaic System
- **System Design**
- **Permitting**
- **Equipment Procurement**
- **Installation**
- **Rebate Processing**

Dear _____:

The Housing Development Corporation of _____ (the "Developer"), on behalf of
_____ LLC (the Corporation), is seeking to select a photovoltaic general contractor for its
_____ project located at _____ Street in the City of _____.

I am therefore requesting interested contractors to submit a Statement of Qualifications and Proposal to our
office by _____.

PROJECT BACKGROUND

The project is a ___ -unit multi-family affordable apartment building that will be managed by _____.

The developer plans to install an approximately ___ kW (DC) photovoltaic system to serve the building's (common electricity meter and/or residential units). The size of the proposed system is based on the estimated annual electricity use of the common systems (interior and exterior safety lighting, elevator, management office cooling and appliances), residential units, the available roof area and project budget. The project expects to have ___ net meters connected to the electricity grid and will be applying for rebates and incentives from _____.

The project is _____ construction type. The roofing system is _____. A roof plan, a plan showing mechanical/electrical rooms, and an electrical one-line diagram are attached.

The project will be permitted by the City/County of _____. Electricity service will be provided by _____. No permits have been applied for or obtained for the photovoltaic system.

Construction on the project will begin in _____, and is expected to be completed by _____.

SCOPE OF SERVICES

The chosen contractor will be expected to provide the following services:

1. Design of the photovoltaic system including roof attachment details, roof racks, electrical one line diagram, panel configuration.
2. Specification of manufacturer of the photovoltaic panels, inverters, attachment hardware, electrical wiring, conduit, etc.
3. Installation of all specified equipment. Labor on the project is/is not required to pay prevailing wages.
4. Permitting of all the components identified above (including clearance from the Fire Department.)
5. Administration of rebates and incentives.
6. Assistance with interconnection/net metering agreements with the utility.
7. Final system commissioning, including maintenance and monitoring training for property management staff.

CONTRACTING TERMS

While the PV portion of the project may be permitted separately from the rest of the project, the selected PV contractor will be expected to work as a subcontractor to _____, the project's General Contractor. There is the possibility that the "PV-Ready" portion of the scope of work (roof stanchions, conduit runs, wiring, etc.) will be under one sub-contract to the General Contractor, while installation of the panels will take place under a separate contract directly with the owner after the building. Details of this arrangement will be finalized once a PV contractor has been selected.

The project owner will reserve the right to alter the size of the PV system and/or metering arrangements depending on price fluctuations of PV equipment, changes to rebate levels, available financing, and utility requirements.

REQUIRED PROPOSAL SUBMITALS

Respondents to this RFP should provide the following:

1. Cost proposal inclusive of all taxes, permitting costs. The cost proposal should be in gross terms, i.e., exclusive of expected rebates.
2. Warranty terms for both equipment and installation.
3. A company resume detailing projects completed, projects under construction, and projects in pipeline. Please include details about the number of units, construction dollar volume, and project

sponsorship. Please highlight the Contractor's experience with the type of project described above, paying particular attention to previous experience with multifamily building types and affordable housing financing structures.

4. Client references for past projects as well as for projects under construction.

5. Proof of possession of appropriate license to design, permit, and install Solar photovoltaics.

6. Description of experience, if any, in managing of prevailing wage documentation and reporting requirements.

7. A statement of bonding capacity, if any.

8. A statement of general liability insurance capacity and limits.

The respondant should, as part of its response, identify any concerns and qualifications in the above requested information or proposed scope of work.

I look forward to receiving your response.

Sincerely,

Project Manager

INDEX